ENCYCLOPEDIA OF
CANADIAN
HOME DESIGNS

by SELECT HOME DESIGNS

371
Home & Cottage Plans

HOME PLANNERS

Table of Contents

FEATURES

HOME PLANS

About the Cover: Craftsman is a beloved style everywhere. This choice, our Design SHS010230, shown in detail on page 174, is an exquisite example.
Photo by Bob Greenspan

Vancouver Offices
(publication inquiries, advertising)
Open Monday through Friday
8:30 a.m. to 5 p.m. PST
301-611 Alexander Street
Vancouver, B.C., Canada V6A 1E1
Telephone: 604-879-4144
Fax: 604-251-3212

Toll-free Plan Line:
(plan orders & inquiries only)
1-800-663-6739
Open from 8:00 a.m to 8:00 p.m. (EST) Monday through Friday

Web address:
www.selectaplan.com

E-mail:
info@selecthomedesigns.com

Chief Operating Officer and Publisher
Steve Riley

Quality Control/Production Manager
Regan Swallow

Production Administrator
Jay Peck

CADD Systems Administrator
Warren Noyes

Shipping/Fulfillment Supervisor
Truong Le

Account Manager
David Sandhu

Advertising Sales
Ontario East
Advertising Account Manager
Canadian Media Connection
1000 Yonge Street, Lower Level
Toronto, Ontario, M4W 2K2
Phone: 416-964-3247   Fax: 416-964-0964

Western Canada
Advertising Account Manager
Select Home Designs
301-611 Alexander Street
Vancouver, BC, V6A 1E1
Phone: 604-879-4144   Fax: 604-251-3212

U.S. Office
3275 West Ina Road, Suite 110
Tucson, Arizona 85741
Telephone: 520-297-8200

Circulation
Tom Low
Telephone: 520-297-8200, ext. 120

First printing, September 2000

10 9 8 7 6 5 4 3 2 1

Printed in United States of America
Library of Congress Cataloque Card Number 00 106720
ISBN (softcover): 1-881955-79-6

Looking For The Right Site?

HERE'S HOW...

Think of any building site, no matter how small, as a three-dimensional puzzle, into which you have to fit an essential new piece—your home. Ignore any of the puzzle's other parts and you could easily end up with the right house on the wrong lot, or vice versa. Here are six vital questions to answer.

what's the lay of the land?

The topography, or physical makeup, of a site has lots to do with the type of house you can put on it. Which direction, if any, does the land slope? Where does water drain? Are there trees you want to save? Will you need to do any extensive grading or excavation, and possibly invest in costly retaining walls? How will the site affect architectural features—decks, for example?

Among the 371 plans featured, you can find the right house for just about any terrain. A relatively flat site, for example, easily accommodates a one-storey home, and if it slopes gently to the rear, you might even be able to pick up bonus walk-out living space below. The same goes for most two-storey and 1½-storey houses.

Multi-level homes fit a greater variety of sites. You can step a split-level down a hill for instance, or nestle a two-storey among the trees. (At the same time, don't overlook the possibilities of an "orphan" or "infill" site in a good neighborhood. Among our home plans, you might just discover one that perfectly suits it—and get a great deal on a piece of land that others have written off as unbuildable.)

where's the sun?

One of the first things a designer wants to know when he or she sizes up a site is how it relates to the points of the compass. Plotting exactly when the sun shines on a lot, as it moves from east to west each day, helps determine the orientation of a home's living areas.

Ideally, rooms like the kitchen and breakfast area benefit most from an eastern exposure, where they'll bask in morning sunlight. On the other hand, west-facing areas that see action during the afternoon and evening—family and living rooms, for example—will remain bright later in the day. Also, bear in mind that the midday sun in the northern hemisphere shines from the south, which means a home's north side will get no direct sunlight. Often, this is prime territory for bedrooms, because they'll be darker and cooler both morning and evening.

what can the sun do for you?

Because the sun beats down on a home's southern exposure all day long, you'll be able to capture its energy and, in the process, take a big load off your heating bills. Whether you're thinking about building a passive solar design or installing active solar collectors, or if you just want to get an energy-saving boost from the sun, a home's south face is the most important of all.

That's why it's a good idea to visit a site several times—at different hours of the day—before you sign on the dotted line. Consider these points if you're looking for a place in the sun.

◆ Trees can add to a home's solar potential, or they can nullify it. Deciduous trees that will shade the south side of your house are a big plus. They'll help keep it cool in the summer, when you don't want solar heat gains; in winter, they'll accommodatingly shed their leaves and let sunlight through.

Evergreens have a place, too, but they should be on the north side where they can buffer winter winds. Evergreens can also stop the sun from scorching a home's east and west exposures.

◆ Terrain has a lot to do with solar potential. The best place for sunlight is halfway up a south-facing slope. Sites that face north or are at the bottom of a hill are usually shady and chilly, or just plain cold, during the winter months.

Regardless of the slope it's on, a site at the top of a hill is the coldest of all, because it's buffeted by winds from all directions.

◆ Winds steal heat in the winter, but

they can also help cool a house during the summer. Because the coldest winds usually blow from the north, a site sheltered in this direction is often a good place to put a solar-oriented house.

how's the view— or views?

When's the last time you climbed a tree? Shinnying up to the lower branches of a big tree (all right, you can use a ladder if you want) gives you an excellent chance to check out the views from the upper floors of a two-storey or multi-level home.

On the other hand, seeing other sites may not be what you have in mind; in that case, a plan that turns its back on a busy thoroughfare or the neighbor's garbage cans may be more up your alley.

Also, look for ways to create privacy later on. More often than not, you'll be able to, but if it's important, pay close attention to the plan and the site and the way they work together, especially in a crowded neighborhood.

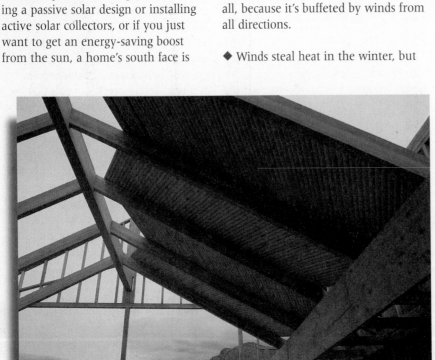

what about outdoor living?

The outdoor areas around a house fall into three categories: public spaces (driveway and front yard, for instance); semi-public or service areas (a garden or children's playground are two good examples); and private spaces, like decks or patios where you can lounge in the sun or entertain friends away from the view of neighbors and passersby.

Good public areas allow for two things: access from the street to the main entrance and parking for vehicles—your visitors', as well as your own. Plan to locate semi-public areas near the home's secondary entry. Low fences or walls here can partially screen clutter.

In colder climates, you might want to position private outdoor living areas on the south side of your home; for warmer locations, a spot on the north side may be more comfortable. With either, think about how fences, plantings, and the house itself can assure privacy.

what do the code words say?

Finally, keep in mind that a community's building code and zoning ordinances may have a lot to do with where you can put your home.

First and foremost, go down to the local building department and find out what setbacks the ordinances require. (Setbacks govern how close a house can come to the street and adjacent property lines.) Some ordinances specify that a house be no nearer than 5 feet from its property lines (called a side setback) and no fewer than 30 feet from the street (front setback). In other communities, the numbers might be completely different.

Once you know the setbacks, you can draw a line within and parallel to the property lines on all sides. This is what designers call the building envelope—it defines the total area in which you're allowed to build.

Other codes and ordinances can affect what you build and where. For example, some communities mandate that a house take up no more than 25-50% of the property it sits on. Similarly, many ordinances restrict the height of residential buildings, typically measured from the roof crest to the ground. In addition, a growing number of local governments have enacted ordinances that regulate total square footage, effectively eliminating smaller (and sometimes larger) homes from the housing mix.

It's tempting to ignore building codes and zoning ordinances, especially if they're outdated or unreasonably restrictive. Forget it. Many communities don't take violations lightly. Penalties include extra fees, fines, even mandatory demolition (think for a second about tearing down what you've already built).

Stick to the rules. If you've got a sound case for doing something differently, check with local officials. You might be able to get a variance, or formal OK to do it your way.

The 10-Second Commute

Planning For An Efficient Home Office

According to a recent survey, upwards of 60 million North Americans now work out of their homes, either as home-based employees of a larger company or as self-employed individuals. Among their ranks are artists, writers, salespeople, marketers, instructors and a host of others who find that the "ten-second commute" from living space to working space is a most convenient and agreeable situation. Gone are the long, tiresome drives to work and back home. And an expensive, uncomfortable business wardrobe can be relegated to those days when clients simply must be met face-to-face. However, the move from business office to home office involves a serious change in lifestyle with numerous considerations. If you are considering such a move, you'll need to take a hard look at the options for creating the best home-office environment you can afford.

Analyze Your Needs

Before you make any decisions about working in a home office, you need to look at when and how your office will be used. By analyzing the amount of time you will spend in your new space and how much space you'll need, you can design (or redesign) an area that will work perfectly for you.

For some people, the home office will only be used on a part-time basis while the outside business office acts as a primary workplace. For others, it will become the sole, full-time, completely equipped business office. Many may find that they have no interest in working at home on a part- or full-time basis, but that they need home office space for paying bills, working quietly at a hobby or studying. All three of these circumstances are viable reasons for setting up a home office, though they may not all require the same design or configuration.

You'll also need to look at how much space you'll need for your home office. Will you have sole rights to the space or will you share the work area with another family member or business partner? How much space is available for your office? If you are converting an existing room for home-office space, this is a major consideration. If you are building a new home, or adding on to an existing home, you can develop the amount of space you think you'll need and plan for expansion space for future needs. The amount of space you need depends directly on the type of work or business you'll be conducting in that space. Straightforward office work can take place in a relatively small space with room for a desk, computer table, filing cabinets and storage spaces. Other kinds of work may require more space for meetings or equipment—computer hardware, fax and copy machines, scanners and the like. An artist would want extra room for specialized materials and appliances to produce a finished product, as well as room to glue, paint, cut and create. The important

Upwards of 60 million North Americans now work out of their homes.

OPPOSITE PAGE: With custom-wood cabinetry, this den becomes a home office to be proud of. Photo by Bri-Mar Photography

LEFT: This inviting home office combines creature comforts with modern technology. Photo by Raef Grohne Photographer

BELOW: A golfing theme personali▩▩ this home office to provide a comfortable working ▩▩▩▩nt. Photo by Raef Grohne Photographer

OVERLEAF: Far from family distractions, this artist's loft also receives plenty of natural light. Hearth & Home cabinets by Aristokraft

thing is to allow as much space as possible without crowding your ability to perform your work.

Where To Put Your Home Office

Generally, you'll want to set up your home office in an area of the house that is far from distractions like pets and children. It should be a room far from the main traffic flow of the house and separated from rooms that are likely to be noisy (don't even consider trying to work in a room next to your teenager's stereo!). It's important to see this space as a work place, so that when you put yourself there, you are mentally prepared to work. Secondly, when you shut down for the evening, it's easier to leave the "office" behind in its own space and move on to more leisurely pursuits.

If you are setting up a home office in your current residence, there are some typical spaces that can easily be converted into usable space. An unfinished attic usually presents a large area that is away from daily family activities and allows for any number of working-space configurations. A basement or part of a basement is equally versatile for the home office. If the basement is a walk-out type, it offers the option of a separate outside access for clients. Sometimes unused space in a garage can be converted into office space with a few walls and a little decorating. This, too, may offer the possibility of an outside entrance. One problem with each of these areas is that they are often unheated, uninsulated spaces and may require extensive work and expense to make them comfortable enough to use.

Other areas to consider for the home-office conversion include dens, studies, balcony lounges, guest bedrooms or even out-of-the-way areas of larger rooms such as living rooms or great rooms. Room dividers can help create separate space in the last instance. It may be necessary for the home office to perform in more than one way if converted from one of these rooms or areas. For instance, if the guest bedroom is made into a home office, you may find yourself working while Aunt Edna takes her afternoon nap a few feet away during her annual two-week visit. Obviously, it is better if the home office is not destined to serve more than one purpose; however, for most homeowners space is a limited luxury and must be apportioned in the most efficient manner.

Those who are planning to build a new home are able to plan accordingly for a home office, even if it is not to be used immediately. Select Home Designs offers floor plans that include dens or studies and some even feature home offices as part of their design. Remember that bonus space, allowed for in many Select plans, can be developed later into office space when you are ready to make the move to working at home.

The Room

When considering a space for a home office, look for an area that contains plenty of natural light. Large windows or skylights can make the difference in a small space and provide an easy-on-the-eyes kind of light that is difficult to duplicate with artificial light. If the windows and skylights can be opened, you'll appreciate the ventilation and cooling effects of a breeze on a nice,

balmy day. Be sure, however, not to position your computer in such a way that direct light falls on the monitor. You might enjoy the warmth of the sun on your back, but you will be frustrated by your inability to see what's on the computer screen.

If you are forced to rely mainly on artificial light, consider a dropped ceiling in your home office with suspended lighting to provide even distribution of light and sufficient brightness for the overall office area. Task lighting to further illuminate specific areas of the office will provide the extra light necessary for reading, writing, drawing, and other close-work assignments. There are many varieties of task lighting available—from the expensive and chic track lighting to the standard drafting lamp. You probably already have an idea of what works best for you, but shop around and "test drive" several before you sink much money into any.

Since space is a major consideration, look for an area that provides enough room for all of the furniture and equipment you'll need for your work. This will include office furniture like desks, filing cabinets, storage cabinets for materials, and chairs, plus any other items you need that are specific to your business. Have a plan for expanding and adding new equipment and furniture. The single-drawer filing cabinet may be sufficient for now, but in a year or two you may have the need for two or three more. It's great if you have enough room to set up activity areas in your office: a production area, a record and filing area, a computer area and so on. For most people, this is not possible, but with a little creativity and the use of screens or free-standing bookcases, you may be able to divide your office into pockets of space that serve different needs.

Floor and Wall Coverings

Easy-care and durable are the bywords in home office decorating. This does not discount the possibility of a beautiful space— it only requires that elements of that space be tough enough to withstand your daily routine. It is advisable, in fact, to create an environment that is both comfortable and aesthetically pleasing to make the time you spend in your home office as pleasant as possible and to impress visiting clients.

Vinyl, ceramic or clay tile coverings work well for floors and clean up more easily than most types of carpets. However, some of the newer brands of carpeting seem to be equally durable and easy to clean. If carpeting is your choice, select one that has a short nap in a darker neutral color.

If you have a computer, it may be advantageous for you to eliminate carpeting and fabric drapes—static being one of the foremost enemies of electronic equipment. Vinyl or metal blinds serve well for window coverings. They are relatively inexpensive, easy to care for, professional looking and are available in a wide range of styles and colors to complement your decor. They also allow you to control the amount of natural light coming into the office to suit your tastes and workability.

Furniture

The amount and type of office furniture you need for your home office is largely a personal matter. For most people a desk or other central workspace, a comfortable working chair, some lamps and filing cabinets are the basics. Many prefer to have a separate writing and computer space that is equally accessible from one central area. An L- or U-shaped unit with a spot for the computer and a surface area for writing, plus a swivel chair, solves the problem nicely for most situations. Depending on your available space and needs, you may find that a couch or lounge is handy for reading and brainstorming. Make it a sleeper sofa if your office must perform double-duty as a guest room.

Anyone who has spent any time at all sitting at a desk or computer terminal knows that the single most important piece of furniture in your office is your work chair. If you can afford to spend money on only one item, this should be it. Look for good back support, adjustability and durability. Try out several in the store or ask for a home trial for a few days. Most reputable office furniture dealers will gladly allow this.

Workspaces are easier to care for if covered in any of the many laminate products available on the market. These surfaces provide long-lasting, maintenance-free performance and are both beautiful and affordable. They are a great option for artists, handcrafters, draftsmen or anyone whose work sometimes creates a mess.

If there is a possibility that clients may visit your home office from time to time, you'll want to spend some extra money on decorating with a presentable-looking desk and other primary furniture. Keep things as neat as possible by utilizing modern filing systems and other office storage products.

Storage
The one element that never seems to be in sufficient supply in any home is storage. You'll find this to be even more the case for your home office. Establish as much storage space as possible and be scrupulous in weeding out unnecessary files and other items that take up precious space.

Bookshelves can hold technical and research manuals, sound equipment, TVs and VCRs, and other often-used items. Built-in cabinets are great for storage; a closet can be lined with shelves and dividers for the same purpose. Other furniture items like chests and armoires neatly hide and store large items and also provide cozy touches in an otherwise sterile atmosphere.

Necessary Extras
Today's manufacturers are attuned to the growing number of people working out of their homes and have responded with some great products that will enhance your home office and make your business run more smoothly. These include intercom systems, many types of phone and answering systems, personal fax and copy machines, scanners and a myriad of personal computer systems. Though all of these electronics are not essential to all businesses, they certainly provide convenience and all-important responsiveness to client needs.

Other amenities you might want to consider include a wet bar with refrigerator for entertaining clients (and appeasing yourself), a home safe (for important papers and cash), good sound system, TV and VCR.

The Wires and Wherefores
If you are truly serious about conducting business from home, it is critical you ensure your computer and information lines are up to speed. For example, with the increased importance of the internet as a forum for generating and conducting business, you won't want to be held back because your home has insufficient wiring capacity to ensure quick and easy access and reliable service. With the correct wiring, you will also have easier and more powerful ways to share internally and externally sourced data from your home computer (or computers). The following minimum wiring requirements are recommended for a typical home:

WIRE TYPE	QUANTITY	DESCRIPTION	USED FOR
High capacity telephone/data wire (Category 5)	1	4 twisted pairs of high-capacity wire enclosed in an insulated sheath	Will handle normal telephone signals for phones, faxes and modems. The increased capacity of this new wire type will handle video and data signals from computers
Coaxial cable (RG 6)	2	Heavily shielded and insulated copper core carries signal	Normally used to deliver video signals, is also capable of handling computerized, interactive services to and from the home.

Wires need to be home run (running all wires together vertically through a central plastic pipe) to a junction box with access to available electrical power, and accessible consumer outlets for system connection.

With a little planning and the right space in your home, you can have an office that provides all the convenience of a large corporate office in a space that's as comfortable as well, your own home!

This page: A home office need not be sterile. With comfortable furnishings and personal effects, a home office will always be a welcome retreat.
Photos by Bizzo Photography

What Color Is Your World?

Enhancing Your Rooms With Paint

We are told the human brain can recognize 7 million different colors, a fact you may appreciate if you've ever tried to pick out exactly the right shade of white for a room. Decorating or redecorating a house can be a daunting undertaking but, with the help of a few guidelines, the results can be stunning.

What you really need to know can be summarized by the color wheel on page E11. All colors are a combination of three primary colors—red, yellow and blue. Complementary colors are directly opposite each other on the wheel, while related colors are next to each other. Three colors that are an equal distance apart are called triad colors. White added to a color makes it lighter; black added makes it darker.

You might choose to decorate with just one color in a variety of intensities or shades. This can result in a very sophisticated look and is effective in small spaces. For a little more contrast, select one main color and use related colors in smaller amounts. Complementary colors also work well together, but if the shades aren't chosen carefully or if it's overdone, the

Benjamin Moore Paints

Using paint and a home-made foam applicator, you can create faux terra cotta tile and give a facelift to virtually any flooring. See a Benjamin Moore paint dealer for instructions.

effect can be disturbing rather than exciting.

Before choosing colors for your rooms, there are several questions to ask. What mood would you like to create? How will the room be used? Are there facets of the room you'd like to enhance or minimize? What colors are in the furnishings?

Let's attempt to answer each of these questions, with the understanding that ultimately you can do anything you want as long as it's pleasing to you. If you can't stand blue, don't use it anywhere just because it's recommended below!

What mood would you like to create?

Warm colors make a room seem smaller and more intimate and will enhance available light in rooms on the shady side of the house. Cool colors are fresh and soothing and especially appropriate for rooms with a southern exposure. Light shades energize a room, making small dark areas appear larger and more cheerful. Use complementary colors for drama. For harmony within a room or to unify adjoining rooms, use related colors.

How will the room be used?

- **Kitchen:** Blue is cool and refreshing; green is a natural, healthy color; and yellow brightens a room and may suggest a lemon-fresh scent.
- **Bedroom:** Golden yellows enhance the glow of sunrise. Green encourages relaxation, as do blue and purple. The latter are also sophisticated. Pinks and peaches are flattering to both rooms and people.
- **Living Room:** Warm colors encourage conversation. Add bright colors for drama and elegance.
- **Dining Room:** Red is the best—it stimulates the appetite! Gold is also great, or consider black for a truly dramatic effect.
- **Bathroom:** Pink and peach make everyone's skin look better; yellow has just the opposite effect. Add white accents—on fixtures perhaps—for a fresh, clean atmosphere.
- **Nursery:** To provide babies with a stimulating environment, forget about pink or blue. Surround them with bright colors and strong contrasts. Or highlight the pastel colors with bold accents.

Encourage your child to write on the walls by creating a one-of-a-kind blackboard with Benjamin Moore's Crayola© Chalkboard Paint. The paint, one of several F/X (special effect) finishes, can also be used on the floor, a tabletop or even a floor cloth.

COLORS CAN BE:
Primary—red, blue and yellow
Secondary—combination of two primary colors
Tertiary—combination of a primary and a secondary color
Related—next to each other on the color wheel
Complementary—directly opposite each other on the color wheel
Triad—three colors equidistant from each other on the color wheel
Warm—containing yellow and red
Cool—containing green and blue
Neutral—beige, white and gray

Are there facets of the room you'd like to enhance or minimize?

Use contrasting colors to highlight an attractive molding or a beautiful art object. If a room is architecturally boring, create interest by painting one wall in a contrasting color. Hide a defect, such as an ugly radiator or exposed pipes, by painting it the same color as the walls.

Lighter tints reflect light more effectively, and can make a small room seem larger. For the opposite effect, use dark colors to make a room more cozy. To widen a narrow room, use a warm dark color on the short walls and a cool, lighter color on the long walls. The ceiling will appear higher if you use light paint above a chair rail and a darker shade below. Conversely, painting a high ceiling a dark color will make it seem lower.

(continued on next page)

What colors are in the furnishings?

Always take into account furniture, wall hangings and other accessories. Decide whether to create drama by using contrasting colors or to harmonize with colors in the furnishings. If you're not going to change a floor covering, you might want to design your color scheme around the colors it contains.

Wood panelling and furniture will add warmth to the overall effect while green plants will cool down bright colors.

Color Selection

Natural light makes bright colors seem even more brilliant. Keep this in mind when selecting colors for a south-facing room, which will receive sunlight all day long. Softer, lighter colors will become richer, while bright colors might become overwhelming. On the other hand, a west-facing breakfast room will not receive direct sunlight when it is most frequently used, so would benefit from bolder, more vibrant colors.

The type of artificial lighting used affects how things look at night. Incandescent light has a yellow cast and works well with warmer, darker colors, making a room seem more inviting. Fluorescent light contains blue and enhances bright colors and white. Halogen bulbs provide a strong white light, which is good with bold colors but washes out softer ones. Color selection should be made under the actual lighting conditions

Colorwashing is a technique designers use to disguise imperfections on wall surfaces, to lighten colors that are too dark or too bright, or even to give new life to old, brightly colored wallpaper. Color A Stroke of Brilliance, available at Benjamin Moore dealers, illustrates this and other easy-to-achieve paint techniques.

Benjamin Moore Paints

Benjamin Moore Paints

Bring the garden indoors to a room light with laughter and ready for girl talk. This ragged wall in Benjamin Moore's Crayola® Carnation Pink paint lends interest and depth on which the painted flowers can blossom.

of the space to be painted. The fluorescent light of the paint store will have a different effect on paint colors than does the lighting in your home. Special effect lighting, such as spot or track lighting can also distort color. And natural light changes the paint color, depending on the time of day.

Shades of white undergo the least variation under different lighting conditions. Pale shades also tend to remain true. However, these share a tendency to reflect nearby colors, such as tones in the carpet.

Color should not be checked in an empty room. Objects absorb and reflect color in different ways and will change the appearance of color on the walls and ceiling.

When using dramatic, daring colors, experiment first. Paint a large sheet of poster board and view it in different parts of the room under the changing lighting conditions for that space.

Benjamin Moore's "Tuscan Treatment" is a faux paint technique derived from the art of frescoing. Using drywall compound for texture and four shades of glaze for color, it is easy to add old world charm to new drywall or old plaster.

Benjamin Moore Paints

Decorative Finishes

Consider adding interest to a painted wall with wallpaper borders or panels. Stencilling is another option and can be done with homemade stencils as well as store-bought.

There are also many painting techniques for adding texture and variety to walls. *Positive methods* are those in which additional layers of paint are added after the base coat has dried. *Negative methods* involve removing some of the paint while it is still wet.

In SPONGING, sponges are used to apply one or more colors over a neutral base coat. Gently dab paint onto the wall, being careful to intermix darker spots (full sponge) with lighter (empty sponge) to ensure evenness over the entire wall. If desired, add different shades of the first color or one or more contrasting colors.

RAGGING uses a lint-free material, such as cotton, burlap or crumpled newspaper either to remove paint that is still wet, or to add a second coat in a contrasting shade.

RAG-ROLLING involves dipping a rag in paint, wringing it out gently and twisting it into a cylinder. Roll it up and down the wall, slightly overlapping the rows.

DRAGGING is a good way to add texture to doors and woodwork. Over a neutral base coat, add a coat of a mixture of paint and glaze, combining shades of the same color. While it is still wet, drag a dry brush over the surface, moving in a straight line from top to bottom with no stopping along the way.

Dragging also is an effective technique for walls. Consider such alternatives as: dragging one color vertically, a second horizontally; using the rubber side of a squeegee, notched, for a graphic pattern; or drawing squiggles or curves instead of straight lines.

COLORWASHING is an easy way to dress up less-than-perfect walls, to enhance plaster or stuccoed walls or to soften any finish. Apply the wash with a sponge or a 3" brush, leaving sponge or brush marks to add interest and dimension. This technique can also be used over wallpaper to tone down its colors or patterns.

SMOOSHING is a negative method that uses plastic drop sheets to create a marble-like texture. Spread a thin plastic drop sheet over the wet glaze and pat, rub or wrinkle with your hands. Pull the plastic off and discard. Repeat with fresh sheets of plastic.

SPECIALTY PAINTS are available to give you the look of stucco and plaster. Or, for a child's room or a playroom, consider chalkboard paint, which can be written on with chalk. Frame with wood, if desired, and add a rail to hold chalk and an eraser.

HINTS & TIPS

Experiment on sample boards before attempting any technique.

Choose from a wide selection of professional patterning tools or common household items like combs, spatulas, rulers, plastic wrap, etc. Divide brushes and rollers with rubber bands or masking tape or cut them to make a pattern.

When combining paint and glaze, make sure to use either water-based (latex) or oil-based (alkyd) products for both components—don't mix them. Use latex paints for positive methods, where fast drying can be a benefit. The slow drying of alkyd paints is ideal for negative methods.

Negative techniques go faster with two people—one to apply, the other to remove.

The color you apply last is the color you will see the most and vice versa.

Colors appear lighter when mixed, so always choose colors a little darker than your desired color.

For a frosted or cloudy look, use a light glaze over a dark base. Dark glazes applied over light bases usually provide the truest color results.

Is B For Boudoir

...or is it "Bedroom"?

Perhaps it's impossible for people to get involved with anything without giving it a name. This results, no doubt, from our obsession with analysis and examination, leading to a report of the findings—an impossible task without the use of words. A glance at any recently drawn floor plan reveals a plethora of labels—some are easily identifiable; others serve only to confuse.

Consider the many varieties of calling cards attached to the room once known as the **living room**. Two that come to mind immediately are state-of-the-art appellations these days: **gathering room** and **great room**. While **gathering room** seems easy enough—a place where people gather, **great room** (and the even—er—grander **grand room**) causes a slight mental stutter. Did the term grow out of some architect's notion of grandeur or is it descriptive of the size and scope of the room's dimensions. And will we be expected to do great things in such a room? It's a bit overwhelming to ponder.

Another living-area term that causes confusion among those who dare to care is **keeping room**. Presumably it's a descendant of a word used to describe some kind of room in a castle, but it may be best not to dwell on what an Arthurian nobleman might have kept here. And do you need a **family room** if you have no family?

Drawing room, **parlor** and **sitting room** bring to mind the setting for a British novel. It's difficult to imagine these rooms without lots of Victorian furniture, Persian rugs and large-mantled fireplaces. Interestingly, **drawing room** is actually a shortened form of **withdrawing room**, clearly a room to which one can withdraw. Its roots are buried in a past century's polite society—this was usually the room where the ladies went after dining while the men repaired elsewhere for cigars and brandy.

A **morning room** need not be used only in the morning, but is a sort of **sitting room** that can be used by the whole family. Of course, for actually talking, they may want to settle in the **conversation room**. To provide an escape from the rest of the family, most homes now offer a **study**—what was once called a **den**. I wonder—how many books are required before this room becomes the **library**?

Thanks to the French, we have the term **boudoir**, though why anyone would choose to refer to a **bedroom** in this way is unfathomable. The word originates from "bouder," meaning to pout or sulk, and suggests opulent design details reminiscent of Scarlett O'Hara.

Things are just as bad outside. A home might have a **veranda** in the South or a **piazza** in Europe, but is there any real difference? Add to this a **loggia** or a **portico** and the common garden variety **porch**, **patio**, **terrace** or **balcony** and one might rejoice in never again setting foot out-of-doors. And let's not forget the grand-sounding **porte cochere**—what Mother used to call the **breezeway**.

Escape back inside only to be confronted beyond the front door with **vestibule**, **foyer**, **entryway** and the ever-popular **hall**. Is there no residential solace?

Mealtimes are not exempt from this phenomenon. The **dining room** seems reserved for formal occasions, with a **breakfast room** more convenient for everyday eating—and not just for breakfast either. The **kitchen** is usually closely connected to the **dining nook**—except when the whole area is called a **country kitchen**.

Wax nostalgic for the 1950s and 1960s (those Happy Days of homes), when the most exotic room any family might have had was the **rumpus room**. People ate in the dining room, slept in the bedroom, lived in the living room and rumpussed in the rumpus room. Now we have the choice of a **leisure room**, **hearth room**, **activities room** or **media room**.

Indeed, architecture and nomenclature have come a long way since those days of the dark and dreary cave dwellings of our distant ancestors, but any further consideration of names would require withdrawing to the **lounge** and reposing on the **couch**. Or is it a **davenport**?

Photo by Bob Greenspan

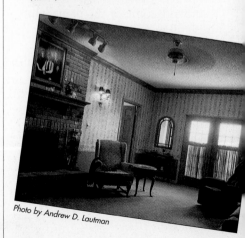

Photo by Laszlo Regos

Photo by Andrew D. Lautman

A-DOOR-ABLES The Gateway to Your Haven

Steel entry door and Radius Half View decorative glass design from Stanley Door Systems

A-DOOR-ABLES

Few architectural features can create a higher personal statement than a well-appointed entry. Finding the perfect door for your new home can be either a simple choice or threaten to overwhelm you with confusion. Should you go with the old tried-and-true wooden door? Or venture out into the worlds of steel and fiberglass? And what about windows—how many, how big and what style?

A thoughtfully chosen front door can reinforce homey feelings of welcome, comfort and security. They can also provide an opportunity for creative self-expression, whether with stained-glass sidelites, a carved surface, a unique paint job or fancy hardware. With your new door, you are presented with a blank canvas with which to convey the message "This is where I live."

(above) Pinecrest Inc. presents #445 from the Black Forest Collection

(left) By choosing a variety of specialty windows by Loewen (1-800-563-9367 or www.loewen.com), you may make a truly dramatic entry statement.

(below) Door style 220-3 from the Knotty Alder Series by Craftsmen in Wood, Mfg.

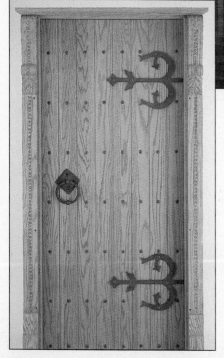

What material should I choose?

Wooden doors have been the material of choice for hundreds of years. There are two types still very common: the panel door and the batten door.

A batten door is made up of several vertical wooden planks placed side by side and held together by shorter horizontal boards, called battens. This style of door started a long time ago in the Euphrates River valley and is still in use today. But the serious drawback to batten doors is the wood's tendency to swell or shrink when it absorbs or releases moisture. When the boards dry out, gaps open up between them, allowing drafts in the cold winter months. In more humid climates, the boards expand, causing the door to swell and bind. Batten doors work best in sheds or storage buildings, where an airtight seal isn't critical.

(continued on page E18)

(above) Door no. 4533
from Bend Door Co.,
part of the JELD-WEN family

Whether you prefer the simple
elegance of a single door, or
deep embossed paneled double
doors highlighted by sidelites
and an overhead transom—
Loewen (1-800-563-9367 or
www.loewen.com) Entrance
Systems will grace any entry.

A-DOOR-ABLES

In colonial times there was a shift toward a newer design called the panel door. Though more difficult to make than batten doors, panel doors resist warping, swelling and sticking. They can also be decorated with carvings, or enhanced with fanlites above the door, narrow sidelites flanking the door and pediments supported by pilasters. However they were decorated, panel doors set the standard from the late 1700s until the late 1970s. They are available today in a wide variety of styles and sizes. From simple six-panel doors made of fir, pine, oak or mahogany, your choices are many. Adding a bit to your confusion, today's wooden doors are also available with a multitude of window options. Transoms, sidelites, half- or full-height panels of leaded glass—again, the choices are diverse.

Weather Shield's Signature Series doors combine the look of True Oak™ with the performance of steel

The Advent #2860 by Simpson Door Company

(below) The warmth and natural beauty of Bonneville Windows and Doors (418-387-1000 or www.bonnevillewd.com) french doors will bring a new dimension to your home. For ease of maintenance, they can be clad with aluminum on the outside.

All Bonneville Windows and Doors (418-387-1000 or www.bonnevillewd.com) french doors come standard with a brass-finish handle and multipoint-locking mechanism, consisting of two latches and a deadbolt lock to ensure security.

*Pease Industries introduces the Ever-Strait®
Fiberglass Door System #E411, shown here
with two S412 sidelights and R04 toplight*

*Personalize your entry from the full range of Loewen (1-800-563-9367 or www.loewen.com)
door styles, glass inserts and options that are second to none.*

*Bonneville Windows and Doors (418-387-
1000 or www.bonnevillewd.com) steel entry
doors are an invitation to live in a comfortable
stylish environment, sealed with quality.
Choose from a vast selection of doors and
decorative glass, set off with lateral panels,
transoms or varied architectural forms.*

As stated earlier, wooden doors were the standard until the late 1970s. Then along came the insulated steel door. Actually patented in 1961 by David Pease, steel doors are easy to maintain—they don't warp, crack, or swell and one or two coats of paint takes care of them for several years. Steel doors are also better barriers against fire and intruders than the average wooden door. In the 1980s, steel doors surpassed wooden doors in annual sales.

The variety of product offered by steel door manufacturers has equaled that of wooden door companies, thus giving you more diversity to pick from.

Another alternative to wood is fiberglass. These doors can be textured with a wood-grain pattern and, unlike steel, can be stained to mimic wood. They are also highly resistant to corrosion, a factor to consider if you live near saltwater. Additional benefits to fiberglass doors over wooden doors:

they offer up to five times the insulation value of comparable wood doors and will not dent, split, crack or warp like wood.

In the end, no matter how you frame it, what is important is that your door looks good, keeps the weather out and makes you feel secure. With the variety of materials, detailing, sizes and shapes, you can give your front entry a very personal look while protecting your home in the bargain.

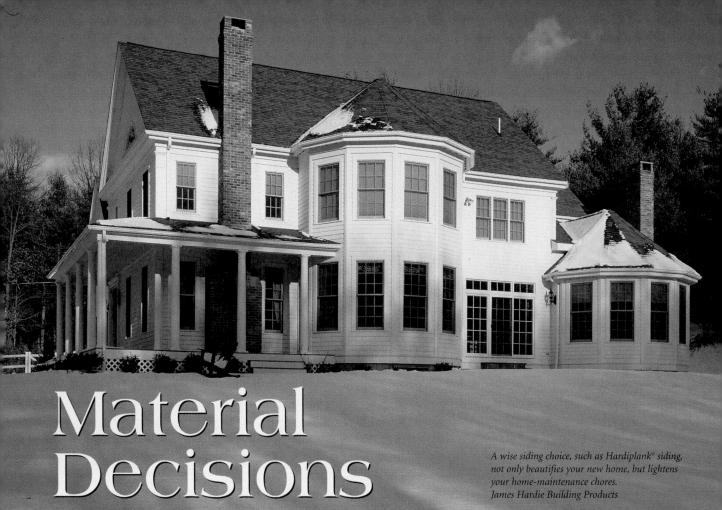

A wise siding choice, such as Hardiplank® siding, not only beautifies your new home, but lightens your home-maintenance chores.
James Hardie Building Products

Material Decisions

When seeing a house for the first time, nothing is as important to that initial emotional reaction than the look and feel of its exterior. In fact, most homeowners make primary decisions about the residence they will buy or build based on appearance, which directly reflects the material from which it is built. The various siding materials that are available for residential housing offer beautiful, practical choices in an almost unlimited selection of styles and colors.

Though determined somewhat by the style of house, the type of materials used for the exterior is largely a matter of personal choice. The choice is also based on availability, level of maintenance and the climate of the area in which the home is to be built. Following is a review of what siding materials are available and what you can expect from each of them.

Wood

Wood, in one form or another, covers more homes than any other type of exterior wall covering. Wood siding is available in two forms: natural wood, which is generally cedar or redwood, and engineered wood, which is produced by processing individual wood fibers or chips. Cedar or redwood siding is available in machine-sawn shingles, hand-split shakes and boards, which are available in beveled, shiplap, or tongue-and-groove design. While natural wood siding is usually easy to install, it is for the most part relatively expensive and should be ordered with a pre-primed coating on all six sides. Engineered wood siding is available in sixteen-foot lengths and in similar profiles as natural wood siding. It is available either smoothed or with an embossed texture and is available generally with a twenty-five year warranty.

One feature of wood siding, which is both an advantage and a disadvantage, is that it requires paint or stain to protect its finish. This means that the exterior color of a home can be changed from time to time at the preference of the owner. However, it also requires hours of labor or expensive paint contracting.

Horizontal wood siding is an excellent choice for Victorian and farmhouse designs. To see floor plans for this home, Design SHS010194, see page 151.

Photo by Raef Grohne Photographer

Horizontal and Vertical Wood Siding

Undressed horizontal wood-siding boards range in thickness from a half inch to one inch and are anywhere from four to twelve inches wide. Once in place on the exterior of a home, their total width ranges from 3⅛ to 10¼ inches. Wood siding is available in many patterns: the well-known clapboard, tongue-and-groove and various types of shiplap. It is a very popular choice in areas that lend themselves well to home styles like Cape Cod and farmhouse designs.

Vertical wood siding is generally considered a more rustic option and is usually of a local, rough-sawn species of wood. Available patterns for vertical siding include tongue-and-groove, shiplap and channel shiplap. This unique exterior choice is rarely painted, but should be treated with water repellent before installation and may be stained or bleached for a natural weathered look. The boards should be narrower than those that would be used for horizontal siding—usually less than eight inches.

Cedar Shingles

A popular choice for home exteriors in the 1920s and 1930s, cedar shingles are now making a comeback. They have many advantages over other types of wood siding: they require little maintenance beyond staining at installation, enjoy a long lifetime (often over 40 years), and lend a charming appearance to a home's facade. They also can be obtained with a fire retardant. However, cedar shingles are expensive and take time and experience to install correctly. Shingles are usually found in red or white cedar, and range in lengths from 16 to 24 inches. They are the exteriors of choice for many Bungalow and Craftsman-style homes.

Masonry Products

Masonry exteriors include brick, stone and stucco products. Besides being wonderfully durable and versatile, they are available in thousands of varieties of shapes, colors and textures. Masonry products are usually more expensive than their wood counterparts, but they are much longer-lasting and need little or no maintenance.

Brick

An elegant choice for home exteriors—especially traditional homes—brick is fireproof, impervious to inclement weather and maintains its solid grace with little upkeep.

Above: Vertical wood siding is often used as an accent on wood-sided homes. To see floor plans for this home, Design SHS010195, see page 152.
Photo by Andrew D. Lautman, Lautman Photography

Below: Cedar shingles create a lovely design feature at gable ends in this farmhouse plan. To see floor plans for this home, Design SHS010172, see page 135.
Photo by Bob Greenspan

Brick makes an elegant choice for traditional homes and is virtually maintenance-free.   *Photo by Living Concepts Home Planning*

Most of the brick used in exteriors of homes is produced in colors of red, buff, grey or cream and in many different textures. The patterns formed by the brick units and the mortar, which hold them together, give this material an almost unlimited number of appearances. Mortar joints can be formed in many different ways to provide even further decorative (and sometimes functional) appearances. Nearly 100% of the brick used for residential construction is modular brick. Modular bricks are found in sizes from four to six inches in thickness, two to five inches in height and eight to twelve inches in length. Concrete building brick often has the appearance of clay brick and retains all of its positive features, but is lighter in weight and somewhat less expensive.

Current trends in residential brick tend toward weathered—or aged-looking—brick. Home builders are drawn to the antique appearance, especially for use in Colonial and Early American homes. There are two ways to achieve this "look." One means is to procure actual used or reclaimed brick, a method that has gained considerable popularity, particularly in cities with urban renewal projects, where old brick buildings are being demolished and materials are recycled. Another option is to use hand-formed or irregular-cast bricks, which provide the same elegant "aged" finish. These bricks are more expensive than regular modular brick, but offer an excellent option for those interested in achieving a distinctive material for their home's exterior.

Stone

Stone walls may be constructed entirely of natural stone or may be a dramatic facade to concrete masonry or wood frame. This natural material is fireproof, resistant to decay and its various colors and textures provide gorgeous exterior alternatives. It should be noted, however, that stone is quite expensive and very labor intensive to install. Many choose to use it only on portions of a home's exterior as a decorative device.

Two types of stone are available for housing exteriors—natural stone and manufactured stone. Common natural stone products include granite, sandstone and limestone. Granite is a very hard material that can be smooth or left in a coarse finish. It comes in shades of black and white as well as variations of pink, green and yellow. Sandstone, while an attractive choice, is porous and may have to be treated to improve its insulation properties. It comes in colors ranging from brown and tan to rust. Limestone is more efficiently used in dry rather than wet climates, because it tends to deteriorate in humidity. Its most popular colors are white, dark grey and tan.

Manufactured stone is a veneer material made from lightweight concrete that has the appearance of natural stone. It may also be made from fiberglass. It is versatile, lighter in weight than stone, and can be applied over almost any kind of surface. It is a great alternative in areas where natural stone is not readily available and is more waterproof and weatherproof than the real thing—although some people do not like what they describe as an "imitation" look.

Stucco

Comprised of sand, cement, limestone and water, stucco can be applied to just about any kind of exterior wall construction—wood frame and concrete block being the most common. It is a common exterior choice for homes in British Columbia and the Prairie Provinces. It is also available in a synthetic fiberglass-based form from a number of manufacturers. This man-made material can be sprayed onto a prepared surface, accepts paint more readily, cracks much less at stress points and can withstand the ravages of time and weather better than the natural product.

Vinyl

Vinyl siding is available in designs to match virtually all architectural styles. The cost of vinyl varies according to thickness and color, but it is relatively inexpensive. Vinyl is long lasting, but its color may fade and cannot be recoated or replaced. It can also develop a "chalky" look from weathering. Vinyl can buckle if installed improperly and it becomes less resistant to impact when subjected to extreme cold; it is easily damaged by hail as well. Vinyl also expands and contracts more than other materials, and this must be allowed for during installation. However, warranties against blistering, cracking, chipping and other damage can extend up to fifty years.

Aluminum and Steel

Aluminum and steel siding are sold in interlocking strips to give the appearance of clapboard. They are easy to install, lightweight, fire resistant, and rot and insect resistant. One drawback is that the metal, unless well backed by insulation, absorbs heat in summer and loses inside heat in winter.

The cost of aluminum siding can vary according to thickness, pattern, length and finish. Hail and oxidation can affect its surface. Vinyl-coated aluminum resists impact but it is not practical to recoat it. This siding is durable and can have extended warranties, which do not cover impact damage.

Steel siding is fairly popular as a residential siding. It comes in a range of colors and textures and resists dents better than aluminum, making it more suitable in the hail-belt regions of the country. It is not a good choice, however, in areas near salt water or where there is heavy air pollution. Any breaks or nicks in the surface finish must be touched up properly and promptly or it will rust. Steel is much heavier than aluminum and may require professional installation.

Fiber Cement

One of the most highly recommended types of manufactured siding is fiber-cement. This type of siding is 90% Portland cement mixed with finely ground sand, natural cellulose fibers, additives and water, combined and cured through a unique process to give one of the most

durable sidings available. Fiber-cement has the look, feel and workability of natural wood. However, it won't rot, split, warp, buckle or swell. This siding product also has a dimensional stability that allows it to hold paint up to 3 or 4 times longer than wood or wood-based products, which translates to one of the lowest maintenance options available to homeowners. Fiber-cement is also moisture-proof and resistant to termites.

Fiber-cement comes in a wide variety of offerings to suit all architectural styles. Most are designed to simulate the look of wood panels or clapboard. One of the most respected, leading manufacturers of fiber-cement siding also produces lap siding options that have the look of fresh-cut cedar, shingles with the look of cedar, and many traditional styles such as Colonial siding, which has the unmistakable character of a smooth-channel lap shadow line. One drawback with fiber-cement is that, in some areas, not all contractors are familiar with this product. However, with the rapid acceptance of fiber-cement, this is becoming less of an issue.

Any manufactured siding you buy should come with a comprehensive warranty. For example, one of the leading fiber-cement manufacturers offers a fifty-year limited transferable product warranty. Protected by such a warranty, from a reliable and well-known manufacturer, you can be sure you'll be spending your future weekends barbecuing and not painting and scraping.

Stone accents grace the facade of this traditional home and bring out the beauty of its entry.
Photo by Karen Stuthard

Right: Stucco is a long-lasting product that works well on European-style homes. The synthetic version weathers better than natural stucco.
Photo by Living Concepts Home Planning

Below: Fiber-cement products such as Hardiplank® siding has the warmth of wood without the constant upkeep.
James Hardie Building Products

Future Trends

According to North American housing industry experts, traditional materials like wood have become less desirable due to factors already mentioned such as cost, performance and availability. The present building boom has exacerbated the situation—an increased demand for natural materials (reducing available stands of older trees) has significantly driven up costs, making natural wood unaffordable for many. New laboratory-created materials and wood products created from younger trees will continue to be necessary as the Canadian population increases, with different regions of the country relying on particular types of products. Homeowners will profit if manufacturers, distributors and dealers continue to provide low-maintenance, easy-to-install and natural-looking siding products.

All Things Aside

Research all the possibilities before you decide on a final siding for your new home. You'll likely discover many factors that influence your decision—budget, availability of materials, ease of maintenance. Be sure to ask about the energy efficiency of the various types of siding. Some are better insulators than others and some are not practical for certain areas of the country. You'll also have to live with whatever you choose for the length of time you occupy your home, so choose something that you like—and choose something that will be easy for you to maintain. In addition, keep in mind that choices you make now will affect the resale value of your home in the future.

Comparing Siding Choices

Product	Pros	Cons
Wood & Wood-Based Siding Products	Natural product Natural appearance	Needs periodic repainting or refinishing Can weather unevenly if left unfinished Will often swell, warp or buckle Termite and insect damage Combustible
Shingles	Appearance Durability Weather-exposure flexible	Can weather unevenly Slow to install Expensive
Masonry Products	Low maintenance Durable Many varieties and colors Natural and synthetic options available	Often more expensive May be difficult to install
Vinyl	Low maintenance Fast installation Lifetime warranty	Will melt when exposed to significant heat source Unsightly overlapped seams Can be damaged by flying debris Color can fade over time Can't change color Requires professional installation
Steel and Aluminum	Long life Low maintenance	Color can fade over time May require specialized repainting Susceptible to dents Scrapes and nail-holes can cause corrosion and rust Requires professional installation
Fiber-Cement	Look and feel of natural wood Won't warp, split rot, buckle or swell Holds paint 3 to 4 times longer than other products Resists weather damage Resists damage from flying debris Non-combustible Extensive warranty Resists insects and woodpeckers	Not all siding installation contractors are familiar with the product

Welcome Home!

Finding just the right-size Victorian home to build was a challenge for Al and Patricia Bolum of Langley, B.C. It needed to have enough bedrooms and plenty of gathering space to accommodate the needs of the family, which includes two children.

"We were particularly attracted to the wrap-around porch and the entry of this design," says Patricia Bolum. "And it was just the perfect size for us, without being overly large."

Spacious formal spaces and open family and breakfast rooms inhabit the interior, while a covered porch surrounds the house the Bolums selected. Patricia likes to decorate the porch with hanging plants and loves the way light is filtered in through windows in all areas of the home.

Bedrooms on the second floor include a large owners suite and three family bedrooms—more than enough room for everyone. Bedroom 2 even sports a lovely window seat.

The plan (Design SHS010253) was built generally true to its original design, though the Bolums did customize a few things to their taste. For instance, the hutch space in the dining room gained side windows to admit a bit more light into the dining room. And the small window in the kitchen was replaced by additional cupboard space. They also chose to lower the snack bar in the kitchen, providing a cleaner, more even line to the breakfast room.

Al did a portion of the interior trim work himself—including door trim and baseboards—to help hold down construction costs. In the future, the Bolums might consider more exterior trim, such as filigree work between the posts on the porch, and other Victorian-style trim.

Work-saving features became a focus for the Bolums when choosing some of the main features of the home: maintenance-free vinyl siding and in-pane grilles in the windows.

The home is five years old and is still the pride of the Bolum family. Patricia says, "We're just happy with everything about the house."

For more information about this home, see page 190.

Photo by Raef Grohne Photographer

This home, as shown in the photograph, may differ from the actual blueprints. For more detailed information, please check the floor plans carefully.

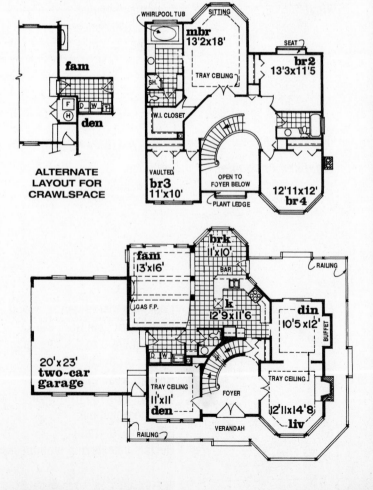

Plan Facts • How To Order Home Plans

SELECT HOME DESIGNS QUALITY

Within this directory of home plans from Select Home Designs, you will find a large variety of new designs as well as hundreds of our most popular builder-proven plans. We offer construction documents created for today's building methods, developed by our design and production teams with a single goal of producing the finest drawings and materials lists available. More than 350,000 new homes have been built from our plans; nearly two thirds have been sold to industry members such as real estate companies, land developers and builders—folks who have a discerning eye for high-quality drawings.

On your specific instructions, each set of detailed construction drawings is individually printed to allow the best reproduction possible. Placing your order is the first, all-important step toward completion of a quality-built new home. Plans convey not only design ideas, but also exactly what must be done in terms of foundation and wall placement, area configuration, structural materials, location of electrical outlets and specifically all of the items, in precise detail, that must be used in the construction of your new home. Plans are drawn using ¼-inch scale (dimensioned in feet and inches).

HOW TO SEARCH FOR A PLAN

To help you navigate through the plan sections, the designs in this volume are arranged in order of size (square footage), except for Designer's Choice, Cottages, Garages and Grade Level/Basement Entry homes, which have their own sections. Prices are conveniently located on page E30. As with construction expenses, the larger and more complicated the house, the more it costs to design . . . accordingly, the higher the price for blueprints. Remember, however, even our most expensive plan is thousands of dollars less than a custom design.

Within each size group, you'll find a large variety of styles to suit your preferences and property conditions. Many are easily changed to accommodate specific conditions. For instance, if you have a sloping site and choose a plan with a basement foundation, it is an easy matter for a builder to change the walls to provide a walk-out basement. Similarly, exterior finishes, such as stucco, can be changed to siding, usually without modifying the plan. Room descriptions may not be as you might like them, yet, except for kitchens and baths, rooms can usually be transformed with ease. For example, you may wish to change a formal dining room to a casual eating area or a den. Keep this flexibility in mind as you look through the sections. It may help you choose a design that, at first glance, seems inappropriate.

THE PLAN PACKAGES

For your convenience, we have created four plan package options: the **MASTER, STANDARD, MINIMUM** and **PROJECT PLANPAKS.** Each is designed for a particular set of circumstances.

Today's building regulations, along with the multitude of trade specialists involved in the building process, demand several sets of construction drawings for each house. Some can be shared, but others such as those going to regulatory agencies, financial institutions and suppliers will be retained by them. Your contractor will want a set of his own and you'll want a set to keep for your reference.

In order to have sufficient sets, we recommend you order the **STANDARD PLANPAK,** which offers eight complete sets of blueprints, notes and standard details. In some locations, such as rural townships where building regulations are less restrictive, the **MINIMUM PLANPAK,** containing five sets, may be sufficient. The **PROJECT PLANPAK** contains one set of blueprints and is only available for our garage plans and yard/garden projects.

The **MASTER PLANPAK** is the most versatile option, because it allows reproduction of an unlimited number of sets and allows changes to be made on its erasable vellum. It is produced in response to your order. The original drawing is plotted on a reproducible and erasable vellum (sometimes called a sepia or mylar) which is a special durable paper. When changes are needed, a professional can erase the original information and easily add new details, eliminating the need to redraw the plans. After the revisions have been made, any number of the revised sets may be copied to complete the construction process.

Builders wishing to build several houses of the same design will find the **MASTER PLANPAK** the most useful and economical choice. A limited license to make revisions and extra copies for one year accompanies each order.

NOTE: The license provided with the **MASTER PLANPAK** does not include the right to re-sell the plan and limits the construction of more than one dwelling to one year from the date of purchase. To avoid copyright license infringement after this date, it is necessary to contact Select Home Designs to renew the license for extended use.

TO BUILD IN REVERSE

You may wish to build one of our plans in reverse of the way it is shown. This is easy to do—simply order one or two extra sets of "mirror reverse" prints in addition to your regular order. The reversed sets come with the lettering and dimensions backward. Reverse prints are particularly useful in visualizing how the house will appear on your lot and can be extremely important to the builder with siting the house on your lot. However, they cannot be read easily and require the regular sets to build with. For some regions where mirror reverses are not accepted by the building authorities, we have produced reverse plans that are available with dimensions and lettering completely re-drawn, resulting in a plan that is "right reading." You will see this logo on many plans, which indicates that the plan is available in reverse, yet right reading. There is an additional fee of $125 on all PLANPAKS, when you order these prints.

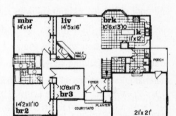

Plan Facts

OUR EXCHANGE POLICY

Since blueprints are printed in response to your order, we cannot honor requests for refunds. However, we will exchange your entire first order for an equal or greater number of blueprints within our plan collection within 90 days of the original order. The entire content of your original order must be returned to our offices before an exchange will be processed. If the returned blueprints look used, redlined or copied, we will not honor your exchange. Fees for exchanging your blueprints are as follows: 20% of the amount of the original order. . .*plus* the difference in cost if exchanging for a design in a higher price bracket or *less* the difference in cost if exchanging for a design in a lower price bracket. (**The MASTER PLANPAK is not exchangeable.**) You will be responsible for postage and handling—see page E30 for details. Shipping and handling charges are not refundable.

REGIONAL BUILDING REQUIREMENTS

All our pre-drawn plans are designed to meet or exceed national and provincial building standards in effect at the time they were drawn. Our strict program of quality control assures the highest quality blueprints. However, local building regulations, increased concern over safety and energy consumption, non-standard building conditions, such as high snow loads and wind loads, seismic requirements, complex foundation or structural specifications exceeding nationally recognized building codes may result in the need to provide a report and/or "seal" from an engineer or architect in your area. Although required infrequently, this service is the responsibility of the plan buyer and may be obtained for an additional fee locally from a qualified professional. For guidance, contact your local building department.

Because codes and requirements can change and may vary from jurisdiction to jurisdiction, Select Home Designs cannot warrant compliance with any specific code or regulation. All pre-drawn plans can be adapted to your local building codes or regulations. It is the responsibility of the builder to see that the structure is built in strict compliance with all governing municipal codes.

ITEMIZED QUANTITY MATERIALS LIST

A list of materials is the second most important construction document, next to the blueprints themselves. Our itemized list of materials contains all lumber dimensions, quantities and specifications, plus a handy framing summary for easy estimating and ordering. Other sections include window and door schedules, interior millwork, insulation, interior finish, cabinetry, electrical fixtures, plumbing fixtures and other valuable information.

This information will help you get faster, more reliable bids from your contractor and building supplier—and helps avoid the expense of unused material and waste. If you are a professional builder, you can save the time and money it takes to prepare building estimates. They will also be of great help in material pricing, purchasing and job scheduling.

Due to the wide variety of building practices and availability of materials from region to region, some adjustments may be necessary to suit local circumstances. Similarly, mechanical details (heating, plumbing, electrical installation) must be supplied by local specialists. Periodically, a plan may not have a corresponding materials list available. Any questions should be directed to our sales representatives before proceeding with construction. Also, any changes made to your plan may affect existing material quantities and specifications.

ESTIMATING PACKAGE

In order to assist you in developing a more accurate estimate of the material costs before actually purchasing the construction drawings, we now offer an Estimating Package for many of our plans. This package contains the complete itemized list of materials and quantities together with a detail sheet, which shows all four views of the house, floor plans, total square footage of finished floor space and width and depth. (Finished area does not include garage, basement and bonus space.) Please ask if an Estimating Package is available for the plan you have chosen.

PLAN PRICES

All prices are valid for twelve (12) months from the date of publication. We will continue to accept plan orders placed thereafter, subject to price adjustments, if any.

We welcome the opportunity to provide no-obligation quotations on an individual project basis, including custom presentation work, revisions to pre-drawn plans, custom design, engineering and metric conversion. Simply call our toll-free number or, if you prefer, use our fax line.

RE-ORDERS

If you find you did not request a sufficient number of sets when you placed your original order, you may purchase additional identical sets at the extra set price. Your order must be placed within thirty (30) days of the original invoice date. Please quote your invoice number when re-ordering.

TO ORDER PRE-DESIGNED PLANS BY MAIL OR FAX

For mail or fax orders (fax line 604-251-3212), please fill out the order form on page E30 and mail to the address on the order form or fax to 604-251-3212. If time is of the essence, you may call on our toll-free number, 1-800-663-6739, and speak with one of our friendly customer service representatives who will help you place your order. Please be sure to note the key code in the lower right hand corner of the order form and be ready to supply this information when the representative asks for it. For Customer Service, call toll-free 1-800-898-3878.

PHOTOGRAPHS

We archive a selection of pictures for each new plan publication to show the results which others have achieved when building one of our designs. May we share the pride you have in the new home you have built from our plans? Send us photographs to be considered for future publication (at least one exterior front view), together with your name, address and telephone number. If your house photo is chosen for publication on a cover, we'll reward you with a cheque for $250.

To Order Call Toll Free 1-800-663-6739

Plan Facts

ABOUT COPYRIGHTS

Federal law protects the intellectual property of architects and home design firms. This protection gives the copyright owner exclusive rights that only they are entitled to. These rights include the right to make copies, the right to distribute copies, the right to create adaptations and the right to license and publicly display the protected work. It is unlawful for anyone to exercise any of these exclusive rights without the consent of the copyright owner.

It is often mistakenly assumed that making a few changes to a plan will protect the user from copyright infringement. It is also incorrectly assumed that the purchaser may build more than one house from the sets of drawings. In all cases, the buyer of Select Home Designs plans is purchasing a restricted license for the specific purpose of building one house and may not make copies, resell or build more than a single dwelling. The only exception is the MASTER PLANPAK license, which permits the purchaser to build more than one dwelling, make copies and changes for a period of one year from the date of purchase.

In order to avoid the possibility of inadvertently infringing on the rights of the copyright holder, please keep these points in mind:

1. Don't copy designs or floor plans from this or any publication or electronic medium (such as CD-ROM or the Internet) or from any existing home.
2. Blueprints cannot be copied or reproduced.
3. Construction drawings cannot be redrawn without permission.
4. Revised plans cannot be reused.
5. All parties, including designers, architects, home builders, subcontractors, real estate agents, engineers, building departments, blueprinters and the purchaser may be held responsible for infringement.
6. Don't use Select Home Designs plans to build more than one house.

All plans appearing in this publication are protected by copyright law. Reproduction by any means of these illustrations or construction documents, whether in whole or in part, or preparation of derivative works thereof, without prior written permission, is strictly prohibited. The purchase of a set of home plans in no way transfers any copyright or other ownership interest in it to the buyer, except for a limited license to use that set of home plans for the construction of one and only one dwelling. Building more than one house from Select Home Designs MINIMUM, STANDARD or PROJECT PLANPAK constitutes copyright infringement.

The purchaser of the MASTER PLANPAK is granted a limited license to make modifications to the plans and to construct more than one house for a period of one year from the date of purchase. Use of these plans in either original form, or as derivative works, for resale, distribution, or otherwise transferred to any person, other than the original purchaser is prohibited. In order to continue using the MASTER PLANPAK for the construction of additional houses beyond the one-year limit, builders must extend the limited license granted with the MASTER PLANPAK through the payment of an annual renewal fee of $399.

Above: Photo by Bizzo Photography, see page 31

Photo by Andrew D. Lautman, Lautman Photography see page 175

PRICE SCHEDULE
(Prices guaranteed through December 31, 2000)

Tier	Master PlanPak® erasable/reproducible vellums	Standard PlanPak® 8 sets of blueprints	Minimum PlanPak® 5 sets of blueprints	Project PlanPak® 1 set of blueprints
P1	$95	$55	$40	$20
P2	$110	$70	$55	$35
P3	$130	$90	$75	$55
P4	$150	$110	$95	$75
P5	$190	$150	$135	$115
P6	$230	$190	$175	$155
A1	$485	$385	$345	N/A
A2	$530	$430	$395	N/A
A3	$585	$485	$445	N/A
A4	$675	$575	$515	N/A
C1	$740	$640	$575	N/A
C2	$805	$705	$635	N/A
C3	$855	$755	$685	N/A
C4	$905	$805	$735	N/A
L1	$955	$855	$785	N/A
L2	$1005	$905	$835	N/A

Options for plans in Tiers A1–L4
Extra Set(s)—additional identical blueprints
When ordered within 30 days of original purchase $50
Mirror-Reverse Blueprints
To build in reverse of plan shown. Lettering and dimensions appear backward $50
Right Reading Reverse (if available)
To build in reverse of plan shown. Lettering and dimensions appear right reading.
Additional fee to all PlanPaks $125

Materials List with plan order
Details all materials needed to build your home..............$69
Estimating Package/Materials List
Includes front, rear and side exterior views, floor plan(s) and materials list for pricing prior to buying plans..............$89

Options for plans in Tiers P1–P6
Extra Set(s)—additional identical blueprints
When ordered within 30 days of original purchase................$10
Mirror-Reverse Blueprints
To build in reverse of plan shown. Lettering and dimensions appear backward $10
Materials List with plan order, Tier P5–P6
Details all materials needed to build your project $25
Materials List included with plan orders for Tier P1–P4 projects

Call Toll Free 1-800-663-6739
Monday through Friday 8 AM - 8 PM Eastern
Our answering service can place orders after hours or on weekends.
Metro Vancouver residents call 604-879-4144. Voice mail message center available 24 hours, seven days a week!

Plans by Fax
604-251-3212
Fax 24 hours, seven days a week!

Plans by e-mail
selecthomedesigns@msn.com
e-mail 24 hours, seven days a week!

Visit our Web site at sales@selecthomedesigns.com
For Customer Service, call toll free 1-800-898-3878
Plans by Mail
In Canada, mail to:
Select Home Designs
Suite 301, 611 Alexander St.
Vancouver, B.C. V6A 1E1

In the U.S., mail to:
Home Planners
3275 West Ina Road, Suite 110
Tucson, Arizona 85741

ORDER FORM

PLEASE RUSH ME THE FOLLOWING:

_____ Master PlanPak® for plan _____ $ _____
_____ Standard PlanPak® for plan _____ $ _____
_____ Minimum PlanPak® for plan _____ $ _____
_____ Project PlanPak® for plan _____ $ _____
_____ Extra set(s) $ _____
_____ Sets of mirror reverse prints $ _____
Right-reading reverse (if available) $ _____

Itemized Quantity Materials List with plan order
Details all materials needed to build your home $ _____

Estimating Package/Materials List without plan order for plan_____ $ _____
If available, includes 4 views, floor plans, and list of materials for pricing before you buy plans.

Garage/Craft Cottage/Garden Studio/Gazebo, plan _____ $ _____
Garage/Craft Cottage/Garden Studio Materials List. Price Tier P5–L4. $ _____

SHIPPING AND HANDLING
For delivery outside of North America, call for quote. $25.00
Canadian residents add G.S.T. or the applicable Harmonized Sales Tax. $ _____
B.C. residents add provincial sales tax. $ _____
Residents of AZ & MI add appropriate sales tax. $ _____

TOTAL $ _____

YOUR ADDRESS
Name _____
Street _____
City _____ Province or State _____
Postal Code or Zip _____ Country _____
Daytime telephone number _____

For Credit Card Orders
Please fill in the information below:
Credit Card Number _____
Expiration Date _____
Check one:
❑ Visa ❑ MasterCard ❑ American Express
Please check appropriate box:
❑ Licensed Builder-Contractor ❑ Homeowner

SELECT HOME DESIGNS

Order Form Key
SHT01

INDEX

INDEX

DESIGN	PRICE	PAGE	RIGHT READ REVERSE	MATERIALS LIST	ESTIMATING PACKAGE
SHS010187	A4	146		Y	
SHS010188	A4	147		Y	
SHS010189	C1	148		Y	
SHS010190	C2	148	Y	Y	
SHS010191	C1	149		Y	Y
SHS010192	A4	150		Y	
SHS010193	C1	151		Y	
SHS010194	A4	151		Y	Y
SHS010195	C1	152		Y	Y
SHS010196	A4	152		Y	Y
SHS010197	A4	153		Y	
SHS010198	A4	153			
SHS010199	A4	154	Y	Y	
SHS010200	A4	154		Y	
SHS010201	A4	155			
SHS010202	C1	156	Y	Y	Y
SHS010203	C1	157	Y	Y	Y
SHS010204	A4	158	Y	Y	
SHS010205	A4	158	Y	Y	
SHS010206	C1	159	Y	Y	Y
SHS010207	C1	160		Y	
SHS010208	C1	161		Y	Y
SHS010209	C1	161	Y	Y	
SHS010210	A4	162		Y	
SHS010211	A4	163		Y	
SHS010212	C2	164		Y	
SHS010213	A4	165		Y	Y
SHS010214	A4	165		Y	
SHS010215	A4	166		Y	
SHS010216	C1	166		Y	
SHS010217	A4	167		Y	
SHS010218	A4	167		Y	
SHS010219	C1	168	Y	Y	Y
SHS010220	C1	168		Y	Y
SHS010221	A4	169		Y	
SHS010222	A4	170		Y	
SHS010223	C1	170	Y	Y	Y
SHS010224	A4	171		Y	Y
SHS010225	A4	171		Y	
SHS010226	A4	172		Y	
SHS010227	A3	172			
SHS010228	C1	173	Y	Y	Y
SHS010229	A3	173			
SHS010230	A4	174	Y	Y	
SHS010231	A4	174		Y	
SHS010232	C1	175	Y	Y	Y
SHS010233	C1	176	Y	Y	Y
SHS010234	A4	177	Y	Y	
SHS010235	C1	177	Y	Y	Y
SHS010236	A4	178		Y	
SHS010237	A4	178		Y	
SHS010238	C2	179		Y	Y
SHS010239	C1	180		Y	Y
SHS010240	C1	180	Y	Y	Y
SHS010241	A4	181			
SHS010242	A4	182	Y	Y	Y
SHS010243	A4	183		Y	
SHS010244	A4	183		Y	
SHS010245	A4	184		Y	Y
SHS010246	A3	185			
SHS010247	A4	186		Y	
SHS010248	A4	186		Y	
SHS010249	A4	187		Y	
SHS010250	A4	188		Y	
SHS010251	C2	189	Y	Y	Y
SHS010252	C2	190		Y	Y
SHS010253	C1	190		Y	Y
SHS010254	C2	191	Y	Y	Y
SHS010255	C1	192		Y	
SHS010256	C1	192		Y	
SHS010257	C1	193		Y	Y
SHS010258	C2	194	Y	Y	Y
SHS010259	C1	194		Y	
SHS010260	C1	195		Y	
SHS010261	C1	196		Y	Y
SHS010262	C1	197		Y	
SHS010263	C3	198		Y	
SHS010264	A4	198		Y	
SHS010265	C1	199		Y	
SHS010266	C1	200	Y	Y	
SHS010267	C1	201		Y	
SHS010268	C1	202		Y	
SHS010269	C1	203		Y	
SHS010270	C2	204		Y	Y
SHS010271	C1	205		Y	Y
SHS010272	A4	206			
SHS010273	C1	207		Y	Y
SHS010274	C1	208		Y	
SHS010275	C1	208		Y	Y
SHS010276	C1	209		Y	
SHS010277	C1	210		Y	
SHS010278	C3	211		Y	
SHS010279	C1	211		Y	
SHS010280	C1	212		Y	
SHS010281	C1	212		Y	
SHS010282	C2	213		Y	Y
SHS010283	C2	214		Y	Y
SHS010284	C3	214		Y	
SHS010285	C2	215	Y	Y	Y
SHS010286	C1	215		Y	
SHS010287	C2	216		Y	Y
SHS010288	C4	217		Y	
SHS010289	C2	218		Y	
SHS010290	C2	219		Y	
SHS010291	C2	220		Y	
SHS010292	C2	221	Y	Y	Y
SHS010293	C3	221	Y	Y	Y
SHS010294	C3	222		Y	
SHS010295	C3	223			
SHS010296	L1	224		Y	Y
SHS010297	L1	225	Y	Y	Y
SHS010298	L1	226		Y	
SHS010299	L1	227		Y	
SHS010300	C4	227		Y	Y
SHS010301	A2	228		Y	
SHS010302	A2	228		Y	Y
SHS010304	A2	229		Y	
SHS010305	A2	230		Y	
SHS010306	A2	230		Y	
SHS010307	A2	231		Y	
SHS010308	A2	231		Y	
SHS010309	A2	232		Y	
SHS010310	A3	232		Y	
SHS010311	A3	233		Y	
SHS010312	A3	233		Y	
SHS010313	A1	234		Y	
SHS010314	A1	235		Y	
SHS010315	A2	236		Y	
SHS010316	A1	236		Y	
SHS010317	A1	237		Y	
SHS010318	A1	238		Y	Y
SHS010319	A1	238		Y	Y
SHS010320	A2	239	Y	Y	
SHS010321	A2	240		Y	
SHS010322	A2	241		Y	
SHS010323	A2	241		Y	
SHS010324	A2	242		Y	
SHS010325	A2	242		Y	Y
SHS010326	A2	243		Y	Y
SHS010327	A2	244		Y	
SHS010328	A2	245		Y	
SHS010329	A2	246	Y	Y	
SHS010330	A2	246		Y	
SHS010331	A4	247		Y	Y
SHS010332	A2	248		Y	Y
SHS010333	A2	249		Y	
SHS010334	A2	249		Y	
SHS010335	A2	250		Y	
SHS010336	A2	251		Y	
SHS010337	A2	251		Y	
SHS010338	A2	252		Y	
SHS010339	A2	252		Y	
SHS010340	A3	253	Y	Y	
SHS010341	A3	254		Y	
SHS010342	A3	255		Y	
SHS010343	A2	255		Y	
SHS010344	A4	256	Y	Y	Y
SHS010345	A3	256		Y	Y
SHS010346	A3	257	Y	Y	
SHS010347	A3	258		Y	
SHS010348	A4	258		Y	Y
SHS010349	A4	259	Y	Y	Y
SHS010350	A3	259		Y	
SHS010351	A3	260		Y	
SHS010352	A3	260		Y	
SHS010353	A3	261		Y	
SHS010354	A3	262		Y	
SHS010355	A3	263	Y	Y	Y
SHS010356	C1	263		Y	
SHS010357	C2	264	Y	Y	Y
SHS010358	A4	265	Y	Y	Y
SHS010359	P5	266		Y	
SHS010360	P6	266		Y	
SHS010361	P5	267	Y	Y	
SHS010362	P6	267		Y	
SHS010363	P5	268		Y	Y
SHS010364	P6	268		Y	Y
SHS010365	P4	269		Y	
SHS010366	P5	269		Y	Y
SHS010367	P4	270		Y	
SHS010368	P5	270		Y	
SHS010369	P4	271		Y	
SHS010370	P5	271		Y	Y
SHS010371	P6	272		Y	Y
SHS010372	P6	272		Y	Y

DESIGNER'S CHOICE

This home, as shown in photograph, may differ from the actual blueprints. For more detailed information, please check the floor plans carefully.

Photo by Bob Greenspan

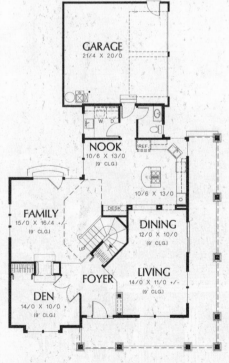

GARAGE
21/4 X 20/0

NOOK
10/6 X 13/0
(9' CLG.)

REF

W D

10/6 X 13/0

FAMILY
15/0 X 16/4 +/-
(9' CLG.)

DESK

DINING
12/0 X 10/0
(9' CLG.)

FOYER

LIVING
14/0 X 11/0 +/-
(9' CLG.)

DEN
14/0 X 10/0
(9' CLG.)

Available reverse

right reading

PLANT SHELF

BR. 3
10/6 X 13/0

FAMILY BELOW

LINEN

DN

BR. 2
12/4 X 11/0

VAULTED MASTER
12/0 X 15/0 +/-

Design SHS010001

First Floor: 1,371 square feet
Second Floor: 916 square feet
Total: 2,287 square feet
Width: 43'-0" **Depth:** 69'-0"
Price Schedule: A4

The decorative pillars and the wraparound porch give a perfect introduction to this charming bungalow. Inside, from the foyer where an angled stairway leads to the second level, French doors lead to the den that shares a see-through fireplace with the two-story family room. The large island kitchen includes a writing desk, corner sink, breakfast nook and an efficient utility room. Upstairs, the owners suite is a real treat with its French-door access, vaulted ceiling and luxurious bath. Two secondary bedrooms and a full bath complete the second floor.

SELECT HOME DESIGNS

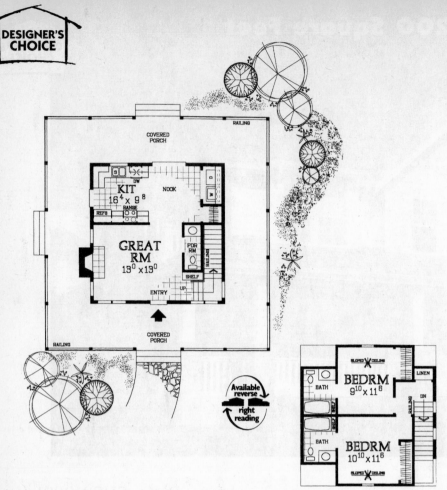

Design SHS010002

First Floor: 586 square feet
Second Floor: 486 square feet
Total: 1,072 square feet
Width: 40'-0" **Depth:** 40'-0"
Price Schedule: A4

This quaint, country-style cottage would make a fine vacation retreat. Balusters and columns deck out the wraparound porch, while the glass-paneled entry offers an elegant welcome. With a cozy fireplace and plenty of views in the great room, the interior is warmed by more than just heat—it enjoys a charming sense of the outdoors. A well-organized kitchen has its own door to the wraparound porch, as well as a dining nook that also leads outdoors.

Available reverse right reading

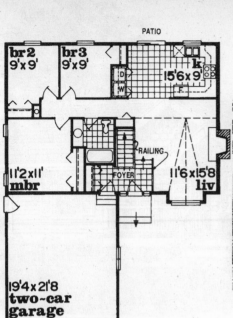

Design SHS010004

Square Footage: 1,000
Width: 38'-0" Depth: 48'-4"
Price Schedule: A1

This compact, three-bedroom design offers all the amenities of a larger home. Railings which separate the foyer and basement stairs enhance the spaciousness of the entry. The country kitchen offers wrapping U-shaped counters and a double sink with a window. Bedrooms revolve around a three-piece owners bathroom with a soaking tub. The living room has a fireplace, and sliding glass doors lead outside to the patio.

Design SHS010003

Square Footage: 1,054
Width: 42'-8" Depth: 26'-8"
Price Schedule: A2

The interior holds many amenities unusual for a plan of its size. The front porch protects the entry, which opens directly to a large living room with a masonry fireplace. It is complemented by a formal dining room open to the galley kitchen. Bedrooms share a full hall bath and have wall closets of ample size. If you choose, Bedroom 3 could double as a den or home office.

Design SHS010005

Square Footage: 1,092
Width: 64'-0" **Depth:** 32'-0"
Price Schedule: A2

Compact, yet efficient, this one-story home opens with a quaint covered porch that leads to a convenient floor plan. The great room has a vaulted ceiling and warming hearth for cozy winter blazes. The step-saving galley kitchen is pure country with space for a family-sized dining area and sliding glass doors to the rear deck. The owners bedroom has an angled entry and windows overlooking the rear yard. It shares a full bath that has a split entry with two family bedrooms (note the art niche at the entry to Bedroom 2). If you choose the crawlspace option, you'll gain space for a washer and dryer and a spot for a built-in media center. The two-car garage is reached through a side door in the kitchen.

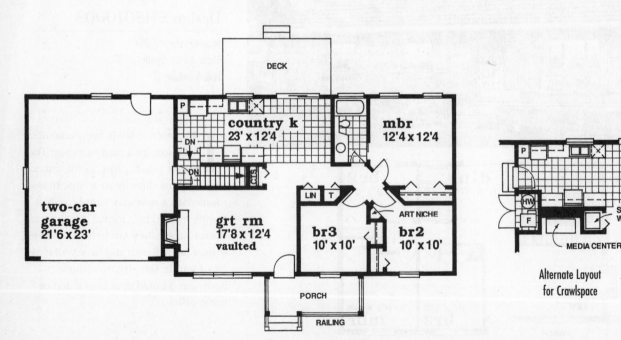

DECK

P

country k
23' x 12'4

DN

DN

CTS

mbr
12'4 x 12'4

two-car garage
21'6 x 23'

grt rm
17'8 x 12'4
vaulted

LIN   T

br3
10' x 10'

br2
10' x 10'

ART NICHE

PORCH

RAILING

P

HW

F

STACKED W/D

MEDIA CENTER

CTS

Alternate Layout
for Crawlspace

Design SHS010006

Square Footage: 1,108 square feet
Unfinished Lower Level: 620 square feet
Width: 38'-0" **Depth:** 31'-0"
Price Schedule: A2

raftsman styling and a welcoming porch create marvelous curb appeal for this design. A volume ceiling in the living and dining rooms and the kitchen make this home appear larger than its modest square footage. The owners bedroom offers a walk-in closet, full bath and a bumped-out window overlooking the rear yard. Two additional bedrooms also boast bumped-out windows and share a full bath. The lower level allows for a future bedroom, a den and a family room.

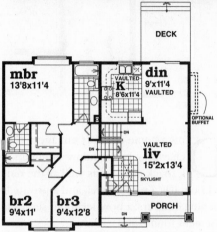

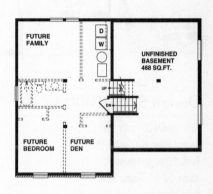

Design SHS010007

Square Footage: 1,080
Width: 42'-0" **Depth:** 48'-0"
Price Schedule: A2

circle-head window and brick facade adorn the well-balanced exterior of this compact three-bedroom home. The living room boasts a fireplace, a vaulted ceiling and a wet bar. The nearby country kitchen has a snack-bar counter that separates it from the living room. Sliding glass doors lead out to the rear yard. Bedrooms include two family bedrooms with a shared hall bath and an owners bedroom with a walk-in closet and a private bath. A laundry room sits just off the two-car garage.

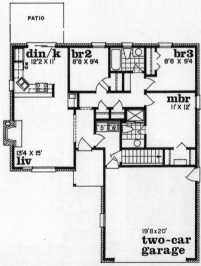

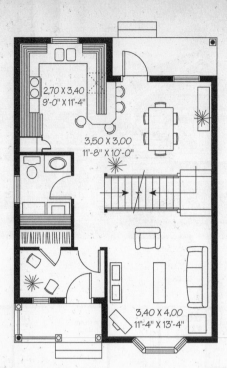

2,70 X 3,40
9'-0" X 11'-4"

3,50 X 3,00
11'-8" X 10'-0"

Available
reverse
right
reading

3,40 X 4,00
11'-4" X 13'-4"

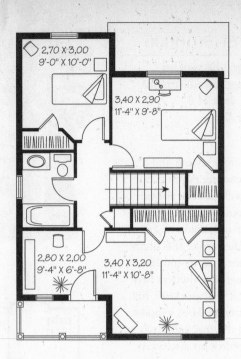

2,70 X 3,00
9'-0" X 10'-0"

3,40 X 2,90
11'-4" X 9'-8"

2,80 X 2,00
9'-4" X 6'-8"

3,40 X 3,20
11'-4" X 10'-8"

Design SHS010008

First Floor: 620 square feet
Second Floor: 620 square feet
Total: 1,240 square feet
Width: 22'-0" **Depth:** 32'-0"
Price Schedule: A3

Down-home comfort enhances the uptown spirit of this traditional home. A charming bay window brightens the living room. A U-shaped kitchen serves a snack counter as well as the dining area. Upstairs, the second-floor owners bedroom has a reading area and a private balcony. A full bath serves the second-floor sleeping quarters; a powder room serves the first floor. This home is designed with a basement foundation.

Design SHS010009

Square Footage: 1,120
Unfinished Lower Level: 1,056 square feet
Width: 44'-0" Depth: 26'-0"
Price Schedule: A2

This economical, three-bedroom, split-level home offers an efficient floor plan that can be expanded. Brick veneer and siding grace the outside, further enhanced by two box-bay windows and a bay window. The living and dining rooms on the left side of the plan offer a fireplace and buffet alcove. The U-shaped kitchen has loads of cupboards and counter space and connects directly to the dining room. Bedrooms on the right side are comprised of an owners suite with a half-bath and two family bedrooms sharing a full bath. The lower level includes space for a family room with fireplace, one or two bedrooms, and a full bath.

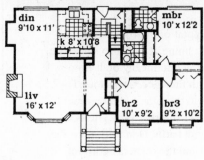

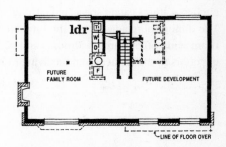

Design SHS010010

Square Footage: 1,184
Unfinished Lower Level: 902 square feet
Width: 38'-6" Depth: 60'-4"
Price Schedule: A2

This affordable home is not only appealing, but is well-suited to a narrow lot. The entry level hosts a skylit foyer and a spacious living room with a box-bay window, a fireplace and multi-paned windows. Up a few steps is the L-shaped kitchen with pantry, breakfast room, island work center and French doors to a rear patio. The owners bedroom at the rear of the plan has a private bath and linen closet, while the two family bedrooms share a full bath. Lower-level space can be developed to include a recreation room or games room, an additional bedroom and a full bath.

Design SHS010012

Square Footage: 1,267
Width: 46'-0" Depth: 50'-0"
Price Schedule: A3

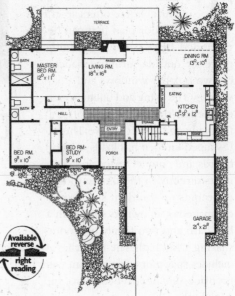

H ere is a charming Early American adaptation that will serve as a picturesque and practical retirement home. It will also serve the small family in search of an efficient, economically built home. The living area, highlighted by the raised-hearth fireplace, is spacious. The kitchen features eating space and easy access to the garage and basement. The dining room adjacent to the kitchen views the rear yard. The bedroom wing offers three bedrooms and two full baths. Don't miss the sliding doors to the terrace from the living room and the owners bedroom.

Available reverse right reading

Design SHS010011

Square Footage: 1,298
Width: 70'-0" Depth: 36'-0"
Price Schedule: A2

A front veranda, cedar lattice and solid stone chimney enhance the appeal of this one-story country-style home. The open plan begins with the great room, which has a fireplace and a plant ledge over the wall separating the living space from the country kitchen. The U-shaped kitchen has an island work counter and sliding glass doors to the rear deck and a screened porch. The owners suite has a wall closet and a private bath with a window seat.

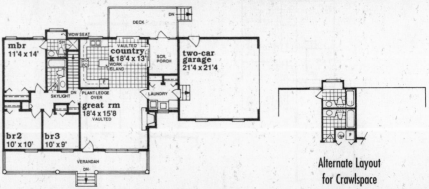

Alternate Layout for Crawlspace

Design SHS010013

Square Footage: 1,293
Width: 42'-0" Depth: 54'-4"
Price Schedule: A2

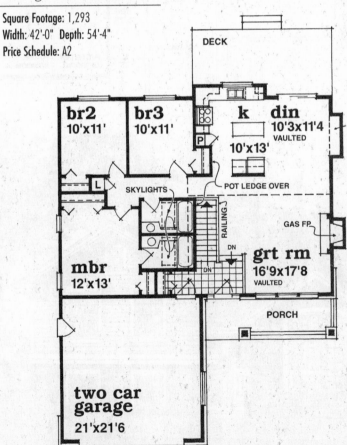

DECK

br2
10'x11'

br3
10'x11'

k

din
10'3x11'4
VAULTED

10'x13'

P

L

SKYLIGHTS

POT LEDGE OVER

RAILING

GAS FP

mbr
12'x13'

DN

DN

grt rm
16'9x17'8
VAULTED

PORCH

two car
garage
21'x21'6

Meeting the needs of first-time homebuilders, this design is, economical to build. Craftsman detailing and a quaint covered porch go a long way to create the charming exterior. Open planning filled with amenities add to the design's livability. The foyer opens to a hearth-warmed great room. Vaulted ceilings and a half-wall separating the stairs to the basement and the foyer add to the spaciousness. An open island kitchen has an adjoining dining room with sliding glass doors to the deck and box-bay buffet space. The owners bedroom adjoins two family bedrooms down the hall. It boasts His and Hers wall closets and a full bath with a soaking tub. Two family bedrooms—or make one a den—share a full bath.

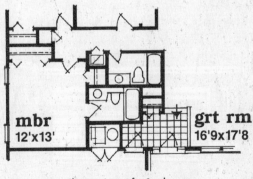

mbr
12'x13'

grt rm
16'9x17'8

Alternate Layout for Crawlspace

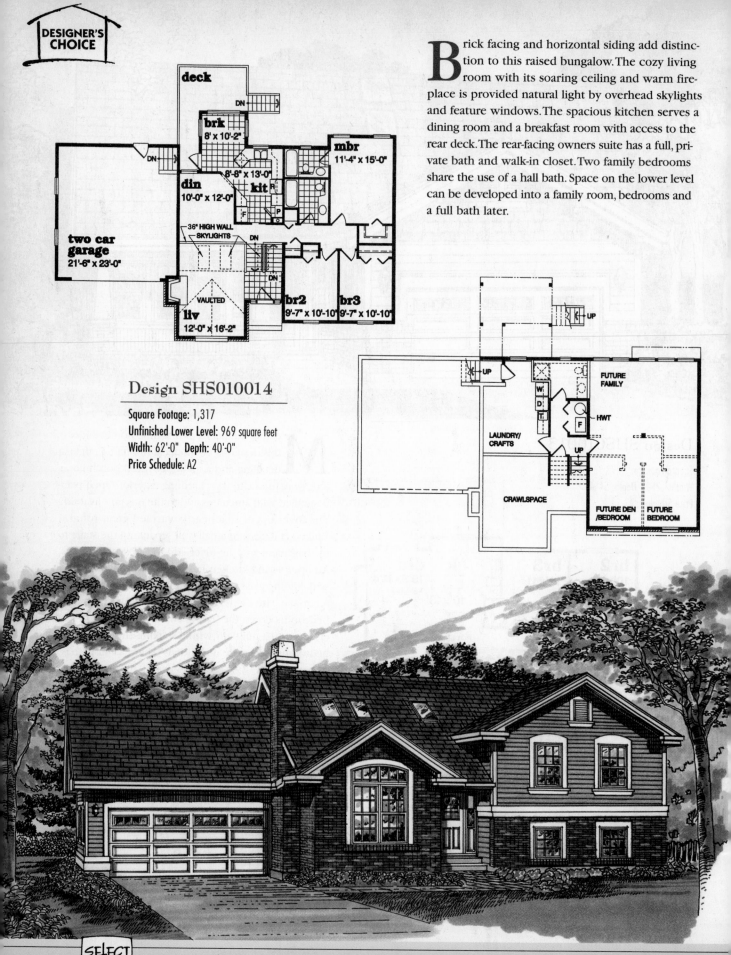

deck

DN

brk
8' x 10'-2"

DN

mbr
11'-4" x 15'-0"

din
10'-0" x 12'-0"

8'-8" x 13'-0"

kit

F

P

two car garage
21'-6" x 23'-0"

36" HIGH WALL
SKYLIGHTS

DN

DN

VAULTED

liv
12'-0" x 16'-2"

br2
9'-7" x 10'-10"

br3
9'-7" x 10'-10"

Brick facing and horizontal siding add distinction to this raised bungalow. The cozy living room with its soaring ceiling and warm fireplace is provided natural light by overhead skylights and feature windows. The spacious kitchen serves a dining room and a breakfast room with access to the rear deck. The rear-facing owners suite has a full, private bath and walk-in closet. Two family bedrooms share the use of a hall bath. Space on the lower level can be developed into a family room, bedrooms and a full bath later.

Design SHS010014

Square Footage: 1,317
Unfinished Lower Level: 969 square feet
Width: 62'-0" **Depth:** 40'-0"
Price Schedule: A2

UP

UP

W
D
T

FUTURE
FAMILY

HWT

F

LAUNDRY/
CRAFTS

UP

CRAWLSPACE

FUTURE DEN
/BEDROOM

FUTURE
BEDROOM

FOR PLAN ORDERING INFORMATION SEE PLAN

DECK

din
10'4x11'4

BUFFET

k

10'x13'

P

br3
10'x11'

br2
10'x11'

SKYLIGHTS

GAS FP

RAILING

DN

DN

mbr
12'x13'

grt rm
13' & 17'x19'8
VAULTED

two car garage
21'x21'6

SKYLIGHTS

L

SKYLIGHTS

mbr
12'x13'

Alternate Layout for Crawlspace

Design SHS010015

Square Footage: 1,319
Width: 44'-0" Depth: 54'-8"
Price Schedule: A2

Charming and economical to build, this brick ranch design is ideal for first-time homeowners or retired couples. A tiled foyer leads past the open-rail staircase to the basement into a vaulted great room. Here a gas fireplace warms the living and entertaining area. The dining room has buffet space and sliding glass doors to the rear deck. An L-shaped island kitchen is nearby and overlooks the rear deck. Three bedrooms include two family bedrooms sharing a full bath. The owners suite has two wall closets and a private bath with a soaking tub. A two-car garage sits in front of the bedrooms to shelter them from street noise.

You have the option of two or three bedrooms. One of the bedrooms could be used as a family room. A half-wall separates the foyer from the living room, which is highlighted by a window seat in its box window, a fireplace and an attached dining room. A U-shaped kitchen features abundant counter space, an angled sink under a corner plant shelf and a sunny breakfast area with access to the rear patio. The family room—or third bedroom—has a bright window seat, also. The owners bedroom has no rival for luxury. It has a bay-window seating area, large wall closet and private bath. Access the two-car garage through the service entrance at the laundry alcove.

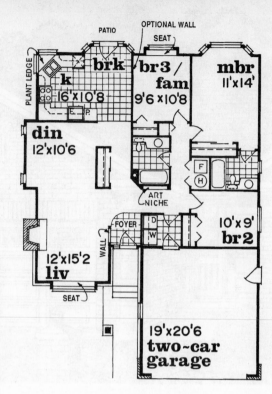

Design SHS010016

Square Footage: 1,336
Width: 40'-0" Depth: 54'-6"
Price Schedule: A2

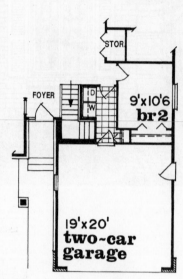

Alternate Layout for
Crawlspace

FOR PLAN ORDERING INFORMATION SEE PLAN

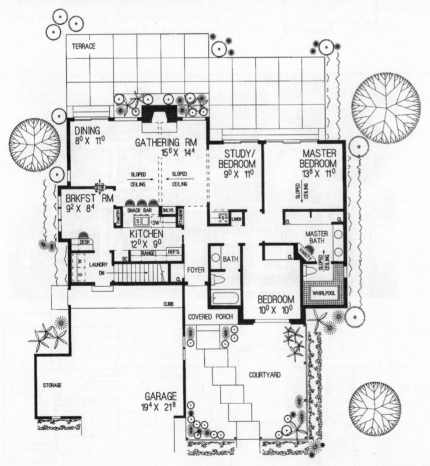

Design SHS010017

Square Footage: 1,387
Width: 54'-0" **Depth:** 52'-0"
Price Schedule: A2

Though modest in size, this fetching one-story home offers a great deal of livability with three bedrooms (or two bedrooms and a study) and a spacious gathering room with a fireplace and a sloped ceiling. The galley kitchen, designed to save steps, provides a pass-through snack bar and has a planning desk and attached breakfast room. In addition to two secondary bedrooms with a full bath, there's a private owners bedroom that enjoys views and access to the backyard. The owners bath features a large dressing area, a corner vanity and a raised whirlpool tub. Indoor/outdoor living relationships are strengthened by easy access from the dining room, study/bedroom and owners bedroom to the rear terrace.

Design SHS010019

First Floor: 995 square feet
Second Floor: 484 square feet
Total: 1,479 square feet
Width: 38'-0" Depth: 44'-0"
Price Schedule: A2

The rustic character of this appealing plan is defined by cedar lattice, covered columned porches, exposed rafters and multi-pane double-hung windows. The great room/dining room combination is reached through double doors off the veranda and features a fireplace towering two stories to the lofty ceiling. A U-shaped kitchen has an angled snack counter that serves this area and loads of space for a breakfast table—or use the handy side porch for alfresco dining. To the rear is the owners bedroom with a full bath and double doors to the veranda. An additional half-bath sits just beyond the laundry room. Upstairs there are two family bedrooms and a full bath.

Design SHS010018

First Floor: 852 square feet
Second Floor: 829 square feet
Total: 1,681 square feet
Bonus Room: 359 square feet
Width: 50'-0" Depth: 36'-0"
Price Schedule: A4

Options abound in this three-bedroom home. There is an optional two-car garage, which you may build or not as you choose. The bonus room, which sits over the garage, may be finished at the initial building stages or left for future development. Living spaces on the first floor are comfortable and roomy. Two family bedrooms and an owners suite reside on the second floor.

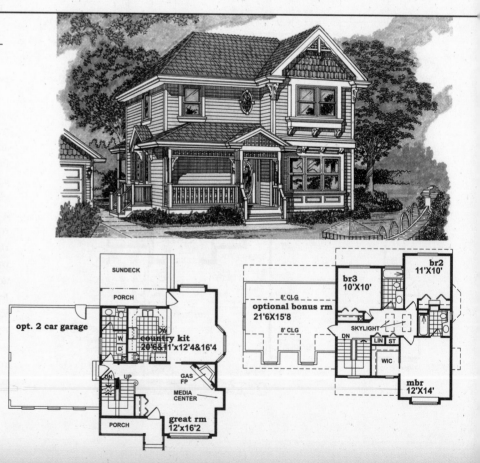

FOR PLAN ORDERING INFORMATION SEE PLAN

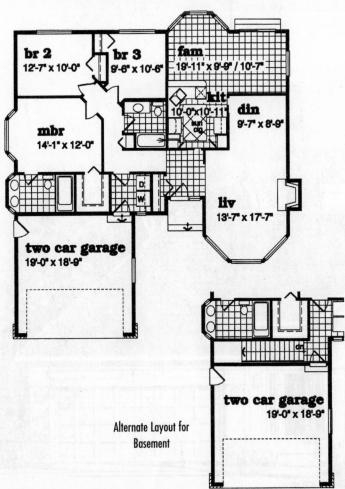

br 2
12'-7" x 10'-0"

br 3
9'-6" x 10'-6"

fam
19'-11" x 9'-9" / 10'-7"

kit
10'-0" x 10'-11"

din
9'-7" x 8'-9"

mbr
14'-1" x 12'-0"

liv
13'-7" x 17'-7"

two car garage
19'-0" x 18'-9"

Alternate Layout for Basement

two car garage
19'-0" x 18'-9"

Design SHS010020

Square Footage: 1,486
Width: 46'-0" **Depth:** 52'-4"
Price Schedule: A2

This ranch design with board-and-batten siding and brick accents has great curb appeal. This is further enhanced by the carousel living room with its fireplace and attached dining area. A step-saving galley kitchen has a sunshine ceiling and adjoins the rear-facing family room with its breakfast bay. Sliding glass doors here lead to the rear yard. Three bedrooms include an owners suite with a large walk-in closet, charming bay window, and bath with His and Hers vanities. The bath is shared by the two additional rear-facing bedrooms. A two-car garage connects to the house at a service entry that contains a laundry alcove. The basement option for this home is 1,566 square feet.

Design SHS010021

Square Footage: 1,699
Width: 52'-8" **Depth:** 49'-0"
Price Schedule: A3

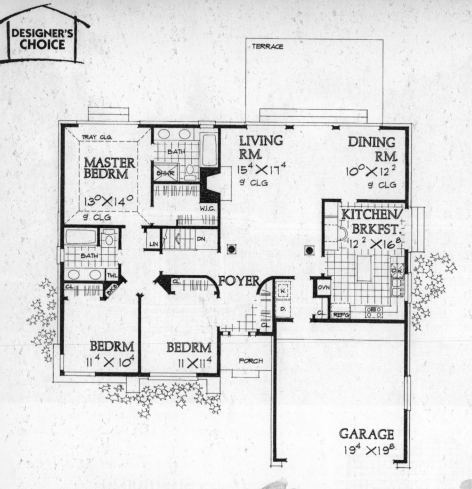

TERRACE

MASTER BEDRM
13⁰ X 14⁰
9' CLG

TRAY CLG.

BATH

SHWR

W.I.C.

LIVING RM.
15⁴ X 17⁴
9' CLG

DINING RM.
10⁰ X 12²
9' CLG

KITCHEN/ BRKFST.
12² X 16⁸

BATH

TWL

CL

LIN

DN

FOYER

W.

D.

OVN

REF'G

CL

BEDRM
11⁴ X 10⁴

BEDRM
11 X 11⁴

PORCH

GARAGE
19⁴ X 19⁸

An efficient, spacious interior comes through in this compact floor plan. Through a pair of columns, an open living and dining room area creates a comfortable space for entertaining, with sliding glass doors guaranteeing a bright, cheerful interior while providing easy access to outdoor living. The L-shaped kitchen has an island work surface, planning desk and an informal eating space. Sleeping arrangements are presided over by the owners suite with its tray ceiling and sliding glass doors to the yard. Two family bedrooms share a full hall bath.

FOR PLAN ORDERING INFORMATION SEE PLAN

Design SHS010022

Square Footage: 1,760
Width: 68'-0" **Depth:** 46'-0"
Price Schedule: A3

This brick one-story design offers a covered rail porch that provides a weather-protected entry to the home. The vaulted foyer carries its ceiling detail into the living room where there is a fireplace and double-door access to the rear patio. The dining room has a tray ceiling and is found to the right of the entry. A screened porch decorates the breakfast room and allows for protected casual outdoor dining. The kitchen is U-shaped with a center work island and large pantry. A nearby laundry room has access to the two-car garage. Look no further than the owners bedroom for true luxury. It boasts a tray ceiling and a full bath with a whirlpool spa, separate shower and double vanity. Family bedrooms have wall closets and share a full bath that separates them.

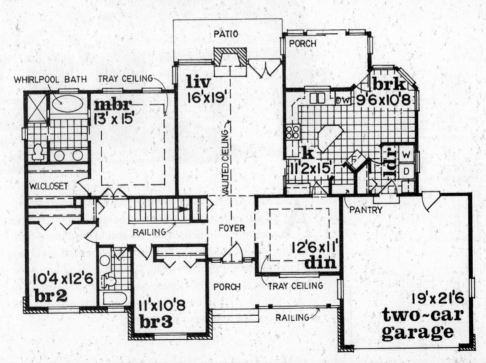

Design SHS010024

Square Footage: 1,911
Width: 56'-0" Depth: 58'-0"
Price Schedule: A4

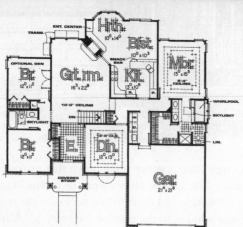

This sophisticated ranch design shows off its facade with fan-lights and elegant arches. Grace pervades the interior, starting with the formal dining room with a twelve-foot coffered ceiling and an arched window. An extensive great room shares a through-fireplace with a bayed hearth room. The well-planned kitchen features a spacious work area and a snack-bar pass-through to the breakfast area. The secluded owners suite offers a coffered ceiling, corner windows, a whirlpool bath and a skylight. On the opposite side of the plan, two family bedrooms—or one bedroom and a den—share a hall bath that has a skylight.

Design SHS010023

Square Footage: 1,879
Width: 50'-0" Depth: 62'-10"
Price Schedule: A3

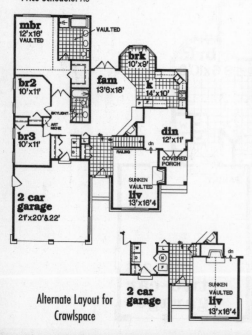

Alternate Layout for
Crawlspace

A contemporary stucco home with keystone and brick detailing is an attractive addition to any neighborhood. It begins with a welcoming foyer, brightly lit by abundant natural light from gabled windows above. Vaulted ceilings throughout the foyer and living room add to the openness of the plan. The living room has a cozy fireplace; the dining room is graced by double doors to the side porch. The owners bedroom offers a walk-in closet and vaulted bath with His and Hers vanities, a whirlpool spa and separate shower.

Photo by Andrew P. Lautman

Design SHS010025

Square Footage: 1,830
Width: 75'-0" **Depth:** 43'-5"
Price Schedule: A4

This charming one-story traditional home greets visitors with a covered porch. A uniquely shaped galley-style kitchen shares a snack bar with the spacious gathering room, where a fireplace is the focal point. The dining room has sliding glass doors to the rear terrace as does the owners suite. This bedroom area also includes a luxury bath with a whirlpool tub and separate dressing room. Two additional bedrooms, one that could double as a study, are located at the front of the home. The two-car garage features a large storage area and can be reached through the service entrance or from the rear terrace.

TERRACE

MASTER
BEDROOM
11'⁰ x 17'⁶

WHIRLPOOL

BATH

GATHERING RM
15'⁰ x 17'⁶

DINING RM
12'⁰ x 9'⁸

VANITY

DRESS RM

PANTRY

KITCHEN
14'² x 12'⁰

GARAGE
21'⁴ x 22'⁴ + STOR

BATH

BOOKS
CABT

FOYER

BRKFST RM
8'⁰ x 10'⁴

STORAGE

BEDROOM
10'⁸ x 11'⁶

STUDY/
BEDROOM
11'² x 11'⁶

COVERED PORCH

RAILING

FACTS AT THE BEGINNING OF THIS ISSUE

SELECT
HOME DESIGNS

Design SHS010027

Square Footage: 1,971
Width: 42'-8" **Depth:** 65'-10"
Price Schedule: A4

Available reverse right reading

Perfect for a narrow lot, this one-story home presents a practical and enjoyable floor plan. From the covered porch and tiled entry, you enter the great room with its dining bay, fireplace and arch-top front windows. The U-shaped kitchen is open to the family room via a snack bar. Both the family room and owners suite open to the patio. The compartmented owners bath has everything: garden tub and separate shower, double-bowl vanity, walk-in closet and linen closet. Two family bedrooms—or make one a den—share a hall bath. A laundry room with access to the garage completes this compact, livable plan.

Design SHS010026

Square Footage: 2,086
Width: 74'-8" **Depth:** 47'-0"
Price Schedule: A4

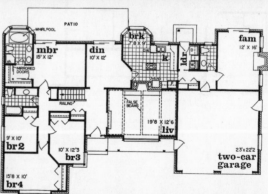

Though a traditional ranch, this one-story home possesses some of the quaint detailing shown in Tudor design. The covered entrance, brick exterior with quoining, and the large box windows add to its appeal. Inside, the sunken living room hosts a beam ceiling and oversized masonry fireplace. The dining room is across the hall and connects to the breakfast bay and kitchen with a built-in oven and center cooktop island. Note the amenities in the owners suite: a dressing room with a mirrored wall closet and a bath with a double-bowl vanity and a whirlpool tub tucked into a windowed bay.

FOR PLAN ORDERING INFORMATION SEE PLAN

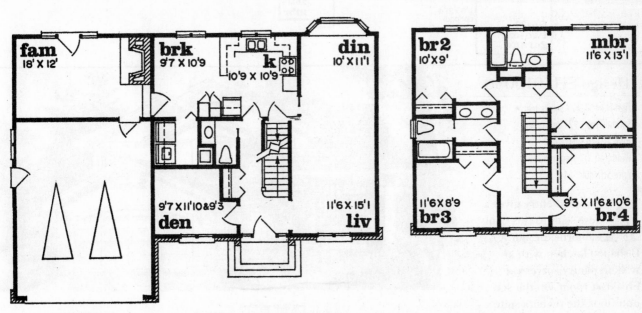

Design SHS010028

First Floor: 1,087 square feet

Second Floor: 850 square feet

Total: 1,937 square feet

Width: 50'-0" **Depth:** 35'-8"

Price Schedule: A3

The floor plan of this house is commodious. Formal living reigns on the right side of the plan, which comprises a living room and a dining room with a bay window. A private den is to the left, near a half-bath off the hallway. The U-shaped kitchen serves the breakfast room and the dining room. The sunken family room features a fireplace and a door to the rear yard. Four corner bedrooms are located on the second floor. The owners suite offers a large wall closet and private bath. Three family bedrooms share a full bath.

SELECT HOME DESIGNS

DESIGNER'S CHOICE

Design SHS010029

First Floor: 1,195 square feet
Second Floor: 893 square feet
Total: 2,088 square feet
Width: 38'-0" Depth: 57'-8"
Price Schedule: A4

Looking for drama and spaciousness? This design has volume rooflines to allow for vaulted ceilings in the living room, dining room and foyer. The gourmet kitchen, hearth-warmed family room and bumped-out breakfast nook form a large casual area for gatherings. Note the sliding glass doors in the family room leading to the rear yard. Positioned close to a full bath, the den can double easily as a guest room. Three second-floor bedrooms include an owners suite with a private bath, vaulted ceiling and window seat. If you like, choose the three-car garage option.

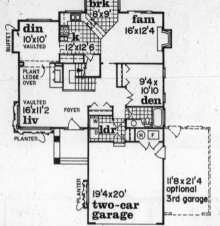

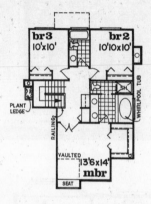

Design SHS010030

First Floor: 1,199 square feet
Second Floor: 921 square feet
Total: 2,120 square feet
Width: 40'-0" Depth: 50'-6"
Price Schedule: A4

An angled entry gives a new slant to this cool California design. A U-shaped kitchen with a walk-in pantry serves the breakfast room. On the second floor, the owners suite includes a walk-in closet and a private bath with a corner whirlpool tub and separate shower. Two additional bedrooms share a full bath.

Alternate Layout for Basement

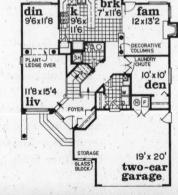

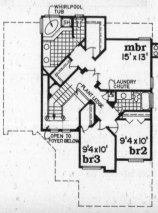

Design SHS010031

Square Footage: 2,112
Width: 63'-4" **Depth:** 54'-10"
Price Schedule: C1

A Tudor exterior with an efficient floor plan is favored by many. Each of the three main living zones in this plan are within a few steps of the foyer for easy traffic flow. Open planning and plenty of glass create a bright environment for the living/dining areas. The L-shaped kitchen with island range and work surface is delightfully open to the large breakfast room. Nearby is the step-saving laundry. The sleeping zone has the flexibility of functioning as a two- or three-bedroom area.

(Floor plan labels:) TERRACE · MASTER BEDROOM 11'⁰x17'⁸ · BATH · WHIRLPOOL · SEAT · DRESS RM · LINEN · BATH · BOOKS CAB'T · GATHERING RM 15'⁰x17'⁸ · DINING RM 12'⁰x9'⁸ · PANTRY · KITCHEN 14'²x12'⁰ · SHELVES · DESK · BEDROOM 10'⁰x11'⁰ · STUDY/BEDROOM 11'²x11'⁶ · FOYER · BRKFST RM 8'⁸x10'⁴ · COVERED PORCH · RAILING · GARAGE 21'⁴x22'⁴ + STOR · STORAGE

DESIGNER'S CHOICE

Design SHS010033

Square Footage: 2,189
Width: 56'-0" Depth: 72'-0"
Price Schedule: C1

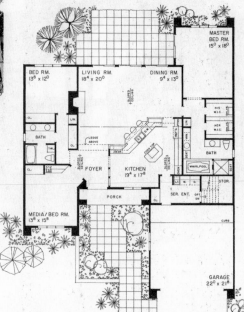

Simplicity is the key to the stylish good looks of this home's facade. Inside, the kitchen opens directly off the foyer and contains an island counter and a work counter with eating space on the living area side. The owners bedroom sports sliding glass doors to the terrace. Its dressing area is enhanced with double walk-in closets and lavatories. A whirlpool tub and seated shower are additional amenities. Two family bedrooms are found on the opposite side of the house.

Design SHS010032

Square Footage: 2,393
Width: 79'-7" Depth: 71'-7"
Price Schedule: C2

Available reverse right reading

Corner quoins, hipped rooflines and a well-designed floor plan make this three-bedroom home highly desirable. From the media room to the family room with its fireplace, this house can be built with the family in mind. The formal dining room and living room work well together for entertaining needs. The large kitchen will easily serve a banquet, while also accommodating those intimate meals. Two family bedrooms share a full hall bath with a double-bowl vanity. The owners bedroom features a large walk-in closet, a compartmented bath, and a garden tub. A two-car garage easily handles the family fleet.

Design SHS010034

First Floor: 1,261 square feet
Second Floor: 950 square feet
Total: 2,211 square feet
Width: 63'-0" **Depth:** 34'-8"
Price Schedule: C1

Though technically a story and a half, the second floor of this charming Tudor-style home offers so much livability, it's more like a two-story plan. The first floor is solidly designed for efficiency and contains a living room with a fireplace, a large formal dining room, a beam-ceilinged family room, an efficient U-shaped kitchen, a study with a sunny bay window, and a covered porch. In addition to a large owners suite, two family bedrooms and a second full bath, the second floor includes a cozy spot that could serve as a home office, a nursery or a play area.

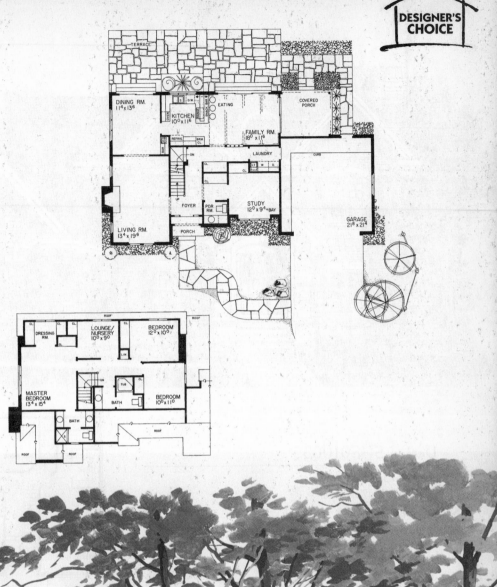

Design SHS010035

First Floor: 1,566 square feet
Second Floor: 1,119 square feet
Total: 2,685 square feet
Bonus Room: 469 square feet
Width: 61'-4" **Depth:** 49'-4"
Price Schedule: C1

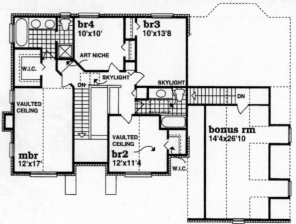

The brick facade of this home is accented with shutters, dentil crown moulding, stone lintels and keystones. The raised foyer spills into a living room with its tray ceiling and the adjoining dining room. The living room has a fireplace; the dining room features a bay window. The gourmet kitchen with its work island has a sunny breakfast room that opens to a rear porch. French doors open to the family room with a coffered ceiling, window seats in twin bays and a cozy fireplace. A study with a beamed ceiling is tucked away behind double doors off the entry hall. A skylit hall introduces the upstairs bedrooms. The vaulted owners suite has an extravagant bath with His and Hers vanities, a whirlpool spa and a separate shower. Additional bedrooms share a skylit bath. A bonus room over the garage makes a perfect studio or in-law suite.

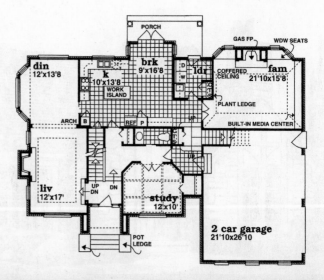

SELECT HOME DESIGNS

FOR PLAN ORDERING INFORMATION SEE PLAN

Design SHS010036

First Floor: 1,536 square feet
Second Floor: 1,183 square feet
Total: 2,719 square feet
Width: 56'-0" **Depth:** 48'-0"
Price Schedule: C1

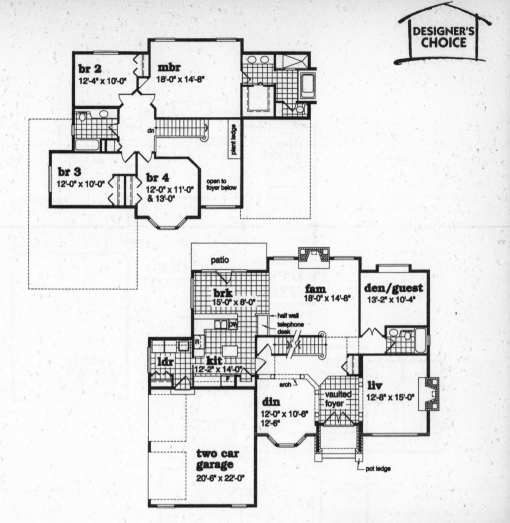

European-style details, such as stonework, a volume roof and a two-story bay, cross the pond to add distinctive touches to this design. The vaulted foyer is flanked by formal spaces—a living room with a fireplace and a dining room with a bay window. Arches help define these spaces. The large family room is also hearth-warmed and lies to the rear near the kitchen and breakfast room. A den or guest room is tucked into the right corner near a full bath. Upstairs, the bedrooms include an owners suite and three family bedrooms. Note the lavish bath with its walk-in closet, dual sinks, and separate tub and shower. A two-car garage is reached through a service entry near the laundry alcove.

Design SHS010037

First Floor: 1,592 square feet
Second Floor: 1,259 square feet
Total: 2,851 square feet
Width: 56'-0" **Depth:** 53'-6"
Price Schedule: C1

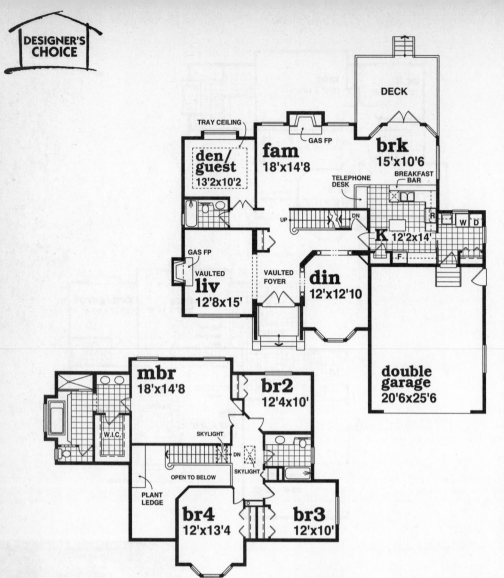

DECK

den/ guest 13'2x10'2
TRAY CEILING

fam 18'x14'8
GAS FP

brk 15'x10'6
BREAKFAST BAR
TELEPHONE DESK

K 12'2x14'
W D
R
F

GAS FP
liv 12'8x15'
VAULTED

VAULTED FOYER
UP
DN

din 12'x12'10

double garage 20'6x25'6

mbr 18'x14'8
W.I.C.

br2 12'4x10'
SKYLIGHT
DN
SKYLIGHT

OPEN TO BELOW
PLANT LEDGE

br4 12'x13'4

br3 12'x10'

A combination of architectural details makes this home elegant: keystone arches, shuttered windows, a two-story bay with a copper roof, and a recessed entry. Formal rooms flank the vaulted foyer—a living room with a fireplace and a dining room with a bay window. The hearth-warmed family room sits to the rear near the island kitchen and breakfast bay. Double doors lead from the breakfast bay to a deck. A den—or guest room—with a tray ceiling has the use of a full bath. Look for the owners suite on the second floor, just off a skylit hall. It features a walk-in closet and private bath with separate tub and shower. The other three bedrooms share the use of a hall bath. A full basement could be finished later for additional space.

FOR PLAN ORDERING INFORMATION SEE PLAN

Design SHS010038

Square Footage: 2,881
Width: 77'-11" Depth: 73'-11"
Price Schedule: C1

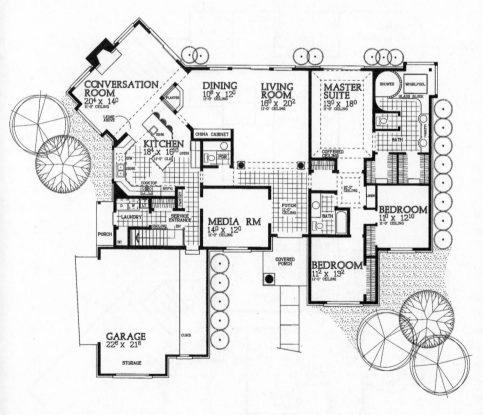

The high, massive hipped roof of this home creates an impressive facade, while varying roof planes and projecting gables further enhance appeal. A central foyer routes traffic efficiently to the sleeping, formal and informal zones of the house. Note the sliding glass doors that provide access to outdoor living facilities. A built-in china cabinet and planter unit are fine decor features. In the angular kitchen, a high ceiling and efficient work patterning set the pace. The conversation room may act as a multi-purpose room. Sleeping quarters take off with the spacious owners bedroom, with a tray ceiling and sliding doors to the rear yard. Two sizable bedrooms accommodate family members or guests.

This home, as shown in photograph, may differ from the actual blueprints. For more detailed information, please check the floor plans carefully.

Photo by BRI-MAR Photography

Design SHS010039

First Floor: 2,152 square feet

Second Floor: 1,936 square feet

Total: 4,088 square feet

Bonus Room: 527 square feet

Width: 104'-4" **Depth:** 57'-10"

Price Schedule: C4

In elegant Tudor style, this estate home has all of the best of luxury living. The vaulted foyer has a circular staircase and gallery above. The living room with its bay window and fireplace is on the left; a cozy den with double-door access is on the right. The dining room is defined by an arched opening and also features a bay window. The U-shaped kitchen features a bar sink and bayed breakfast nook. Enter the sunken family room through decorative columns. You'll find a corner fireplace and sliding glass doors to the rear yard. The second floor holds four bedrooms, one of which is an owners suite with a coffered ceiling and private bath. Family bedrooms share a full bath. Bedroom 4 has a walk-in closet. A bonus room just beyond the secondary staircase allows for 527 square feet of finish-later space.

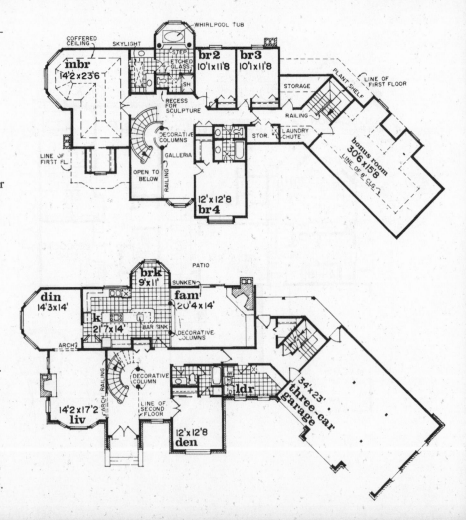

This home, as shown in photograph, may differ from the actual blueprints.
For more detailed information, please check the floor plans carefully.

Photo by Bizzo Photography

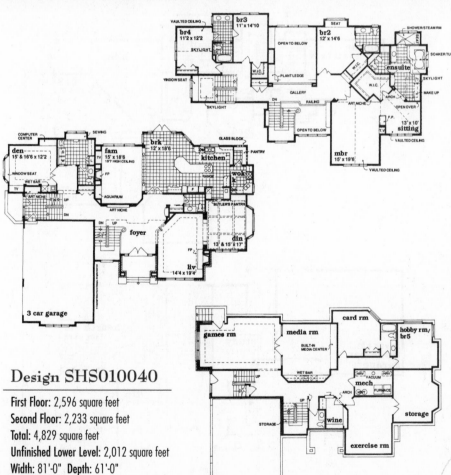

Design SHS010040

First Floor: 2,596 square feet

Second Floor: 2,233 square feet

Total: 4,829 square feet

Unfinished Lower Level: 2,012 square feet

Width: 81'-0" **Depth:** 61'-0"

Price Schedule: L1

This grand, two-story European design is adorned with a facade of stucco and brick, meticulously appointed with details for gracious living. Guests enter through a portico to find a stately, two-story foyer. The formal living room features a tray ceiling and fireplace and is joined by a charming dining room with a large bay window. The family room nearby has a built-in aquarium, media center and fireplace. A den with a tray ceiling, window seat and built-in computer center is tucked in a corner for privacy. Served by two separate staircases, the second floor features a spectacular owners suite with a separate sitting room, an oversized closet and a bath with a shower/steam room and a spa tub. If you choose, you may develop the lower level to include an exercise room, hobby room, card room, game room, media room, wine cellar and large storage space.

SELECT HOME DESIGNS

Design SHS010041

First Floor: 2,473 square feet
Second Floor: 2,686 square feet
Total: 5,159 square feet
Width: 57'-8" **Depth:** 103'-6"
Price Schedule: L1

This unusual stucco-and-siding design opens with a grand portico to a foyer that extends to the living room with a fireplace. Proceed up a few steps to the dining room with its coffered ceiling and butler's pantry which connects to the gourmet kitchen. The attached hearth room has the requisite fireplace and three sets of French doors to the covered porch. The family room sports a coffered ceiling and fireplace flanked by French doors. The second floor boasts four bedrooms, including an owners suite with a tray ceiling, covered deck and lavish bath. Two full baths serve the family bedrooms and a bonus room that might be used as an additional bedroom or hobby space.

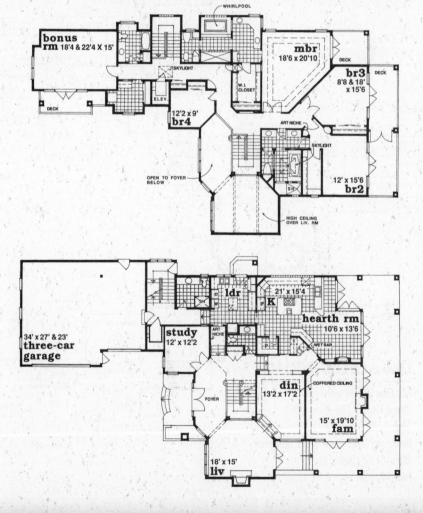

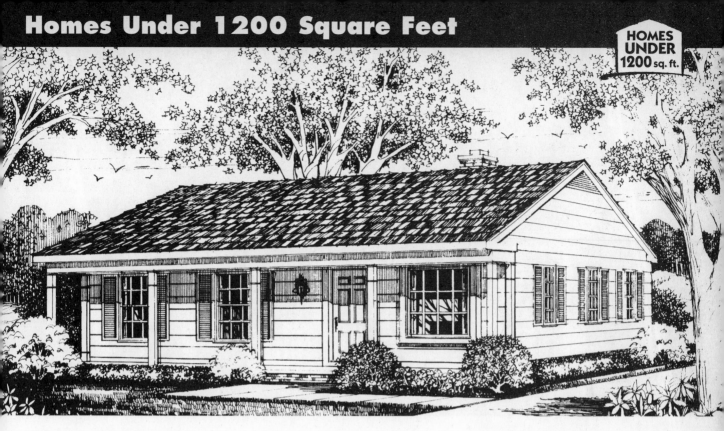

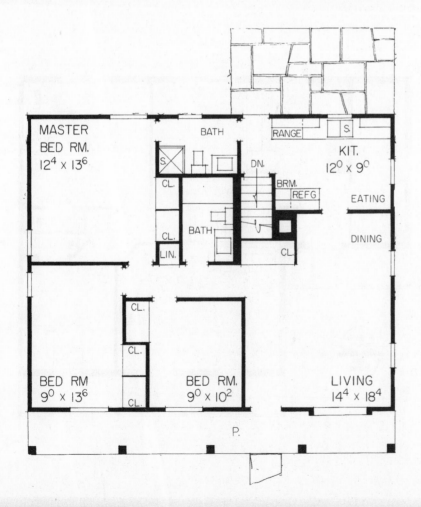

Design SHS010042

Square Footage: 1,080
Width: 36'-0" **Depth:** 28'-0"
Price Schedule: A3

This cozy plan, is just right for a small family or empty-nesters. A covered front porch shelters visitors from inclement weather. An ample living room/dining room area leads the way to a rear kitchen overlooking a terrace. Two full baths serve three bedrooms—one an owners suite. The kitchen includes informal eating space. Stairs lead to a full basement that may be developed as desired.

Available reverse — right reading

SELECT
HOME DESIGNS

Design SHS010043

Square Footage: 920
Width: 38'-0" Depth: 28'-0"
Price Schedule: A1

Compact yet comfortable, this country cottage has many appealing amenities. From the covered front porch that invites relaxed living, the entrance opens onto the living room with access to the dining room and snack bar at the rear. Two bedrooms are secluded to the right of the plan; kitchen, bathroom and laundry facilities are located on the left side. A second porch off the kitchen provides room for more casual dining and quiet moments. This home is designed with a basement foundation.

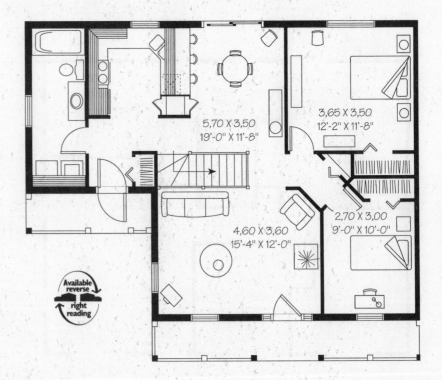

5,70 X 3,50
19'-0" X 11'-8"

3,65 X 3,50
12'-2" X 11'-8"

4,60 X 3,60
15'-4" X 12'-0"

2,70 X 3,00
9'-0" X 10'-0"

Available reverse
right reading

SELECT HOME DESIGNS

Design SHS010044

Square Footage: 924
Unfinished Lower Level (with garage):
646 square feet
Unfinished Lower Level (without garage):
736 square feet
Width: 38'-0"   Depth: 24'-6"
Price Schedule: A1

The front door opens to a cathedral entry with a half-wall separating it from the living room. A fireplace warms this living space. The dining room is attached and has sliding glass doors to a sun deck. The kitchen features a box window over the sink and a U-shaped work area. Two bedrooms sit at the right side of the plan. They share a full bath. If you choose to finish the lower level, you'll gain 646 square feet with the garage or 736 without the garage. One option allows for a bedroom, a full bath and a family room with a fireplace. The other adds another bedroom and a workshop.

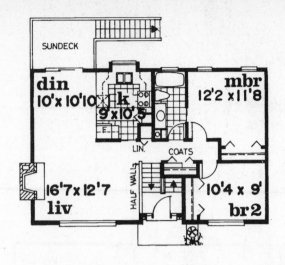

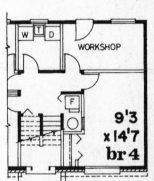

Alternate Lower-Level Layout

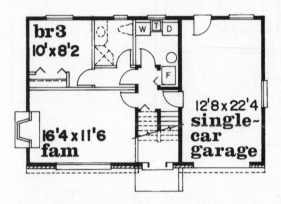

BASIC PLAN

Design SHS010045

Square Footage: 982
Width: 62'-0" Depth: 26'-0"
Price Schedule: A2

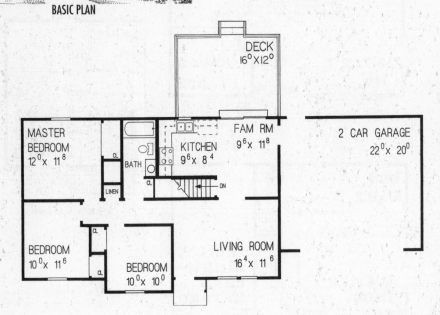

DECK
16⁰ X12⁰

MASTER
BEDROOM
12⁰ x 11⁸

BATH

LINEN

FAM RM
9⁶ x 11⁸

KITCHEN
9⁶ x 8⁴

CL

DN

2 CAR GARAGE
22⁰ x 20⁰

BEDROOM
10⁰ x 11⁶

CL

BEDROOM
10⁰ x 10⁰

LIVING ROOM
16⁴ x 11⁶

D epending on your budget, you can build the basic, low-cost version of this ranch home or the enhanced, upgraded version. The main floor of the enhanced plan is shown here. Both versions have three bedrooms and one full bath, and both include a laundry area. In the basic plan, the laundry area is on the main floor and there is no stairway. The enhanced version includes the stairway and a basement that contains the laundry area. The sliding glass door, two-car garage and rear deck with railing are also optional enhancements. The blueprints show how to build both versions.

ENHANCED PLAN

FOR PLAN ORDERING INFORMATION SEE PLAN

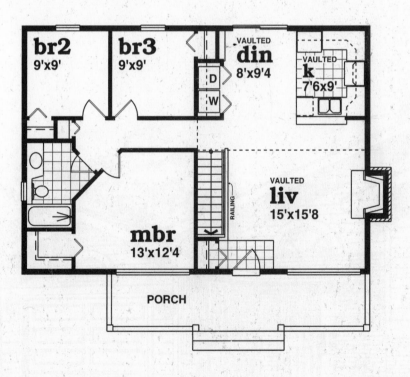

Design SHS010046

Square Footage: 988
Width: 38'-0" **Depth:** 32'-0"
Price Schedule: A1

This economical, compact home is the ultimate in efficient use of space. The central great room features a cozy fireplace and outdoor access to the front porch. A U-shaped kitchen serves both a dining area and a breakfast bar. Sliding glass doors lead from the kitchen/dining area to the rear. The front entry is sheltered by a casual country porch, which also protects the living room windows. The owners bedroom has a walk-in closet and shares a full bath with the secondary bedrooms. A single or double garage may be built to the side or to the rear of the home.

HOMES UNDER 1200 sq. ft.

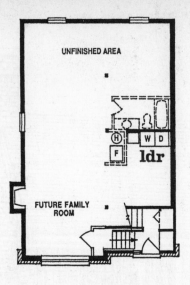

UNFINISHED AREA

ldr

H W D
F

FUTURE FAMILY ROOM

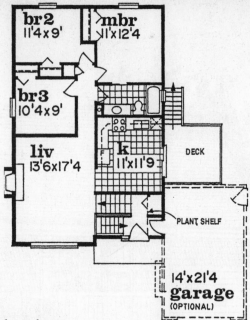

br2 11'4x9'   mbr 11'x12'4

br3 10'4x9'

liv 13'6x17'4

k 11'x11'9   DECK

F

PLANT SHELF

14'x21'4 garage (OPTIONAL)

To accommodate a very narrow lot, this plan can be built without the deck and the garage, though the plan includes the options for both. The lower floor can be finished later into a family room and additional bedrooms and a bath, if you choose. The cathedral entry offers steps up to the main living areas. The living room has a fireplace and leads to the L-shaped kitchen. Here you'll find abundant counter and cupboard space and room for a breakfast table. Sliding glass doors open to the optional deck. Bedrooms include an owners suite and two family bedrooms.

Design SHS010047

Square Footage: 1,007
Unfinished Lower Level: 1,007 square feet
Width: 26'-0" (40'-0" with garage)
Depth: 39'-4" (51'-0" with garage)
Price Schedule: A2

SELECT HOME DESIGNS

FOR PLAN ORDERING INFORMATION SEE PLAN

This small cottage design offers plenty of room for the square footage. The living room enjoys an open layout and flows into the dining area with ease. The U-shaped kitchen is convenient to the dining room. Proceed up a few steps to the sleeping quarters that consist of two family bedrooms, an owners bedroom and a shared bath. Walk down a few steps to the bonus space that allows for future family bedrooms.

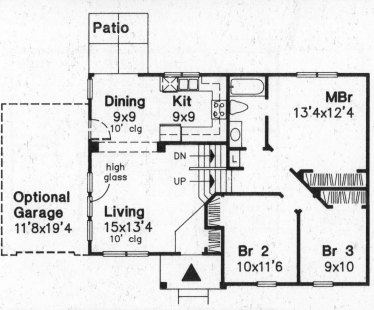

Patio

Dining
9x9
10' clg

Kit
9x9

MBr
13'4x12'4

DN

UP

L

high glass

Optional Garage
11'8x19'4

Living
15x13'4
10' clg

Br 2
10x11'6

Br 3
9x10

Design SHS010048

Square Footage: 992 square feet
Unfinished Lower Level: 532 square feet
Width: 38'-0" **Depth:** 28'-0"
Price Schedule: A1

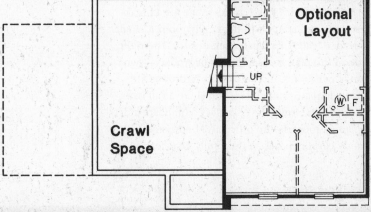

Optional Layout

UP

Crawl Space

W F

Design SHS010049

Square Footage: 1,033
Unfinished Lower Level: 1,000 square feet
Width: 52'-6" **Depth:** 26'-0"
Price Schedule: A2

Build this home with full livability on one level, with the option of expanding to the lower level in the future. Double doors open to the entry where a few steps lead up to the main level. The living room overlooks the cathedral entry and also sports a fireplace. An L-shaped country kitchen has space for a breakfast table and is open to the family room. A single entrance leads to a small deck in back. The right side of the plan is reserved for bedrooms—two family bedrooms and an owners bedroom. All have adequate wall closets and share a full bath. Space on the lower level can accommodate a den or family room, home office and bedrooms. A handy carport protects the family vehicle.

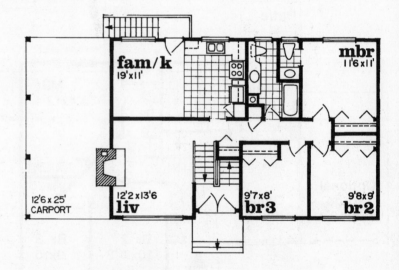

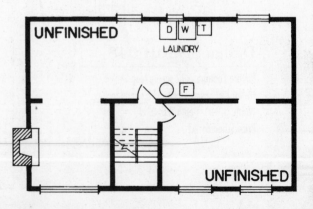

Design SHS010050

Square Footage: 1,100
Unfinished Lower Level: 770 square feet
Width: 40'-0" **Depth:** 34'-0"
Price Schedule: A2

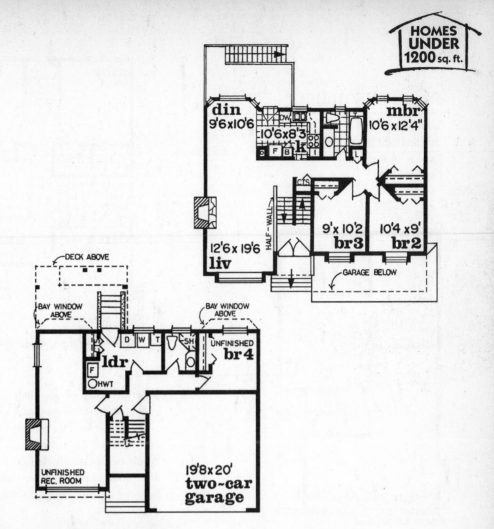

Room on the lower level for future expansion makes this split level as practical as it is appealing. Sharing this level with the two-car garage and laundry room is space for a recreation room, half-bath and fourth bedroom. On the main level, living space includes a living room with fireplace and bayed dining room with deck overlook. A door in the kitchen accesses the rear deck. The owners bedroom is tucked away in a windowed bay at the opposite end of the home. It shares a bath with two family bedrooms with box-bay windows.

FACTS AT THE BEGINNING OF THIS ISSUE

HOMES
UNDER
1200 sq. ft.

Design SHS010051

Square Footage: 1,018
Unfinished Lower Level: 1,018 square feet
Width: 37'-0"   **Depth:** 42'-0"
Price Schedule: A2

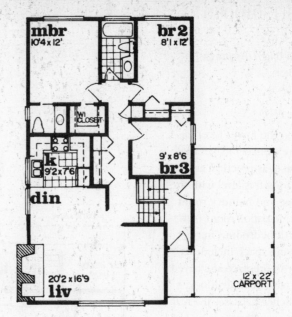

mbr
10'4 x 12'

br 2
8'1 x 12'

w.i.
closet

k
9'2 x 7'6

din

9' x 8'6
br3

liv
20'2 x 16'9

12' x 22'
CARPORT

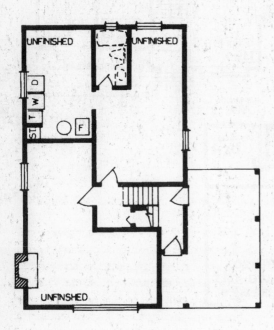

UNFINISHED

UNFINISHED

S T | W | D

F

UNFINISHED

This plan offers a living/dining room with a beautiful view of the front yard and a warming fireplace in the corner. An open kitchen adjoins the dining room and is U-shaped for convenience. An owners bedroom with a walk-in closet and two family bedrooms share a full bath. The lower level has a fireplace and rough-in plumbing so that it can be developed in the future to become a family room, bedroom and bath—or make it a complete in-law suite.

SELECT
HOME DESIGNS

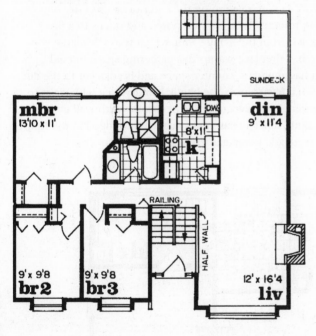

mbr
13'10 x 11'

8' x 11'
k

din
9' x 11'4

SUNDECK

DW

RAILING

HALF WALL

9' x 9'8
br 2

9' x 9'8
br 3

12' x 16'4
liv

This split-level design offers a single-car garage on the lower level along with space for a family room, extra bedrooms or an in-law suite. The main level has a living room with fireplace that overlooks the vaulted foyer and stretches to a dining area. Sliding glass doors lead out to a sun deck at the back. The kitchen features a counter pass-through to the dining room. Bedrooms are on the left side of the plan. They include an owners bedroom with a full bath and two bedrooms with a shared bath.

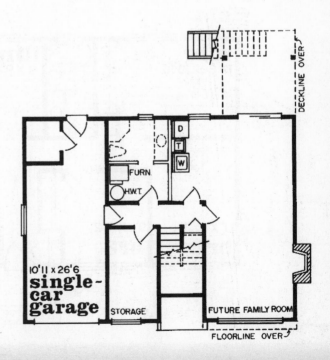

DECKLINE OVER

D
T
W

FURN.

H.W.T.

10'11 x 26'6
single-car garage

STORAGE

FUTURE FAMILY ROOM

FLOORLINE OVER

Design SHS010052

Square Footage: 1,047
Unfinished Lower Level: 712 square feet
Width: 38'-0" Depth: 28'-6"
Price Schedule: A2

Design SHS010053

Square Footage: 1,089
Width: 54'-0" Depth: 29'-4"
Price Schedule: A2

Brick and wood siding work in combination on the exterior of this cozy one-story home. The entry is protected by a covered porch and opens to a foyer with a half-wall separating it from the living room, which features a large window overlooking the front porch. A fireplace warms this gathering space in cold weather. The U-shaped kitchen has abundant counter space and is adjacent to the dining room for convenience. Down a few steps is the handy laundry area with stairs to the basement and access to the single-car garage. Three bedrooms with wall closets share a bath that includes a soaking tub. The basement may be developed in the future to add more bedrooms or to create additional gathering space.

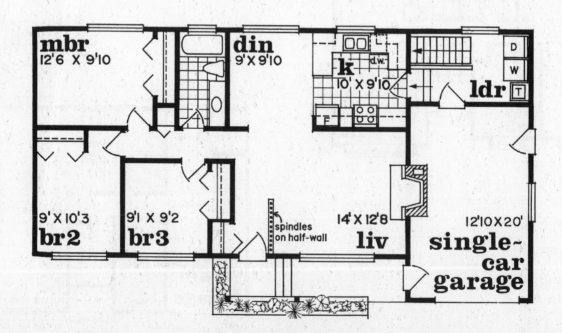

mbr
12'6 X 9'10

din
9' X 9'10

k
10' X 9'10

d.w.

ldr

D
W
T

F

br2
9' X 10'3

br3
9'1 X 9'2

spindles
on half-wall

liv
14' X 12'8

single-car garage
12'10 X 20'

SELECT
HOME DESIGNS

Design SHS010054

Square Footage: 1,114
Width: 48'-0" **Depth:** 31'-0"
Price Schedule: A2

For a starter home, this three-bedroom design retains plenty of style. Horizontal wood siding and shuttered windows bring a look of tradition to its facade. Inside, it holds a livable floor plan. The living room is introduced by columns and has a fireplace and pocket doors that separate it from the large eat-in kitchen. A U-shaped work area in the kitchen is handy and efficient. Access in the kitchen leads to a service area with a door into the single-car garage and stairs to the full basement—perfect for future expansion. Use all three bedrooms for sleeping space, or turn one bedroom into a home office or den. All three bedrooms have wall closets and share the use of a full bath.

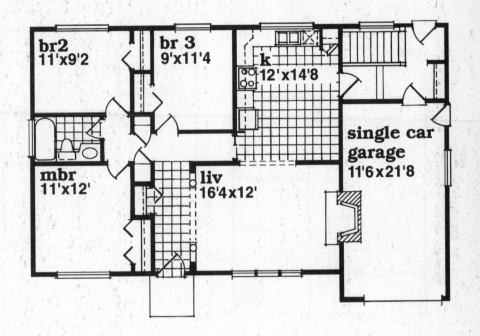

br2 11'x9'2
br 3 9'x11'4
k 12'x14'8
single car garage 11'6 x 21'8
mbr 11'x12'
liv 16'4x12'

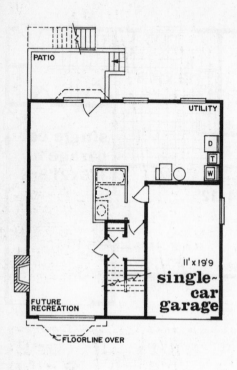

PATIO

UTILITY

D
T
W

FUTURE
RECREATION

11' x 19'9

single-car garage

FLOORLINE OVER

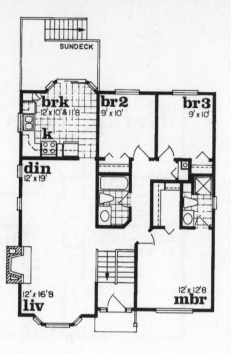

SUNDECK

brk
12' x 10' & 11'8

k

din
12' x 19'

br2
9' x 10'

br3
9' x 10'

12' x 16'8
liv

12' x 12'8
mbr

Design SHS010055

Sqaure Footage: 1,116
Unfinished Lower Level: 765 square feet
Width: 31'-6" **Depth:** 38'-6"
Price Schedule: A2

This delightful wood-sided design offers bonus space on the lower level that can be finished later to include a recreation room with patio access and full bath besides the laundry room and single-car garage. The main level holds a living room with fireplace, formal dining room, L-shaped kitchen with bayed breakfast nook, and three bedrooms. A sun deck can be reached through sliding glass doors in the nook. The owners suite has a walk-in closet and a full, private bath, while family bedrooms share a hall bath.

FOR PLAN ORDERING INFORMATION SEE PLAN

COVERED PATIO | W.I. CLOSET

mbr
11'1 x 11'4

br2
9' x 11'4

liv
17'4 x 12'4

PASS THRU

k
11'2 x 15'5

br3
11' x 9'4

W | D

brk

21'x23'2
two~car garage

Design SHS010056

Square Footage: 1,122
Width: 44'-8" Depth: 48'-0"
Price Schedule: A2

This compact design offers a host of extras beginning with its charming exterior. The focus of the interior is to the rear to capture views—the living room opens to a covered patio through sliding glass doors. It is also warmed by a central fireplace. The kitchen features a breakfast nook and pass-through to the living room. Note the large, built-in pantry. There are three bedrooms—an owners suite and two family bedrooms. The owners suite has a private bath, while the family bedrooms share a full hall bath. Entry to the two-car garage leads through a convenient laundry alcove.

ENHANCED PLAN

Traditional charm is an apt description for this economical ranch home. The kitchen is designed to serve as an eat-in kitchen. The owners bedroom offers a full bath plus ample closet space. A full-sized bath adjoins the other two bedrooms. Options include a one- or two-car garage, a front porch, a rear deck with railing, a box-bay window and a fireplace. The blueprints for this house show how to build both a basic, low-cost version and an enhanced, upgraded version.

BASIC PLAN

Design SHS010057

Square Footage: 1,130
Width: 60'-0" Depth: 28'-0"
Price Schedule: A3

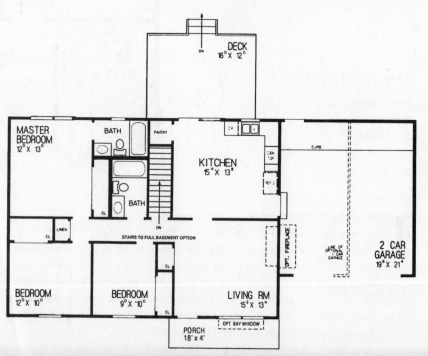

DECK
16° X 12°

MASTER
BEDROOM
12° X 13°

BATH

PANTRY

KITCHEN
15° X 13°

BATH

LINEN

STAIRS TO FULL BASEMENT OPTION

2 CAR
GARAGE
19° X 21°

BEDROOM
12° X 10°

BEDROOM
9° X 10°

LIVING RM
15° X 13°

OPT. FIREPLACE

PORCH
18° X 4°

OPT BAY WINDOW

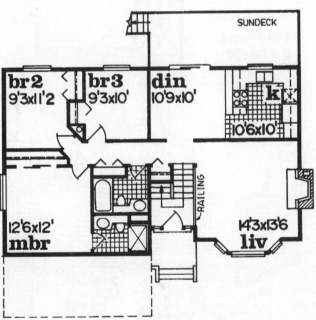

SUNDECK

br2 9'3x11'2

br3 9'3x10'

din 10'9x10'

k 10'6x10'

RAILING

12'6x12' **mbr**

14'3x13'6 **liv**

This bungalow design features woodwork accents and a bumped-out bay window. Inside, stairs ascend to the main floor. The dining room opens to the tiled kitchen and features a sliding door to the sun deck. The living room enjoys a fireplace and a bay window. Down the hall, two family bedrooms share a full bath, while the owners bedroom has its own bath. On the lower floor, a future family bedroom and recreation room with fireplace awaits expansion.

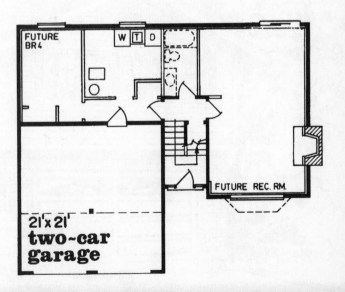

FUTURE BR 4

W T D

FUTURE REC. RM.

21'x21' **two~car garage**

Design SHS010058

Square Footage: 1,150
Unfinished Lower Level: 799 square feet
Width: 44'-0" **Depth:** 36'-0"
Price Schedule: A2

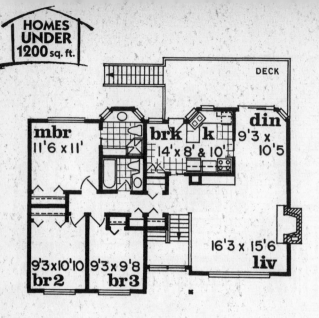

mbr
11'6 x 11'

brk
14' x 8' & 10'

k

din
9'3 x 10'5

br2
9'3 x 10'10

br3
9'3 x 9'8

liv
16'3 x 15'6

DECK

erfect for a hillside lot, this design combines brick and horizontal siding to lovely effect. Double doors with a transom overhead create a fine entry. A few steps up is the main home, with a living/dining room combination. The living room has a fireplace, while the dining room has sliding glass doors to the rear deck. The kitchen and attached breakfast room are nearby and also open to the deck. Three bedrooms are found on the left side of the plan. The owners suite has a private bath with a garden sink and corner shower. Family bedrooms share a full bath. If you choose to develop the lower level, you'll gain 522 square feet and a family room with fireplace, plus a full bath. The laundry room and garage with storage space sit on the lower level.

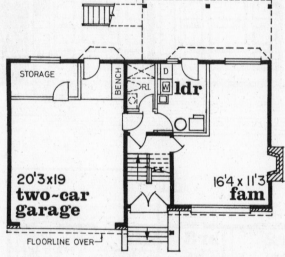

STORAGE

BENCH

R.I.

D W

ldr

20'3x19 two~car garage

16'4 x 11'3 fam

FLOORLINE OVER

Design SHS010059

Square Footage: 1,197
Unfinished Lower Level: 522 square feet
Width: 44'-0" **Depth:** 30'-0"
Price Schedule: A2

FOR PLAN ORDERING INFORMATION SEE PLAN

Design SHS010060

Square Footage: 1,176
Width: 58'-0" Depth: 28'-0"
Price Schedule: A2

The classic ranch exterior of this home opens upon a wonderfully efficient layout. The living room has a warming fireplace and moves smoothly into the dining room. The kitchen offers an open feeling and includes a large island snack bar for casual meals. Three bedrooms grouped to the right of the plan share a full bath with two sinks. Laundry facilities are also included in the bathroom. This home is designed with a basement foundation.

Available reverse right reading

4.50 X 7.90
15'-0" X 26'-4"

4.50 X 3.60
15'-0" X 12'-0"

4.60 X 3.60
15'-0" X 12'-0"

2.70 X 3.70
9'-0" X 12'-4"

3.60 X 3.10
12'-0" X 10'-4"

3.60 X 3.70
12'-0" X 12'-4"

Design SHS010061

Square Footage: 1,200
Unfinished Lower Level: 858 square feet
Width: 52'-0" Depth: 32'-0"
Price Schedule: A2

This well-planned split-level home leaves room for expansion in the future. The foyer opens to steps leading both up and down—up to the first floor, down to expansion space. The main floor holds a living room with a window seat and a railing that separates it from the dining room. Reach the sun deck through sliding glass doors in the dining room. The L-shaped kitchen nearby has an island workspace. Three bedrooms include an owners suite with a full bath and a walk-in closet and two family bedrooms with a shared bath. The lower floor has unfinished space that may be developed into a family room, a full bath, a den and a bedroom.

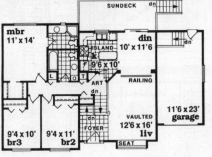

SUNDECK
dn

mbr
11' x 14'

ISLAND
k
9'6 x 10'

din
10' x 11'6

ART

RAILING

dn

9'4 x 10'
br3

9'4 x 11'
br2

FOYER
dn

VAULTED
12'6 x 16'
liv
SEAT

11'6 x 23'
garage

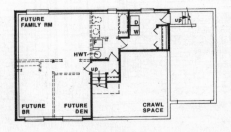

FUTURE FAMILY RM

HWT

D W

up

up

FUTURE BR

FUTURE DEN

CRAWL SPACE

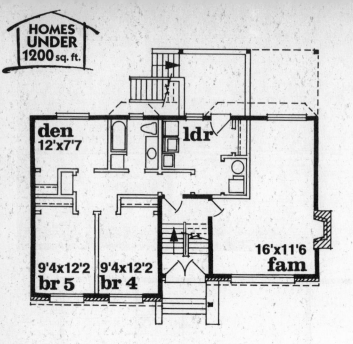

den
12'x7'7

ldr

9'4x12'2
br 5

9'4x12'2
br 4

16'x11'6
fam

This traditional design offers not only a great exterior, but plenty of room for expansion in the future. The main level contains an open living room and dining room, warmed by a fireplace and open to the rear deck through sliding glass doors. The kitchen and breakfast room are reached easily from either the living room or dining room and also have access to the deck. The owners bedroom and two family bedrooms are on the left side of the plan. The owners bedroom has its own bath, while family bedrooms share a full bath. The lower level offers 1,052 square feet of unfinished space for two additional bedrooms, a den, a full bath and a family room with a fireplace. The laundry room is also on this level.

Design SHS010062

Square Footage: 1,194
Unfinished Lower Level: 1,052 square feet
Width: 44'-0" Depth: 30'-0"
Price Schedule: A2

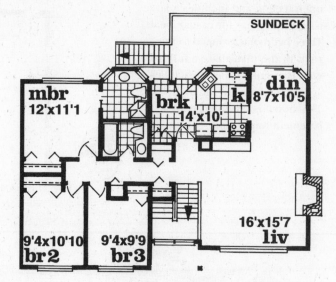

SUNDECK

mbr
12'x11'1

brk
14'x10'

k

din
8'7x10'5

9'4x10'10
br 2

9'4x9'9
br 3

16'x15'7
liv

Design SHS010063

Square Footage: 1,197
Width: 42'-0" Depth: 30'-0"
Price Schedule: A2

This compact, three-bedroom design is ideal as a starter or retirement home. Its siding and brick combination and lovely bumped-out windows give it a cozy, rustic feeling. The bedrooms are positioned along the rear of the home for maximum privacy. Each bedroom has a large window overlooking the rear yard; the owners bedroom is especially spacious. The entry opens directly onto a large living area with a box-bay window and fireplace. The country kitchen contains long, roomy counters, a convenient serving bar and a breakfast nook with a box-bay window. The side door provides quick, easy access to the kitchen and to the basement. If needed, the basement may be finished for additional living space or bedrooms.

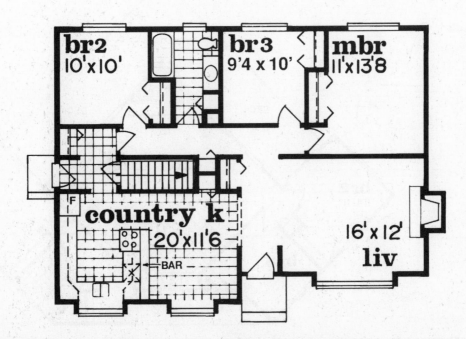

br2
10'x10'

br3
9'4 x 10'

mbr
11'x13'8

country k
20'x11'6

BAR

16' x 12'
liv

D esigned to capture views to the rear of the lot, this home can easily accommodate a narrower lot by angling the plan on the site. Wide sliding glass doors in the living room and dining room open to a wrapping deck that maximizes outdoor living. Note the focal-point fireplace in this open living space. The kitchen sits to the front and offers a large breakfast bar to the living space. The owners bedroom is separated from family bedrooms and has deck access. Bedroom 2 also has deck access. When finished, the lower level offers a fourth bedroom, game room and full bath.

Design SHS010064

Square Footage: 1,180
Width: 64'-6" Depth: 46'-0"
Price Schedule: A2

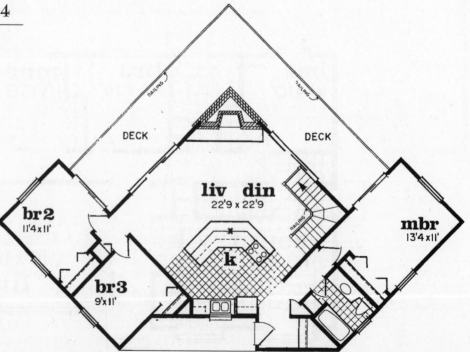

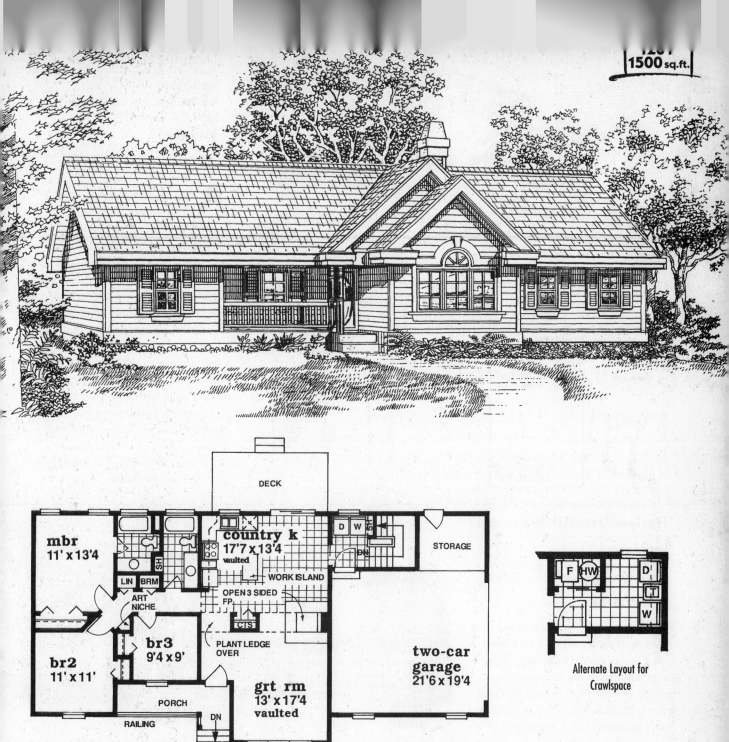

1500 sq.ft.

DECK

country k
17'7 x 13'4
vaulted

D W

STORAGE

mbr
11' x 13'4

SH

LIN BRM

ART
NICHE

WORK ISLAND

OPEN 3 SIDED
FP

CTS

**two-car
garage**
21'6 x 19'4

br3
9'4 x 9'

PLANT LEDGE
OVER

br2
11' x 11'

PORCH

RAILING

DN

grt rm
13' x 17'4
vaulted

F HW D

T

W

**Alternate Layout for
Crawlspace**

Design SHS010065

Square Footage: 1,265
Width: 64'-0" Depth: 32'-0"
Price Schedule: A2

This compact, country home is perfect as a starter design or for empty-nesters. Detailing on the outside includes a covered porch, shuttered windows and a Palladian-style window in the great room. The front entry opens directly into the vaulted great room with its three-sided fireplace, which it shares with the country kitchen. A deck just beyond the kitchen will serve as an outdoor dining spot, accessed easily through sliding glass doors. The kitchen itself is L-shaped and has a handy work island. Three bedrooms include two family bedrooms and a full bath, plus an owners bedroom with a private bath.

SELECT
HOME DESIGNS

Design SHS010066

Square Footage: 1,211
Unfinished Lower Level: 742 square feet
Width: 38'-0" **Depth:** 42'-5"
Price Schedule: A2

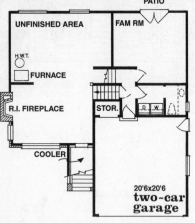

PATIO

UNFINISHED AREA — FAM RM

H.W.T.

FURNACE

R.I. FIREPLACE — STOR. — D W

COOLER

20'6x20'6
two~car garage

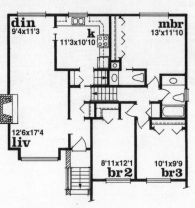

din 9'4x11'3 — **k** 11'3x10'10 — **mbr** 13'x11'10

12'6x17'4 **liv**

8'11x12'1 **br2** — 10'1x9'9 **br3**

Adorned with horizontal siding and brick, the exterior of this home sports details for a rustic, country appeal. The entry is deep-set for weather protection and opens directly to the open living and dining area of the home. A fireplace and box-bay window here are added features. The kitchen's L-shaped configuration is designed for convenience and allows space for a breakfast table. Up a few steps are a full bath and the bedrooms—two family bedrooms and an owners suite with a powder room. Space on the lower level can be developed into a family room with double-door access to a rear patio, a den, a recreation room with a fireplace or extra bedrooms.

Design SHS010067

Square Footage: 1,215
Unfinished Lower Level: 1,215 square feet
Width: 62'-0" **Depth:** 34'-2"
Price Schedule: A2

The main entry to this home is well protected by a columned front porch. The vaulted living room has a warming fireplace. The vaulted ceiling carries over to the country-style kitchen, which features a work island and a generously sized eating area. A deck just beyond is the perfect spot for outdoor dining. The bedrooms up a few stairs include an owners suite with a walk-in closet and full bath. Two additional bedrooms have wall closets and share the use of a main bath in the hallway. The lower level may be developed later as needs grow. It features space for a family room, two bedrooms—or one bedroom and a den—and a full bath. The laundry room is also on this level.

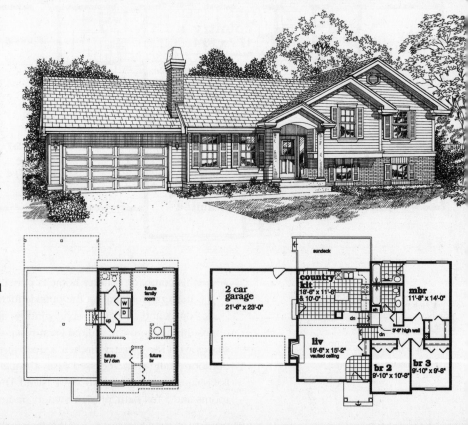

future family room

W D

future br / den — future br

sundeck

2 car garage 21'-6" x 23'-0"

country kit 18'-6" x 11'-6" & 10'-0"

mbr 11'-8" x 14'-0"

3'-6" high wall

liv 18'-6" x 15'-2" vaulted ceiling

br 2 9'-10" x 10'-8" — **br 3** 9'-10" x 9'-8"

FOR PLAN ORDERING INFORMATION SEE PLAN

This attractive siding-and-brick home is not only beautiful, but economical to build. The sunken entry steps up to the living room, warmed by a fireplace. An open railing defines the stairway to the basement, enhancing spaciousness and giving this area a feeling of being much larger. A gourmet kitchen offers a walk-in pantry, a center preparation island with salad sink, and greenhouse windows. Sliding glass doors in the breakfast nook lead to a rear patio. The owners bedroom has a roomy wall closet and separate bath with a shower. Two secondary bedrooms share a bath that includes a soaking tub. A two-car garage sits to the front of the plan, creating privacy and quiet for the bedrooms.

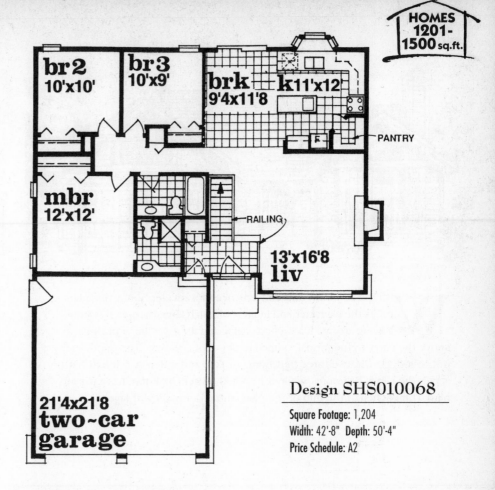

HOMES
1201-
1500 sq.ft.

br2
10'x10'

br3
10'x9'

brk
9'4x11'8

k 11'x12

PANTRY

mbr
12'12'

RAILING

13'x16'8
liv

21'4x21'8
two~car
garage

Design SHS010068

Square Footage: 1,204
Width: 42'-8" Depth: 50'-4"
Price Schedule: A2

SELECT
HOME DESIGNS

Design SHS010070

Square Footage: 1,252
Width: 44'-8" Depth: 50'-8"
Price Schedule: A2

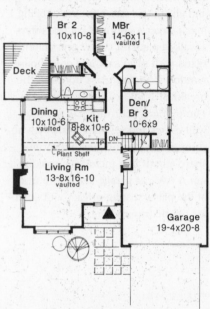

With the economy and convenience of a smaller home, this plan offers the character and interest of much larger homes. It features a living area with a vaulted ceiling and fireplace and a plant shelf above the entry to the formal, vaulted dining room. Sliding glass doors lead out to a deck. Choose three bedrooms or two and a den. A full hall bath serves the family bedrooms, while the vaulted owners bedroom has a private bath. The kitchen at the hub of the plan contains an efficient layout.

Design SHS010069

Square Footage: 1,253
Width: 42'-0" Depth: 52'-0"
Price Schedule: A2

A multi-pane bay window, nestled in a gabled roof, adds charm to this bungalow and gives it a touch of elegance. A large living/dining area is to the left. The living room has a fireplace and bay window; the dining room features a buffet alcove. The kitchen is conveniently located to serve the dining room and enjoys a view over the sink to the rear yard. An owners bedroom and two family bedrooms are on the right side of the plan. The owners suite has a private bath, while the family bedrooms share a full bath that includes a skylight. A two-car garage sits to the front of the plan to help shield the bedrooms from street noise.

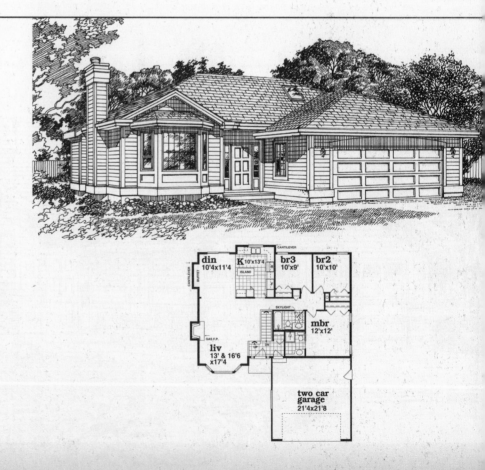

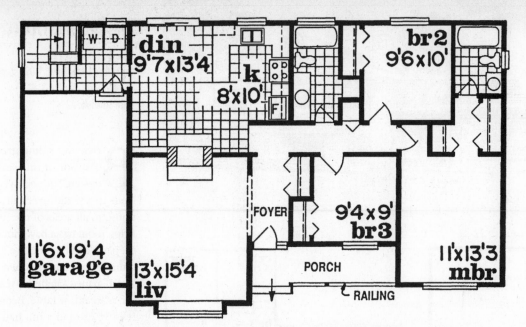

din 9'7x13'4

k 8'x10'

br2 9'6x10'

W D

F

11'6x19'4 garage

13'x15'4 liv

FOYER

9'4 x 9' br3

PORCH

RAILING

11'x13'3 mbr

A covered railed veranda, shuttered windows, siding and wood detailing and a Palladian window all lend their charm to this one-story ranch home. The living room shares a through-fireplace with the dining area and has a box-bay window at the front. A U-shaped kitchen is efficient and pleasant with a window to the backyard over the sink. Garage access is through the laundry room, where you will also find stairs to the basement. The three bedrooms are on the right side of the plan. The owners suite has two wall closets and a private bath. Two family bedrooms share a full hall bath. A single-car garage sits to the side for convenience.

Design SHS010071

Square Footage: 1,233
Width: 54'-0" Depth: 30'-0"
Price Schedule: A2

Design SHS010072

Square Footage: 1,257
Unfinished Lower Level: 1,092 square feet
Width: 55'-0" **Depth:** 43'-9"
Price Schedule: A2

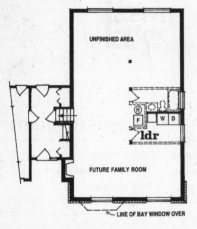

UNFINISHED AREA

ldr
H
F   W D

FUTURE FAMILY ROOM

LINE OF BAY WINDOW OVER

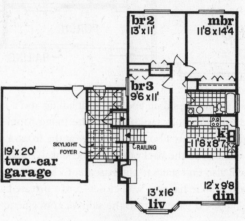

br 2
13'x11'

mbr
11'8 x14'4

br3
9'6 x11'

19'x 20'
two~car garage

SKYLIGHT FOYER

RAILING

k
11'8 x8'7

13'x16'
liv

12' x 9'8
din

Brick and siding grace the exterior of this split-level design. The recessed entry leads to a skylit foyer that directs traffic to all areas of the plan. The living room has a bay window and fireplace and connects to a formal dining room with kitchen access. The L-shaped kitchen saves space for a breakfast table. Bedrooms revolve around a full hall bath with a soaking tub. The unfinished lower level can be developed later into a family room, additional bedrooms, a bathroom and a laundry room.

Design SHS010073

Square Footage: 1,273
Width: 40'-8" **Depth:** 59'-0"
Price Schedule: A3

COVERED RETREAT PATIO SLOPED CLG

LIVING RM
16'8 x 14'0
SLOPED CEILING

MASTER SUITE
12'6 x 14'2
SLOPED CLG

KIT
10'0 x 12'2

LOW WALL

PLANT SHELF ABOVE

LINEN

BATH

LAUNDRY

WALK-IN CLOSET

PANTRY

DINING RM
10'0 x 11'0
TRAY CLG

FOYER

MEDIA/ BEDRM
12'6 x 11'0
8'-0" CLG

MASTER BATH

SHELF

PLANTER

COVERED PORCH

SLOPED CLG

RAILING

GARAGE
19'8 x 21'0

This is a superb home-building candidate for those with a narrow, relatively inexpensive building site. Inside, the rounded corners of the foyer add appeal and foster a feeling of spaciousness. Separate formal and informal dining areas are achieved through the incorporation of a breakfast bar. The kitchen will be a joy in which to work. The spacious living room features a sloped ceiling, a central fireplace and cheerful windows. The owners suite has a sloped ceiling and a high shelf for plants or other decorative items.

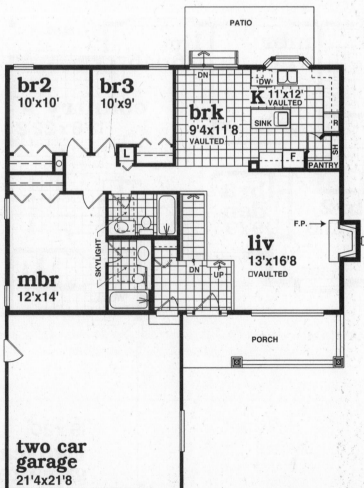

PATIO

br2
10'x10'

br3
10'x9'

brk
9'4x11'8
VAULTED

DN

DW

K 11'x12'
VAULTED

SINK

R

F

PANTRY

SH

L

L

mbr
12'x14'

SKYLIGHT

DN

UP

liv
13'x16'8
□VAULTED

F.P. →

two car
garage
21'4x21'8

PORCH

Design SHS010074

Square Footage: 1,260
Width: 42'-0" Depth: 52'-0"
Price Schedule: A2

This economical-to-build bungalow works well as a small family home or a retirement cottage. The covered porch leads to a vaulted living room with a fireplace. Behind this living space is the U-shaped kitchen with its walk-in pantry and island with utility sink. An attached breakfast nook has sliding glass doors to a rear patio. There are three bedrooms, each with a roomy wall closet. The owners bedroom has a private full bath, while the family bedrooms share a bath. Both baths have bright skylights. A two-car garage sits to the front of the plan to protect the bedrooms from street noise.

Design SHS010075

Square Footage: 1,295
Width: 48'-0" **Depth:** 55'-0"
Price Schedule: A2

This affordable three-bedroom home is not only attractive, but offers all the conveniences. The country kitchen, for example, offers abundant U-shaped counters, a desk/organizer area, a pantry and an eating bar. Sliding glass doors in the country kitchen open to a covered patio—ideal for outdoor entertaining. The living room shares the see-through fireplace with the kitchen and also offers a large window overlooking the rear yard. Direct access from the two-car garage through the laundry room and on to the kitchen is convenient for the family shopper. An owners suite offers a full wall closet and a private bath with a soaking tub. Two additional bedrooms include one that might make the perfect office or guest room.

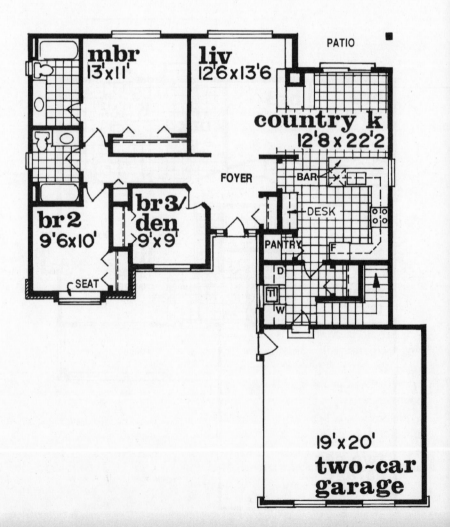

mbr
13'x11'

liv
12'6 x 13'6

PATIO

country k
12'8 x 22'2

FOYER

BAR

DESK

br 2
9'6 x 10'

br 3/
den
9' x 9'

PANTRY

F

D

SEAT

W

19' x 20'
two~car
garage

FOR PLAN ORDERING INFORMATION SEE PLAN

Design SHS010076

Square Footage: 1,282
Unfinished Lower Level: 1,122 square feet
Width: 47'-0" Depth: 27'-0"
Price Schedule: A2

Bold horizontal siding and clean lines make a pleasing exterior for this hillside home. The living and dining rooms flow together for a spacious entertaining area. The living room is warmed by a hearth; the dining room has buffet space. The country kitchen is an ideal gathering spot and allows access to a rear deck. The owners bedroom is tucked into a window bay and features a private bath. Two additional bedrooms share a full bath. The suggested lower level holds laundry space, plus two additional bedrooms, a den and a large family room with fireplace—an additional 1,122 square feet—when finished. A warm sun deck graces the lower level.

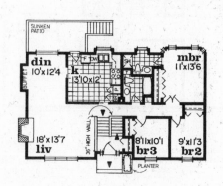

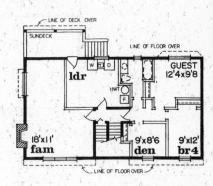

Semi-circular transom windows and decorative columns adorn the front entry of this traditional home. A railing separates the cathedral entry and the living room, which has a bay window. Open space in the formal area, warmed by a fireplace, offers room for entertaining. A buffet nook helps to define the dining room, which is easily served by the nearby kitchen. The lower level offers 514 square feet of space for future expansion.

Design SHS010077

Square Footage: 1,299
Unfinished Lower Level: 514 square feet
Width: 42'-0" Depth: 40'-0"
Price Schedule: A2

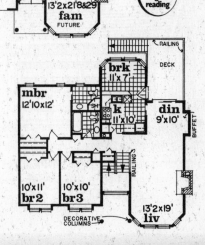

FACTS AT THE BEGINNING OF THIS ISSUE

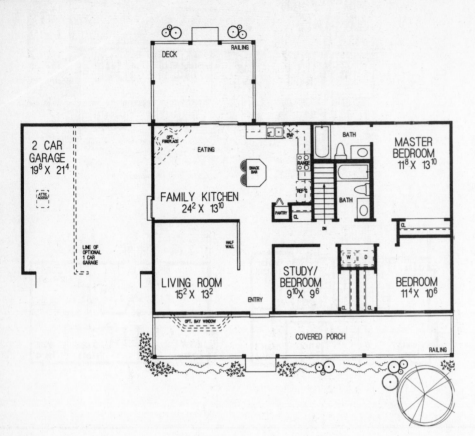

Design SHS010078

Square Footage: 1,317
Width: 66'-0" **Depth:** 34'-5"
Price Schedule: A3

2 CAR GARAGE
19⁸ X 21⁴

ATTIC ACCESS

LINE OF OPTIONAL 1 CAR GARAGE

DECK

RAILING

OPT. FIREPLACE

EATING

SNACK BAR

FAMILY KITCHEN
24² X 13¹⁰

DW

RANGE

REF'S

PANTRY

CL

BATH

BATH

MASTER BEDROOM
11⁸ X 13¹⁰

CL

DN

HALF WALL

LIVING ROOM
15² X 13²

OPT. BAY WINDOW

STUDY/ BEDROOM
9¹⁰ X 9⁶

ENTRY

W   D

CL   CL

BEDROOM
11⁴ X 10⁶

CL

COVERED PORCH

RAILING

All the charm of a traditional country home is wrapped up in this efficient, economical ranch. The time-honored, three-bedroom plan can also serve as two bedrooms plus a study or playroom. The formal living room provides a warm welcome to guests, while the open kitchen and family-room combination offers plenty of space for active family gatherings. This functional interior is packaged in an exterior that features vertical siding, window and door shutters and a crisp brick ledge veneer. A one- or two-car garage may be attached. Other options include a front porch with railing, a bay window and a fireplace.

SELECT HOME DESIGNS

FOR PLAN ORDERING INFORMATION SEE PLAN

Design SHS010079

Square Footage: 1,322
Unfinished Lower Level: 1,031 square feet
Width: 40'-0" **Depth:** 62'-0"
Price Schedule: A2

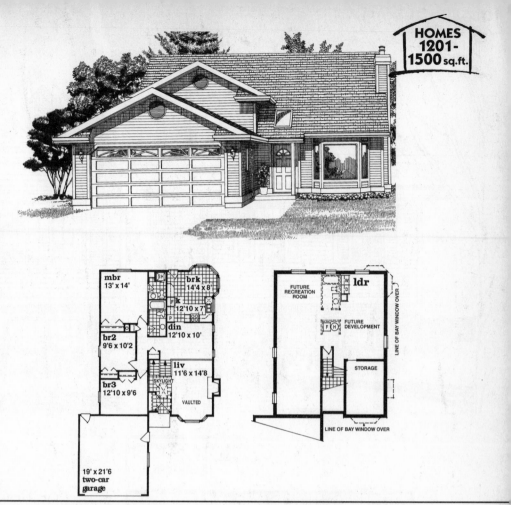

This handsome starter or retirement home offers a wealth of features in a smaller square footage. The vaulted living room, with a fireplace and bay window, shares a level with the skylit foyer. Up a few steps is the railed dining room, which overlooks the living room. The nearby efficient kitchen has a breakfast carousel and access to the rear yard. Bedrooms line the left side of the plan and include an owners suite with a private bath and two family bedrooms sharing a full bath. The lower level has space for a recreation room, a bedroom or home office, a full bath, plus a large storage area and laundry-room alcove.

Design SHS010080

Square Footage: 1,325
Unfinished Lower Level: 1,272 square feet
Width: 38'-0" **Depth:** 56'-0"
Price Schedule: A2

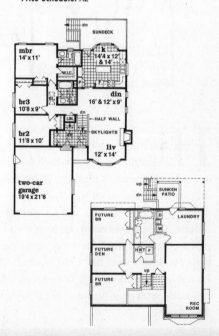

A lovely bay window and a recess entry, complemented by vertical wood siding, enhance the exterior of this split-level design. Skylights brighten the entry foyer and staircase to the main level. A half-wall separates the staircase and the living room. Note the fireplace in the living room. The dining area connects to an L-shaped kitchen with a breakfast bay and access to the rear sun deck. Three bedrooms line the left side of the plan. The owners suite has a full bath and walk-in closet. Family bedrooms share a full bath just off a skylit hall. The lower level contains 1,272 square feet of unfinished space that can be developed into two additional bedrooms, a full bath, a den and a recreation room. The laundry room also on this level offers access to a sunken patio.

FACTS AT THE BEGINNING OF THIS ISSUE

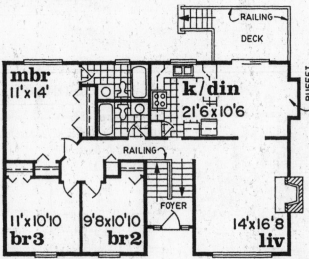

RAILING

DECK

mbr
11' x 14'

k/din
21'6 x 10'6

BUFFET

RAILING

FOYER

11' x 10'10
br3

9'8x10'10
br2

14'x16'8
liv

Design SHS010081

Square Footage: 1,328
Unfinished Lower Level: 1,161 square feet
Width: 44'-0" **Depth:** 28'-6"
Price Schedule: C1

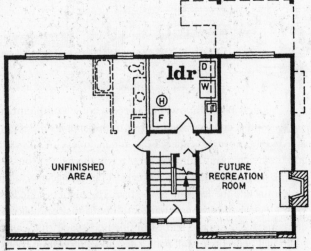

ldr

D
W

H
F

UNFINISHED
AREA

FUTURE
RECREATION
ROOM

Horizontal siding and brick lead to an entry that boasts a half-round window over its door. A cathedral ceiling is found in the foyer, which leads upstairs to the main living level. Amenities include a living room with a masonry fireplace, a dining room with buffet space and sliding glass doors to the rear terrace, and a U-shaped kitchen open to the dinette. The owners bedroom features a large wall closet and private bath. Family bedrooms sit to the front and share a bath. The lower level has 1,161 square feet of unfinished space for a recreation room with fireplace, additional bedrooms, a full bath or even a home office. The laundry room is also found here.

Design SHS010083

Square Footage: 1,332
Width: 63'-6" Depth: 31'-4"
Price Schedule: A2

Brick veneer and siding provide an attractive, low-maintenance option for this ranch home. A weather-protected entry opens to a spacious foyer with a living room on the right and the dining room straight ahead. The living room sports a fireplace and bay window, while the dining room has built-in china cabinet space. The kitchen easily serves the dining room and is U-shaped with ample counters. Sliding glass doors in the dining room lead to a rear patio and the yard beyond. The owners bedroom has a walk-in closet and a private bath with a corner shower. Two additional bedrooms share a hall bath. The single-car garage allows room for a workbench. Note the laundry area that connects the garage to the main house.

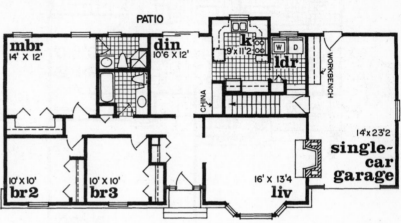

PATIO

mbr
14' X 12'

din
10'6 X 12'

k
9'X 11'2

W D

ldr

WORKBENCH

CHINA

14'x 23'2
single-car garage

10'X 10'
br2

10'X 10'
br3

16' X 13'4
liv

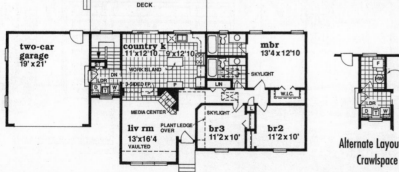

DECK

two-car garage
19' X 21'

country k
11'x 12'10

9'x 12'10

WORK ISLAND

3-SIDED FP

mbr
13'4 x 12'10

SKYLIGHT

MEDIA CENTER

LN

W.I.C.

liv rm
13'x 16'4
VAULTED

PLANT LEDGE OVER

SKYLIGHT

br3
11'2 x 10'

br2
11'2 x 10'

F

BUFFET SPACE

HW

LDR
D T W

Alternate Layout for Crawlspace

Design SHS010082

Square Footage: 1,357
Width; 71'-0" Depth: 30'-6"
Price Schedule: A2

Victorian appointments enhance the facade of this one-story home: horizontal siding, fish-scale details in the gable fronts and simple millwork pieces. The main living area is graced by a vaulted ceiling, a built-in media center and a three-sided fireplace that separates the living area from the country kitchen. The dining space features sliding glass doors to the rear deck. Family bedrooms share a full hall bath with a skylight; the owners bedroom has a private bath. If you choose the crawlspace option, you'll gain buffet space in the country kitchen and extra storage space beyond the laundry room.

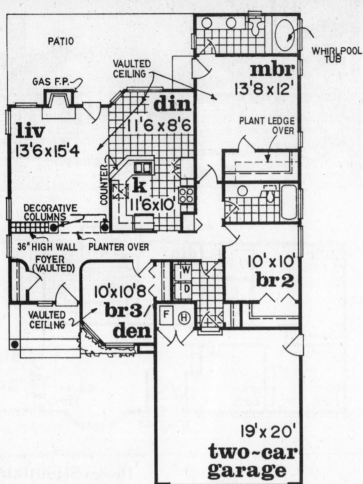

PATIO

VAULTED CEILING

GAS F.P.

WHIRLPOOL TUB

mbr 13'8 x 12'

din 11'6 x 8'6

PLANT LEDGE OVER

liv 13'6 x15'4

COUNTER

k 11'6x10'

DECORATIVE COLUMNS

36" HIGH WALL   PLANTER OVER

FOYER (VAULTED)

VAULTED CEILING

10'x10'8 **br3/ den**

W D

F H

10' x 10' **br2**

19'x 20' **two~car garage**

Design SHS010084

Square Footage: 1,365
Width: 40'-0" Depth: 62'-0"
Price Schedule: C1

This design offers the option of a traditional wood-sided plan or a cool, stucco version. Details for both facades are included in the plans. Although small in appearance the interior offers a very comfortable floor plan. The off-set entry is covered and opens to a vaulted foyer with a coat closet. Decorative columns and a three-foot wall mark the boundary of the living room, which is vaulted and warmed by a gas fireplace. The dining area nearby connects to a U-shaped kitchen with a peninsular counter. Both have cathedral ceilings. A den in the hall might be used as a third bedroom, if you choose. An additional family bedroom has a walk-in closet and a full bath nearby. A vaulted ceiling highlights the owners bedroom. Additional features here include a walk-in closet and a fully appointed bath. A two-car garage remains in the front of the plan and acts as a shield for the bedrooms.

Design SHS010086

Square Footage: 1,360
Width; 56'-0" Depth: 36'-4"
Price Schedule: A2

This beautiful home gives no clue as to how economical it is to build; it holds a rich design with grand amenities. The foyer divides the plan with an open great room and dining room to the rear, kitchen on the left and bedrooms on the right. The vaulted great room has a fireplace. Sliding glass doors in the dining room lead to the rear deck. An L-shaped kitchen is also vaulted and features a box-bay window space for casual dining. One of the family bedrooms serve as a den. The owners suite is also vaulted and has a walk-in closet and private bath.

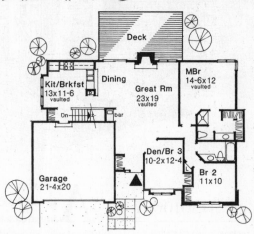

Design SHS010085

Square Footage: 1,360
Width: 64'-0" Depth: 38'-0"
Price Schedule: A2

Small in size, but big on livability, this one-story home has amenities and options usually found only in larger homes. On the right is a vaulted living room with a central fireplace. A bedroom—or make it a den—resides on the left side of this plan. A hall closet holds coats and other outdoor gear. The country kitchen lives up to its name. It features an open-railed staircase to the basement, an L-shaped work counter, a breakfast snack island and a bayed breakfast nook with double-door access to the backyard. The two family bedrooms share a full bath, while the owners bedroom has a private bath.

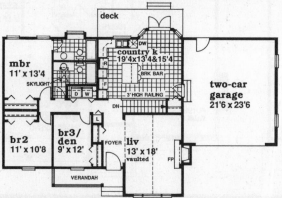

Design SHS010087

Square Footage: 1,363 square feet
Unfinished Lower Level: 848 square feet
Width: 44'-0" **Depth:** 43'-0"
Price Schedule: A2

A columned, covered entry charms the exterior of this three-bedroom, split-entry home. Inside, a 1½-story foyer boasts a dual staircase—one up to the main-floor living area and the other down to the basement. The living area includes a gas fireplace and windows on all walls, ensuring natural light. The adjacent dining room with a buffet alcove exits through a sliding glass door to the rear patio. The roomy kitchen has a raised snack bar, a built-in pantry and is open to a bayed eating area surrounded by windows. A skylight brightens the hall to the three bedrooms. Look for His and Hers closets and a private bath in the owners suite. Future expansion is reserved for space on the lower level.

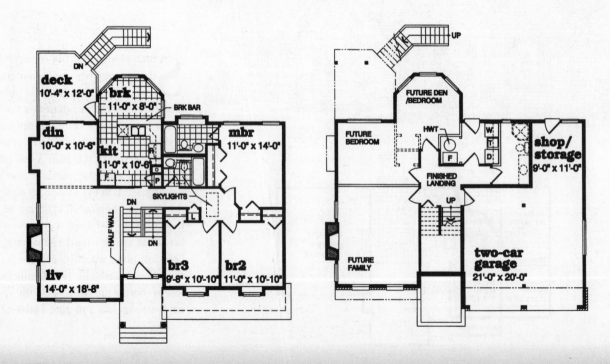

Design SHS010088

First Floor: 674 square feet
Second Floor: 677 square feet
Total: 1,351 square feet
Width: 48'-0" **Depth:** 30'-2"
Price Schedule: A2

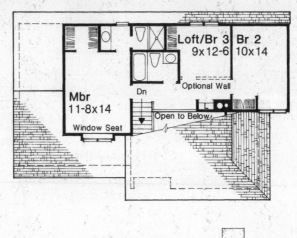

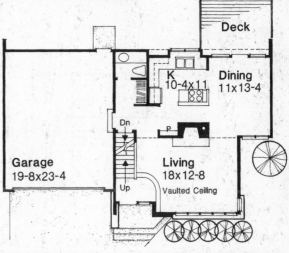

Sweeping rooflines make this modest three-bedroom home appear larger than it really is. Furthering the illusion is a vaulted ceiling in the living room and a balcony overlook from the second floor. A fireplace in the center of the living room acts as a pivotal point around which flows the first-floor traffic. The dining room has sliding glass doors to the rear deck and is served by the L-shaped island kitchen. A half-bath on this level is found near the service entrance. Three bedrooms, or two bedrooms and a loft, are found on the second floor. The owners suite has a private bath.

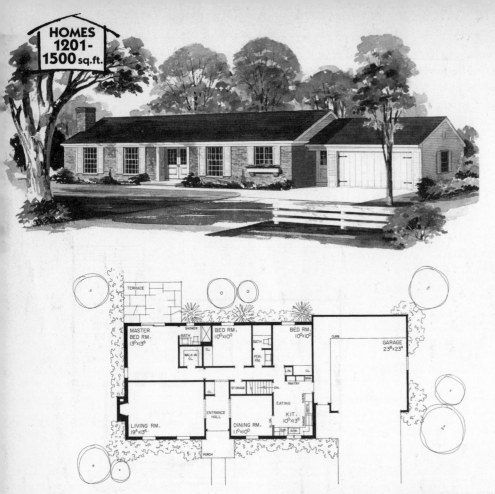

Design SHS010089

Square Footage: 1,387
Width: 74'-9" Depth: 30'-5"
Price Schedule: A3

This finely proportioned home has more than its full share of charm. The focal point of the exterior is the recessed front entry with double Colonial-style doors. The secondary service entrance through the garage to the kitchen is a handy feature. The plan contains three bedrooms, one an owners suite, and two full baths. A living room with fireplace, front kitchen with eating area, and formal dining room make up the living area of the home. There is abundant storage space, plus a basement for additional storage or development in the future.

Design SHS010090

Square Footage: 1,366
Width: 65'-0" Depth: 37'-4"
Price Schedule: A2

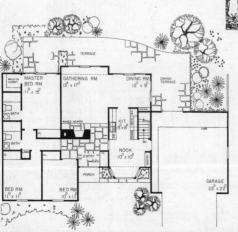

This is a practical, affordable design for families with a strict budget. The large gathering room, open to the dining area, is a center of both casual and formal occasions. Note the raised-hearth fireplace and the adjacent rear terrace. The galley-style kitchen makes great use of available space, opening to a 100-plus-square-foot nook graced with a bay window.

FOR PLAN ORDERING INFORMATION SEE PLAN

Design SHS010091

Square Footage: 1,383
Width: 47'-8" Depth: 32'-6"
Price Schedule: A2

Enhanced by farmhouse details—turned spindles on a covered porch and gable trim—this compact home is as pleasing as it is affordable. The entry opens to a center hall with a living room on one side and dining room on the other. The living room features a box-bay window and warming fireplace. The dining room attaches to the U-shaped kitchen. A handy laundry area with access to the optional two-car garage is nearby. The three bedrooms stretch out along the rear width of the home. The owners suite has a private bath and two wall closets. Two family bedrooms also have wall closets and share the use of a full bath. The basement may be finished later for additional living or sleeping space.

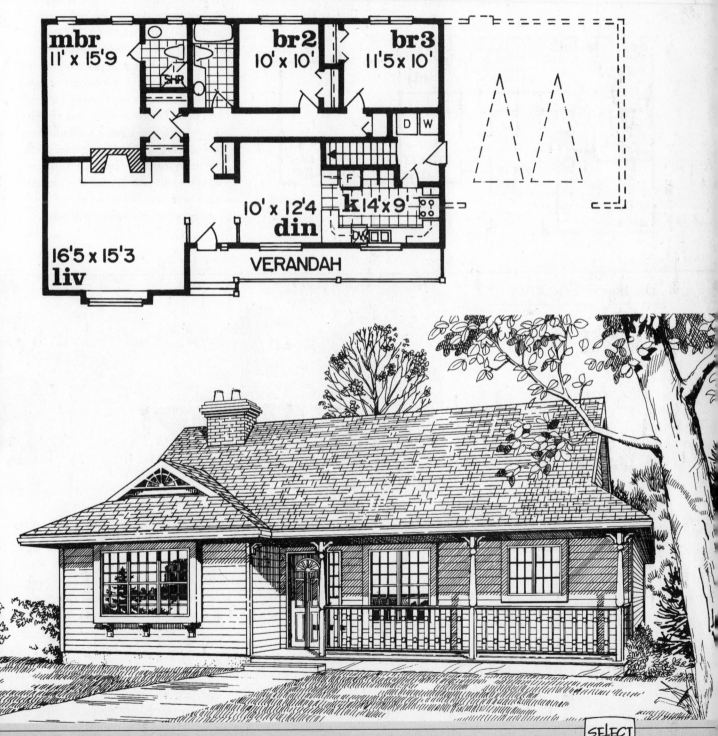

SELECT
HOME DESIGNS

Design SHS010092

Square Footage: 1,399
Width: 69'-0" Depth: 35'-0"
Price Schedule: A2

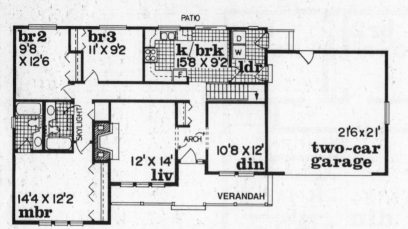

PATIO

br2
9'8 X 12'6

br3
11' X 9'2

k/brk
15'8 X 9'2

ldr

D
W

F

skylight?

12' X 14'
liv

ARCH

10'8 X 12'
din

21'6 x 21'
two~car garage

14'4 X 12'2
mbr

VERANDAH

Classic floor planning dominates this ideal one-story starter home; however, the exterior is worthy of consideration as well. It features a Palladian window, a covered veranda and multi-pane windows. The entry opens to a central foyer flanked by a living room with a fireplace on the left and a formal dining room on the right. Across the hall is the U-shaped kitchen and breakfast room with sliding glass doors to the rear terrace. A laundry area has access to the two-car garage and to the rear yard. There are three bedrooms and two full baths. The owners bedroom has a large wall closet and private bath. Family bedrooms share a full bath.

Design SHS010093

Square Footage: 1,389
Width: 44'-8" Depth: 54'-6"
Price Schedule: A3

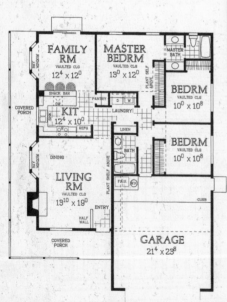

FAMILY RM
VAULTED CLG
12'4 x 12'0

MASTER BEDRM
VAULTED CLG
15'0 x 12'0

MASTER BATH

BEDRM
VAULTED CLG
10'0 x 10'8

SNACK BAR

PANTRY

KIT
12'4 x 10'0

LAUNDRY

LINEN

BATH

BEDRM
VAULTED CLG
10'0 x 10'8

COVERED PORCH

DINING

LIVING RM
VAULTED CLG
13'10 x 19'0

ENTRY

HALF WALL

F.A.U.

CURB

COVERED PORCH

GARAGE
21'4 x 23'8

Simple rooflines and an inviting porch enhance the floor plan. A formal living room has a warming fireplace and a delightful bay window. The U-shaped kitchen shares a snack bar with the bayed family room. Note the sliding glass doors to the rear yard here. Three bedrooms include two family bedrooms served by a full bath and a lovely owners suite with its own private bath.

Design SHS010094

Square Footage: 1,392
Width: 44'-0" **Depth:** 52'-6"
Price Schedule: A2

DECK

br2
10'x12'

br3
10'x12'

din
10'x12'

K
10'x12'

R

BR

F

L

SKYLIGHT   DN

WORK ISLAND

GAS F.P.

MEDIA CENTER

SKYLIGHT

mbr
12'4x14'3

W   D

VAULTED liv
13'x17'2

two car garage
21'8x21'6

DECK

din
9'8x15'6

HOMEWORK SPACE

H

F

GAS F.P.

VAULTED liv
13'x17'2

Alternate Layout for Crawlspace

Traditional corner columns add prestige to this three-bedroom ranch. The vaulted living room features a gas fireplace and a built-in media center. An open kitchen with a work island adjoins the dining room, which contains a large bay window and double French doors leading to the rear deck. An abundance of natural light from the skylights in the main hallways add dramatic effects. The owners suite is appointed with His and Hers wall closets and a private bath. Family bedrooms share a full hall bath. The laundry room has space for a full-sized washer and dryer with cabinets overhead. The crawlspace option allows for a convenient homework space between the dining and living rooms.

Design SHS010095

First Floor: 836 square feet
Second Floor: 581 square feet
Total: 1,417 square feet
Bonus Room: 228 square feet
Width: 42'-0" **Depth:** 33'-6"
Price Schedule: A2

Charming details add to the rustic appeal of this smaller farmhouse design. The covered porch shelters an entry that opens to a center hall with the living and dining rooms on one side and a cozy den on the other. The living/dining room space is warmed by a fireplace. The den has access to a full bath and can double as a guest room. Two bedrooms are on the upper level: an owners bedroom with a wall closet and a family bedroom. Both rooms share a full bath. Bonus space is found on the second floor and can be made into another bedroom or a hobby room when needed.

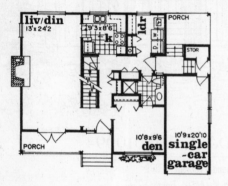

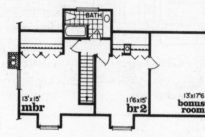

Design SHS010096

Square Footage: 1,408
Width: 70'-0" **Depth:** 34'-0"
Price Schedule: A2

Vaulted ceilings lend a sense of spaciousness to this three-bedroom home. A bright country kitchen boasts an abundance of counter space and cupboards. The front entry is sheltered by a broad veranda. A box-bay window and a spa-style tub highlight the owners suite. The two-car garage provides a workshop area.

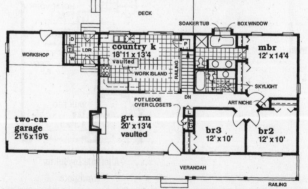

Alternate Layout for Crawlspace

FOR PLAN ORDERING INFORMATION SEE PLAN

Design SHS010098

Square Footage: 1,413
Width: 46'-0" Depth: 55'-6"
Price Schedule: A3

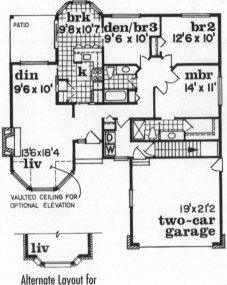

brk 9'8 x 10'7
den/br3 9'6 x 10'
br2 12'6 x 10'
din 9'6 x 10'
k
mbr 14' x 11'
liv 13'6 x 18'4
PATIO
D
W

VAULTED CEILING FOR
OPTIONAL ELEVATION

19' x 21'2
two~car
garage

liv

**Alternate Layout for
Living room**

Dramatic details grace all exterior options for the facade of this cozy one-story plan. The floor plan is spacious and accommodating. It includes a living room with a bay-windowed sitting area and fireplace and the attached formal dining room with a window overlooking the covered patio. An L-shaped kitchen has an adjacent breakfast bay and access to the patio. A nearby flexible-space room can be used as a den or as a third bedroom. The owners suite has a walk-in closet and private bath with shower. One additional bedroom has the use of a hall bath. A utility area holds a laundry alcove and access to the two-car garage. Note the optional living room layout.

Design SHS010097

Square Footage: 1,428
Width: 68'-0" Depth: 38'-0"
Price Schedule: A2

This clever one-story ranch features a covered veranda at the front to enhance outdoor livability. The entry opens to a foyer that leads into a vaulted living room with fireplace on the left and a den or third bedroom on the right. The country kitchen is found to the back and is highlighted by a breakfast bar and sliding glass door to the rear patio. The hallway contains an open-railed stairway to the basement and a laundry alcove, plus a coat closet. Bedrooms are large and have ample closet space. The owners bedroom features a walk-in closet and a full, private bath. Family bedrooms share the use of a skylit bath. A two-car garage handles the family vehicles and faces the front for convenience.

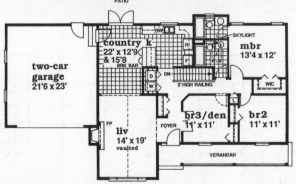

two-car
garage
21'6 x 23'
country k
22' x 12'9
& 15'8
BRK BAR
mbr
13'4 x 12'
SKYLIGHT
liv
14' x 19'
vaulted
FP
FOYER
br3/den
11' x 11'
br2
11' x 11'
WIC
3' HIGH RAILING
VERANDAH
PATIO

Design SHS010099

Square Footage: 1,449
Unfinished Lower Level: 1,222 square feet
Width: 55'-0" **Depth:** 50'-0"
Price Schedule: A2

This lovely split-level home offers full livability on one floor with the possibility of expanding to the lower level at a future time. The main living level includes a large living room with an optional bay window and a fireplace. Bedrooms are to the rear of the plan and include an owners suite with a private bath and two family bedrooms sharing a full bath. The laundry room is at the entry level, where stairs lead to the lower level. When developed, the lower level will include a family room with fireplace, additional bedrooms and a full bath.

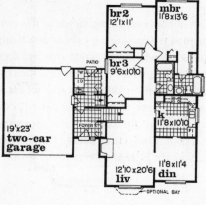

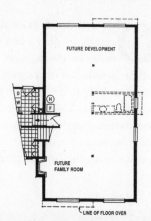

Design SHS010100

First Floor: 743 square feet
Second Floor: 707 square feet
Total: 1,450 square feet
Width: 49'-4" **Depth:** 34'-0"
Price Schedule: A3

Within this compact design lies a wealth of livability. The foyer includes a handy powder room and leads to both the living room, with its central fireplace, and the comfortable kitchen and breakfast nook. The dining area accesses the kitchen and living room. Three bedrooms are located upstairs. The family bedrooms share a full bath, while the owners bedroom features a private bath and a walk-in closet. Additional space is available, which can be made into another bedroom, an office, a studio or used for storage space.

FOR PLAN ORDERING INFORMATION SEE PLAN

Design SHS010101

Square Footage: 1,424
Width: 40'-0"   Depth: 55'-0"
Price Schedule: A2

This affordable three-bedroom starter or empty-nester home offers an efficient floor plan and maximizes square footage. The skylit foyer spills into a vaulted living room, warmed by a hearth and graced with a box-bay window. Just beyond is a vaulted dining room, near the country kitchen. The gourmet will delight in the appointments in the kitchen: a center work island, abundant counter space and a sunny breakfast area with sliding glass doors to the rear garden. The owners bedroom boasts a walk-in closet and a bath with a whirlpool spa. Two additional bedrooms share a bath that includes a skylight. The two-car garage can be reached through a service entrance at the laundry alcove.

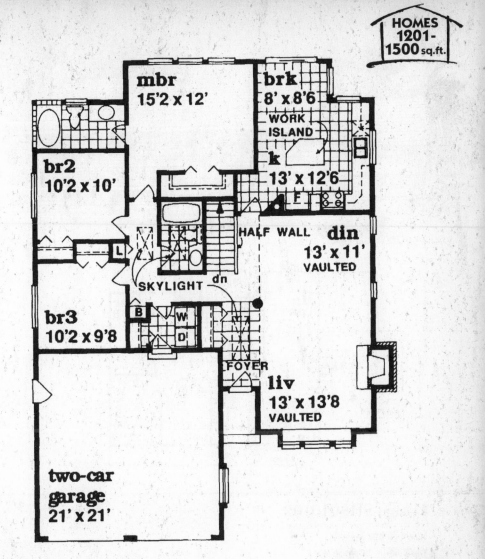

mbr
15'2 x 12'

brk
8' x 8'6

WORK
ISLAND

k
13' x 12'6

br2
10'2 x 10'

HALF WALL

din
13' x 11'
VAULTED

SKYLIGHT

dn

br3
10'2 x 9'8

B

W

D

FOYER

liv
13' x 13'8
VAULTED

two-car
garage
21' x 21'

Design SHS010103

Square Footage: 1,456
Width: 56'-0" Depth: 41'-0"
Price Schedule: A2

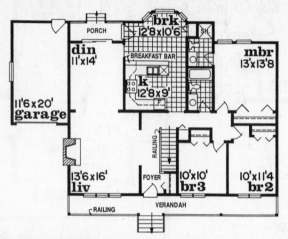

A covered veranda, spanning the width of this three-bedroom home, is a graceful and charming exterior detail. It leads to an entry foyer and the large living and dining space beyond. Here a warming fireplace will act as a focal point. The dining room has a small covered porch beyond sliding glass doors. The U-shaped kitchen has a breakfast bar and serves the dining room and sunny breakfast bay easily. The owners bedroom is one of three at the right of the plan and features a wall closet and a full bath with a shower. Two family bedrooms share a full hall bath.

Design SHS010102

Square Footage: 1,452
Width: 68'-0" Depth: 36'-6"
Price Schedule: A4

This compact three-bedroom home is as economical to build as it is beautiful to behold. Its appeal begins right on the outside with a bay window, a half-circle window over the bay and a railed front porch. The skylit entry foyer leads to a hallway that connects the living areas with the sleeping quarters. The living room is vaulted and has a fireplace, a built-in audio-visual center and a window seat in the bay window. The open dining room shares the vaulted ceiling. The kitchen, with ample work counters, has plenty of room for a breakfast table.

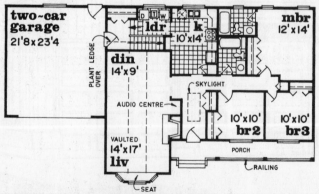

FOR PLAN ORDERING INFORMATION SEE PLAN

RAILING
DECK
12⁰ X 16⁰

DINING RM
8¹⁰ X 10⁸

KITCHEN
8⁰ X 10⁴

RANGE

REF'G

DW

S

MASTER
BATH

S

BATH

MASTER
BEDROOM
13⁶ X 10⁴

CL

CL

CL

OPT. FIREPLACE

RAILING

UP   DN
ENTRY

PORCH

LIVING RM
11⁴ X 14⁸

BEDROOM
10² X 9⁰

BEDROOM
10⁴ X 10⁰

This home offers a living room, a dining room, a kitchen, two baths and three bedrooms. The lower level, with a two-car garage, can be finished in the future to include a family room, a powder room and a utility room. The basic plan may be enhanced with a fireplace in the living room, a brick veneer front, decorative louvers and a rear deck. The blueprints for this house show how to build both the basic, low-cost version and the enhanced, upgraded version.

Design SHS010104

Main Level: 1,028 square feet
Lower Level: 442 square feet
Total: 1,470 square feet
Width: 40'-0"   **Depth:** 26'-0"
Price Schedule: A3

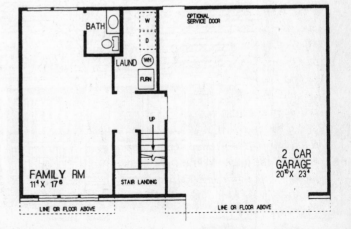

BATH

W
D

OPTIONAL
SERVICE DOOR

LAUND   WH

FURN

UP

FAMILY RM
11⁴ X 17⁶

STAIR LANDING

2 CAR
GARAGE
20¹⁰ X 23⁴

LINE OR FLOOR ABOVE   LINE OR FLOOR ABOVE

Design SHS010105

Square Footage: 1,475
Width: 44'-0" Depth: 43'-0"
Price Schedule: A2

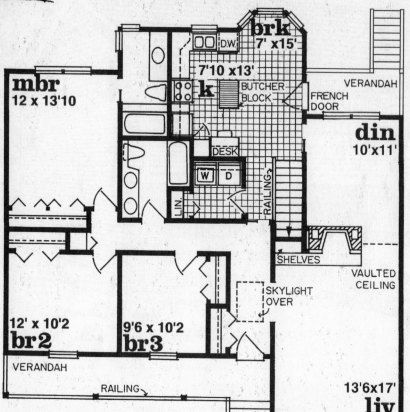

mbr
12 x 13'10

brk
7' x15'

DW

7'10 x13'
k
BUTCHER-
BLOCK

DESK

W D

LIN.

RAILING

VERANDAH

FRENCH
DOOR

din
10'x11'

SHELVES

VAULTED
CEILING

SKYLIGHT
OVER

12' x 10'2
br 2

9'6 x 10'2
br 3

VERANDAH

RAILING

13'6x17'
liv

A railed veranda, turned posts and filigrees complement a lovely Palladian window on the exterior of this home. The foyer is brightly lit by a skylight, and leads to the living room, which has a vaulted ceiling, a fireplace and bookshelves. The dining room overlooks a covered veranda that opens from the breakfast room. A well-organized kitchen features an L-shaped work area and butcher-block island. Clustered sleeping quarters include an owners suite and two family bedrooms sharing a full bath that includes a double vanity.

Design SHS010106

Square Footage: 1,471
Width: 57'-6" **Depth:** 42'-2"
Price Schedule: A2

A gable/cottage roof combination, with horizontal siding and multi-pane windows, lend charm to this affordable family home. The covered entry opens directly to an expansive living room featuring a corner fireplace. The kitchen, dining room and family-room are warmed by a rustic wood stove. Sliding glass doors in the family room area lead out back to a patio and the rear yard beyond. The dining room rests in a bay-windowed area and provides a view to the back. Lovely skylights brighten the hallway and the staircase to the basement.

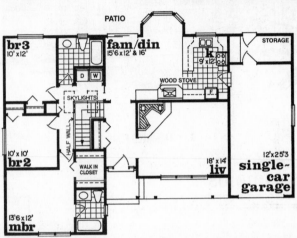

Design SHS010107

Square Footage: 1,485
Width: 65'-10" **Depth:** 37'-4"
Price Schedule: A2

L ow-maintenance brick cladding, quoining and a cottage roof single out this home as a fine traditional design. A flagstone foyer opens on the right to the U-shaped kitchen and bayed breakfast nook and straight ahead to the formal dining and living rooms. Look for a vaulted ceiling with beams, a fireplace and access to the rear patio in the living/dining area. Three bedrooms are on the left side of the plan: an owners suite with a private bath and walk-in closet, and two family bedrooms. Two storage spaces are found in the two-car garage.

ENHANCED PLAN

Design SHS010108

Square Footage: 1,492
Width: 72'-0" Depth: 28'-0"
Price Schedule: A3

Comfort and charm combine in this very affordable ranch plan. A large dining area with a deck door joins the oversized kitchen. An owners bedroom has a private bath; two additional bedrooms share a hall bath. Livability can be enhanced with the optional one- or two-car garage, rear deck with a railing, two angle-bay windows and a fireplace. The blueprints for this house show how to build both a basic, low-cost version and an enhanced, upgraded version.

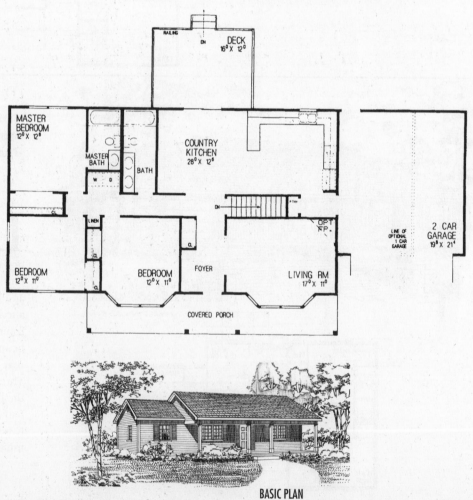

DECK
16⁰ X 12⁰

RAILING
DN

MASTER
BEDROOM
12⁰ X 12⁸

MASTER
BATH

BATH

W D

COUNTRY
KITCHEN
28⁰ X 12⁸

LINEN

CL

DN

OPT
FP

LINE OF
OPTIONAL
1 CAR
GARAGE

2 CAR
GARAGE
19⁸ X 21⁴

BEDROOM
12⁰ X 11⁰

BEDROOM
12⁰ X 11⁰

FOYER

LIVING RM
17⁰ X 11⁰

COVERED PORCH

BASIC PLAN

SELECT HOME DESIGNS

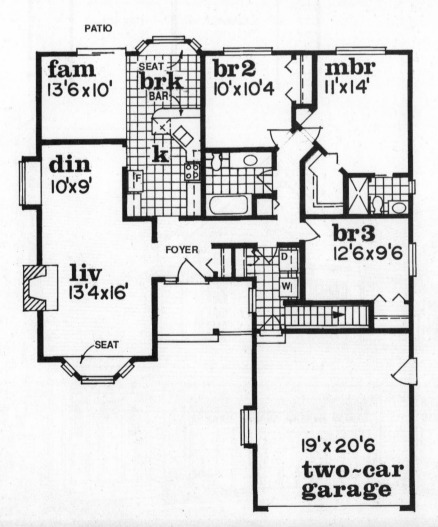

PATIO

fam 13'6 x 10'

SEAT

brk BAR

br2 10'x10'4

mbr 11'x14'

din 10'x9'

k

F

br3 12'6 x9'6

FOYER

liv 13'4x16'

D

W

SEAT

19' x 20'6 **two-car garage**

Design SHS010109

Square Footage: 1,495
Width: 45'-6" Depth: 54'-0"
Price Schedule: A2

This affordable, three-bedroom starter home has a practical layout and an appealing facade, which makes it an attractive choice in a smaller home. A bay window, horizontal siding and a covered entry with turned posts and wood railings are the first noticeable details. Inside, the floor plan minimizes hallways and maximizes the floor area to encourage a sense of space. The living room/dining room combination features a window seat in the bay window and a warming fireplace. The kitchen has a breakfast bar and a bay-windowed eating area. The nearby family room features sliding glass doors to the rear patio. Three bedrooms include two family bedrooms sharing a full bath and an owners suite with a walk-in closet and private bath.

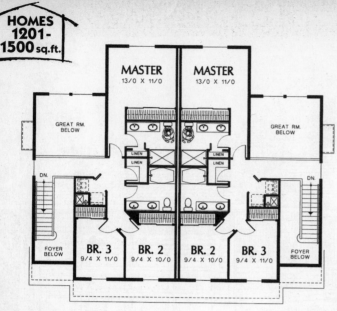

MASTER
13/0 X 11/0

MASTER
13/0 X 11/0

GREAT RM. BELOW

GREAT RM. BELOW

LINEN
LINEN

LINEN
LINEN

DN.

DN.

FOYER BELOW

FOYER BELOW

BR. 3
9/4 X 11/0

BR. 2
9/4 X 10/0

BR. 2
9/4 X 10/0

BR. 3
9/4 X 11/0

Seeing double? No! You're just looking at the smart design of an efficient and comfortable two-story duplex. Inside each unit, a two-story great room offers a warming fireplace for those cool winter evenings. The dining room has easy access to the rear yard, as well as to the C-shaped kitchen. A powder room completes this level. Upstairs, the sleeping zone is made up of a walk-in linen closet, an owners suite with a private bath and two secondary bedrooms sharing a full hall bath that features a dual-bowl vanity.

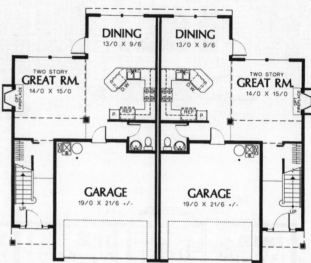

DINING
13/0 X 9/6

DINING
13/0 X 9/6

TWO STORY
GREAT RM.
14/0 X 15/0

OPT. FIREPLACE

TWO STORY
GREAT RM.
14/0 X 15/0

OPT. FIREPLACE

DW

DW

P

REF

REF

P

UP

UP

GARAGE
19/0 X 21/6 +/-

GARAGE
19/0 X 21/6 +/-

Design SHS010110

First Floor: 704 square feet

Second Floor: 782 square feet

Total: 1,486 square feet

Width: 56'-0" **Depth:** 47'-0"

Price Schedule: A2

SELECT HOME DESIGNS

FOR PLAN ORDERING INFORMATION SEE PLAN

2000 sq.ft.

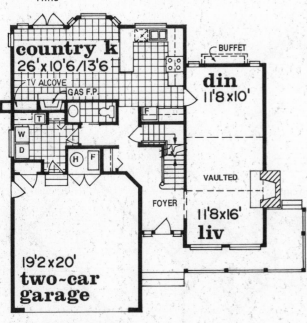

PATIO

country k
26'x10'6/13'6

TV ALCOVE

GAS F.P.

BUFFET

din
11'8 x10'

T

W

D

H   F

VAULTED

FOYER

11'8 x16'
liv

19'2 x 20'
two-car garage

Design SHS010111

First Floor: 963 square feet

Second Floor: 753 square feet

Total: 1,716 square feet

Width: 45'-0" Depth: 44'-0"

Price Schedule: A3

Fish-scale siding and a covered porch with graceful arched woodwork provide stunning curb appeal for this three-bedroom home. The vaulted foyer is brightened by a distinctive second-story bay and spills into the living room and adjoining dining room. These formal areas are graced by a vaulted ceiling and share the warmth of the fireplace in the living room. Optional buffet space is available in the dining room. The country kitchen offers a U-shaped prep area, a bay-windowed eating area, a gas fireplace, a TV alcove and a double door to the rear yard. Second-floor bedrooms include two family bedrooms with a shared bath and an owners suite with a private bath.

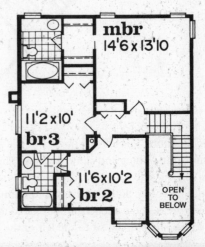

mbr
14'6 x 13'10

11'2 x10'
br3

11'6 x10'2
br2

OPEN
TO
BELOW

SELECT
HOME DESIGNS

Design SHS010112

Square Footage: 1,530
Unfinished Lower Level: 1,440 square feet
Width: 77'-7" **Depth:** 61'-0"
Price Schedule: A3

DECK   DECK

DINING   LIVING
12'   27'-7"   28'-6"(8.7m)12'

BEDROOM   MASTER
11' X 11'-3"   BEDROOM
                            13'-3" X 11'

                KITCHEN

BEDROOM   GARAGE
11' X 9'-1"   BALCONY

Rustic in nature, this hillside home offers a surrounding deck and upper-level balcony on the exterior to complement its horizontal siding and stone detailing. The entry opens to a staircase leading up to the main level or down to finish-later space in the basement. The kitchen is at the heart of the home and has miles of counter space and a pass-through bar to the dining room. Both the living and dining rooms have sliding glass doors to the deck. A corner fireplace warms and lights both areas. The owners bedroom sits to the right of the plan and has a private bath and deck access. Two additional bedrooms with a shared bath sit to the left of the plan. One of these bedrooms has deck access.

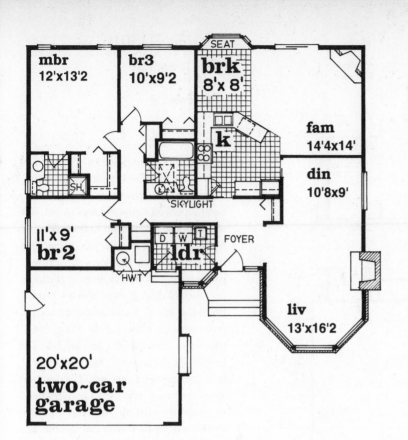

mbr
12'x13'2

br3
10'x9'2

SEAT
brk
8'x8'

k

fam
14'4x14'

din
10'8x9'

SKYLIGHT

SH

11'x9'
br2

D W T
ldr

FOYER

HWT

liv
13'x16'2

20'x20'
two-car
garage

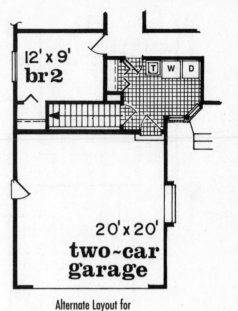

12'x9'
br2

T W D

20'x20'
two-car
garage

Alternate Layout for
Basement

A cozy bay window accents and helps protect the entry of this one-story home. It opens to a foyer with living areas on the right. The formal living room has a fireplace and an attached dining room for formal occasions. Across the foyer is a kitchen with an angled counter, an attached breakfast nook with a window seat and overlook to the family room with its corner fireplace. Bedrooms dominate the left side of the plan and include an owners suite and two family bedrooms sharing a skylit bath. The owners suite has a private bath with a shower and a walk-in closet.

Design SHS010113

Square Footage: 1,511
Width: 46'-0" Depth: 51'-6"
Price Schedule: A3

Design SHS010114

Square Footage: 1,530
Width: 51'-4" Depth: 55'-6"
Price Schedule: A4

TERRACE

MASTER BEDROOM
12⁰x14⁸

BEDROOM
11⁰x11⁰

GATHERING RM.
15⁰x16⁰

TERRACE

DINING RM.
9⁰x13⁴

SLOPED → CEILING

LIN. CL.

DRESSING RM.

WALK-IN CLOSET

BATH

RANGE

ST. DW.

KITCHEN
11⁰x9⁸

PASS THRU

BRKFST RM.
9⁶x8⁰

BATH

TUB

CL.

FOYER

PANTRY

REF'G.

BROOM CL.

LAUND.
W. D.

DN.

CL.

STUDY/BEDROOM
11⁰x11⁰

CL.

COVERED PORCH

CURB

GARAGE
21⁴x21⁴

Available reverse right reading

This charming one-story traditional design offers plenty of livability in a compact size. Thoughtful zoning puts all sleeping areas to one side of the house, apart from household activity in the living and service areas. The home includes a spacious gathering room with a sloped ceiling, in addition to a formal dining room and a separate breakfast room. There's also a handy pass-through between the breakfast room and the large, efficient kitchen. The laundry is strategically located adjacent to the garage and the breakfast/kitchen areas for handy access. An owners bedroom enjoys a private bath and a walk-in closet. A third bedroom can double as a sizable study just off the foyer.

SELECT HOME DESIGNS

FOR PLAN ORDERING INFORMATION SEE PLAN

Design SHS010115

Square Footage: 1,515
Width: 71'-8" **Depth:** 36'-0"
Price Schedule: A3

Whether it's a starter house you are after, or one in which to spend your retirement years, this pleasing farmhouse will provide a full measure of pride in ownership. The contrast of vertical and horizontal lines, the double front doors and the coach lamppost at the garage create an inviting exterior. The floor plan functions in an orderly and efficient manner. The spacious gathering room and dining room have a delightful view of the rear yard and make entertaining a joy. The owners bedroom has a private bath and a walk-in closet. Two additional bedrooms share a full hall bath. Extra amenities include plenty of storage facilities, two sets of glass doors to the terraces, a fireplace in the gathering room, a basement and an attached two-car garage.

TERRACE

TERRACE

STORAGE

MASTER BED RM. 11⁰ x 15⁶

GATHERING RM. 26⁸ x 15⁶

WALK-IN CLOSET

DINING

BATH

CURB

BATH

CL.

CL.

B.CL. RANGE OVEN

DN.

HALL

LINEN

CL. STOR.

ENTRY

KITCHEN 10⁰ x 11⁶

NOOK 8⁴ x 11⁶

PANTRY

GARAGE 23⁴ x 23⁴

PORCH

BED RM. 11⁰ x 11²

BED RM. 10⁰ x 11²

HOMES 1501-2000 sq.ft.

Design SHS010116

Square Footage: 1,538
Width: 54'-6" Depth: 55'-6"
Price Schedule: A3

This compact three-bedroom design offers a wealth of amenities—and you can make one of the bedrooms into a den or home office, if you choose! A skylit foyer spills into a vaulted living room with a bay-windowed seat and corner fireplace. The dining room is open to the living room and connects directly to the kitchen, where there is another bay-windowed seat. An angled snack bar separates the kitchen from the family room; double doors open onto the patio at the back of the house. The owners bedroom offers still another bay window with a window seat and has a walk-in closet and private bath. The family bedrooms—one with a walk-in closet—share a full bath. Note the laundry space in the service entrance to the two-car garage.

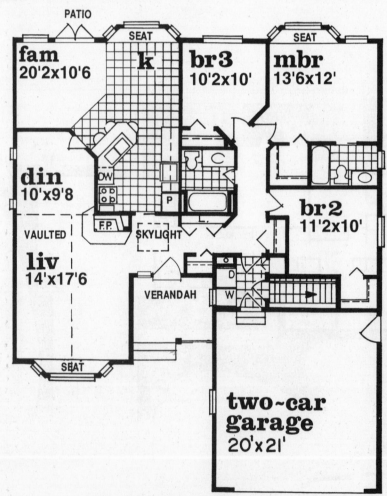

PATIO

fam
20'2x10'6

SEAT

k

br3
10'2x10'

SEAT

mbr
13'6x12'

din
10'x9'8

DW

F.P.

P

SKYLIGHT

br2
11'2x10'

VAULTED

liv
14'x17'6

VERANDAH

D

W

SEAT

two~car
garage
20'x21'

SELECT HOME DESIGNS

FOR PLAN ORDERING INFORMATION SEE PLAN

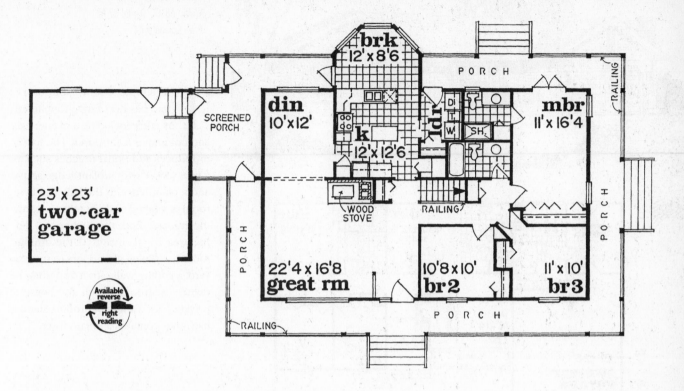

brk 12'x8'6

din 10'x12'

PORCH

mbr 11'x16'4

SCREENED PORCH

RAILING

k 12'x12'6

ldr

D T W

SH.

23'x23' **two-car garage**

PORCH

WOOD STOVE

RAILING

Available reverse right reading

22'4 x 16'8 **great rm**

10'8 x 10' **br2**

11' x 10' **br3**

RAILING

PORCH

This popular design begins with a wraparound covered porch made even more charming with turned-wood spindles. The entry opens directly into the great room, which is warmed by a wood stove. The adjoining dining room offers access to a screened porch for outdoor after-dinner leisure. A country kitchen features a center island and a breakfast bay for casual meals. Family bedrooms share a full bath that features a soaking tub. The two-car garage connects to the plan via the screened porch.

Design SHS010117

Square Footage: 1,541
Width: 87'-0" **Depth:** 44'-0"
Price Schedule: A3

Design SHS010118

Square Footage: 1,566
Width: 68'-0" Depth: 37'-0"
Price Schedule: A4

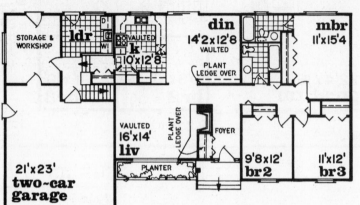

STORAGE & WORKSHOP

ldr

D
W

k
10'x12'8

VAULTED

din
14'2 x 12'8
VAULTED

mbr
11'x15'4

PLANT LEDGE OVER

VAULTED
16'x14'
liv

PLANT LEDGE OVER

FOYER

PLANTER

9'8'x12'
br2

11'x12'
br3

21'x23'
two-car garage

This simple, country, one-story plan has decorative touches at its entry including a planter box and columned front porch. The foyer introduces additional touches such as a coat closet with a plant ledge above and a plant ledge in the hall. The living room is vaulted and contains a warming fireplace. Both the kitchen and dining area are also vaulted; the dining room has sliding glass doors to the rear yard. A roomy wall closet appoints the owners bedroom, which also boasts a private bath. Family bedrooms share a bath that contains a linen closet.

Design SHS010119

Square Footage: 1,577
Width: 76'-0" Depth: 34'-0"
Price Schedule: A3

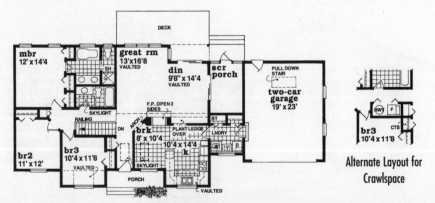

Circle-head windows lend character to the exterior of this country-style, three-bedroom home. The skylit entry foyer leads to a vaulted great room with a centrally located fireplace open to the kitchen and breakfast nook. The formal dining room is also vaulted and has sliding glass doors to the rear deck and to a side screened porch. Both entries to the kitchen/breakfast area are accented—one by an arch and one with a plant ledge. The owners bedroom features three wall closets and a private bath with a separate tub and shower and double vanities. Family bedrooms have the use of a full bath with a skylight.

DECK

mbr
12' x 14'4

great rm
13'x16'8
VAULTED

din
9'8" x 14'4
VAULTED

scr porch

PULL DOWN STAIR

two-car garage
19' x 23'

SKYLIGHT

F.P. OPEN 2 SIDES

RAILING

DN

brk
8' x 10'4

ST

LNDRY

PLANT LEDGE OVER

br2
11' x 12'

br3
10'4 x 11'8
VAULTED

k
10'4 x 14'4

SKYLIGHT

PORCH

VAULTED

br3
10'4 x 11'8

CTS

Alternate Layout for Crawlspace

SELECT HOME DESIGNS

FOR PLAN ORDERING INFORMATION SEE PLAN

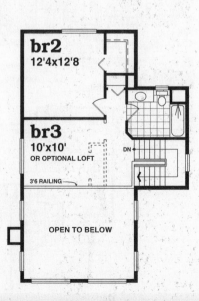

PORCH

mbr
12'4x12'8

din
12'10'

k
8'4x10'

W D

CABINETS

DN

UP

BREAKFAST BAR

great rm
17'x13'6

PORCH

br2
12'4x12'8

br3
10'10'
OR OPTIONAL LOFT

3'6 RAILING

DN

OPEN TO BELOW

Design SHS010120

First Floor: 1,012 square feet
Second Floor: 556 square feet
Total: 1,568 square feet
Width: 34'-0" **Depth:** 48'-0"
Price Schedule: A3

Country comes home to this plan with details such as a metal roof, horizontal siding, multi-pane double-hung windows, and front and rear porches. The recessed front entry leads to a two-story great room, flanked by a breakfast bar and formal dining room with access to both the front and rear porches. The great room is warmed by a fireplace and features a two-story ceiling. The owners bedroom is on the first level and has a private bath and walk-in closet. A half-bath is in the laundry room. The second floor has two additional bedrooms, one with a walk-in closet. If you choose, Bedroom 3 could be turned into loft space. A full bath serves both bedrooms.

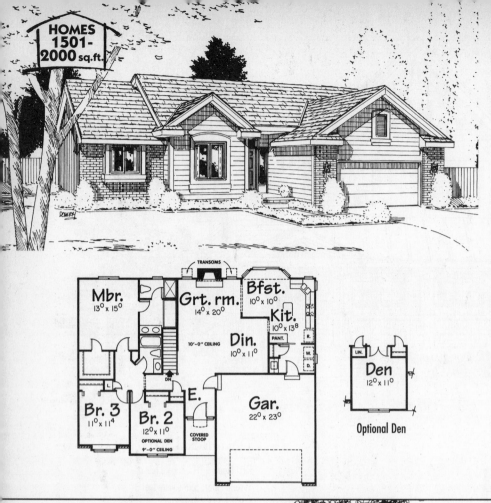

Design SHS010121

Square Footage: 1,579
Width: 53'-4" Depth: 46'-0"
Price Schedule: A3

Simple and sound, this fine one-story choice gives you many options. Build Bedroom 2 as an optional den with double-door access, and you will also gain an additional linen closet. The remainder of the floor plan is eminently livable. The great room and dining room feature ten-foot ceilings. They attach directly to the breakfast room/kitchen area. Besides great work space, this area offers sunlit casual dining and access through a pocket door to the laundry room. The owners suite has fine appointments, including a walk-in closet, a bath with a separate tub and shower, dual sinks and a compartmented toilet. The two-car garage resides to the front to help shield the main house from noise. Please specify basement, block or slab foundation when ordering.

Design SHS010122

Square Footage: 1,583
Width: 50'-0" Depth: 53'-4"
Price Schedule: A3

A carousel roofline, circle-head windows and brick accents highlight the exterior of this distinctive home. The skylit foyer spills over into a vaulted living/dining room combination and then, through pocket doors, to a cozy family room with a fireplace. The kitchen features an angled counter and has a breakfast nook with sliding glass doors to the rear patio. Bedroom 3 could make the perfect den and has a vaulted ceiling over a Palladian window. The owners suite has a skylit dressing area, long wall closet and private bath. Please specify basement or crawlspace foundation when ordering.

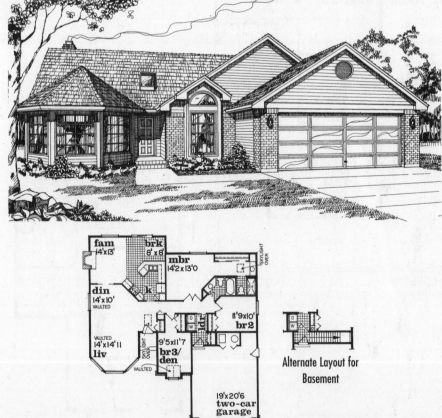

FOR PLAN ORDERING INFORMATION SEE PLAN

Design **SHS010123**

Square Footage: 1,588
Width: 78'-0" Depth: 36'-0"
Price Schedule: A3

The columned front porch of this home conceals a recessed entry that opens to a foyer leading directly into the vaulted great room and dining room. The country kitchen is easily accessed from all main areas of the home. It features a work island and a vaulted ceiling. The bedrooms are down a skylit hall and include an owners suite with a walk-in closet and a bath with a double vanity and a soaking tub. The family bedrooms share the use of a full bath.

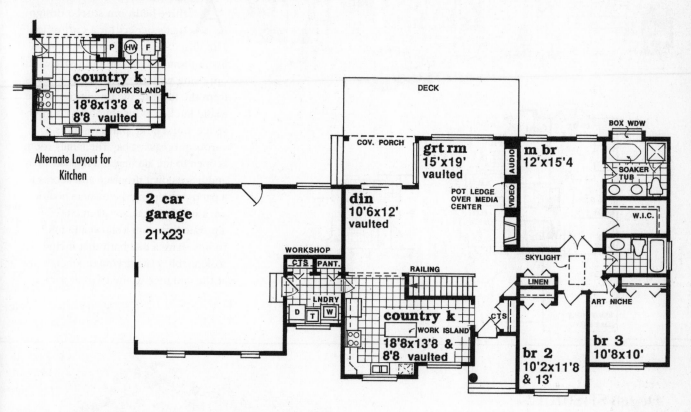

Alternate Layout for Kitchen

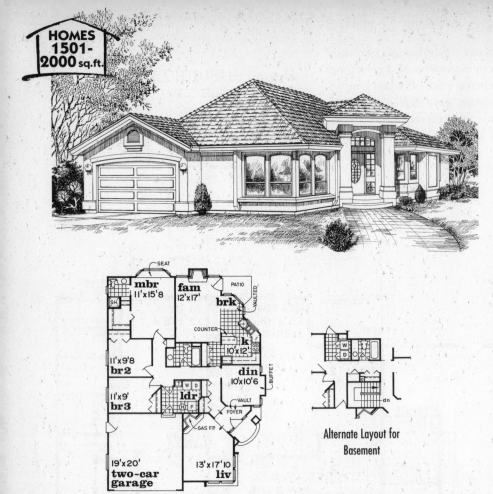

Design SHS010125

Square Footage: 1,613
Width: 40'-0" **Depth:** 56'-6"
Price Schedule: A3

Alternate Layout for Basement

A tall, arched entry introduces this three-bedroom stucco design that's perfect for a corner lot. The raised foyer spills into a sunken living room with a corner fireplace and opposing windows. An archway leads from the foyer to the dining room. The island kitchen, with abundant counter space and a large pantry, serves a carousel breakfast bay. The family room is open to the kitchen and breakfast bay and has its own fireplace and access to a patio. Appointing the owners bedroom are a window seat, a walk-in closet and a private bath with a shower. Family bedrooms share a hall bath that includes a soaking tub. A laundry/mudroom lies just at the entrance to the two-car garage.

Design SHS010124

Square Footage: 1,624
Width: 52'-0" **Depth:** 50'-6"
Price Schedule: A3

This affordable ranch home offers horizontal siding and brick. The entry features transom windows, which bathe the plant ledge in natural light. The living room has a vaulted ceiling, a fireplace and rear-yard access. The formal dining room provides tall, arched windows and easy access to both the foyer and the gourmet kitchen. The breakfast room features a planning desk.

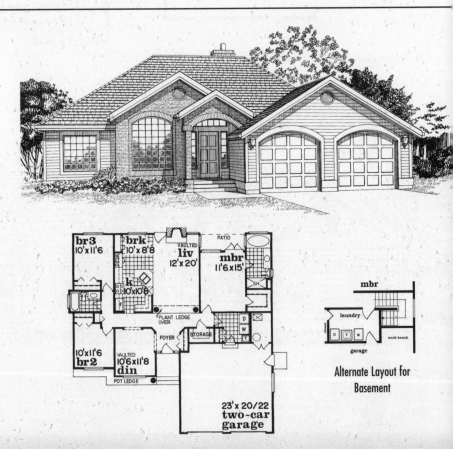

Alternate Layout for Basement

Design SHS010126

First Floor: 886 square feet
Second Floor: 734 square feet
Total: 1,620 square feet
Width: 52'-0" **Depth:** 35'-0"
Price Schedule: A3

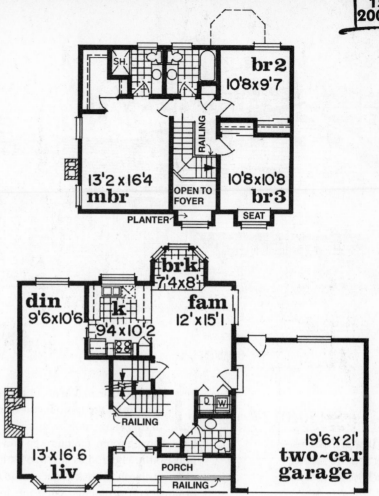

Delightful details color this farm-house-style home. A covered porch, a bay window and dormers all add interesting touches. Inside, the vaulted foyer divides the first-floor plan into formal and informal areas. A living room with its fireplace and attached dining room are on the left; a family room with a bayed breakfast nook is on the right. The U-shaped kitchen sits between the two areas and is graced by a window sink. The laundry alcove leads the way to the two-car garage. Three bedrooms are contained on the second floor. Bedroom 3 has a lovely window seat in a dormer window. The owners bedroom features a walk-in closet and a private bath with a shower. Family bedrooms share a hall bath.

ENHANCED PLAN

Design SHS010127

Main Level: 528 square feet
Upper Level: 576 square feet
Lower Level: 528 square feet
Total: 1,632 square feet
Width: 62'-4" **Depth:** 28'-0"
Price Schedule: A3

Three-level living! Main, upper and lower levels serve you and your family. Start from the bottom and work your way up. A family room with an optional fireplace, study or bedroom, laundry and powder room occupy the lower level. A living room, dining room and kitchen are on the main level. The upper level houses three bedrooms and two baths. This design has great interior livability and exterior charm. A brick veneer front, rear deck with railing and two-car garage are optional enhancements. Blueprints for this house show how to build both the basic, low-cost version and the enhanced, upgraded version.

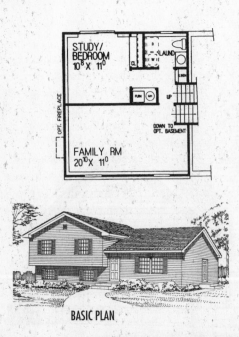

STUDY/BEDROOM 10⁸ X 11⁰
LAUND
OPT. FIREPLACE
FURN
UP
DOWN TO OPT. BASEMENT
FAMILY RM 20¹⁰ X 11⁰

BASIC PLAN

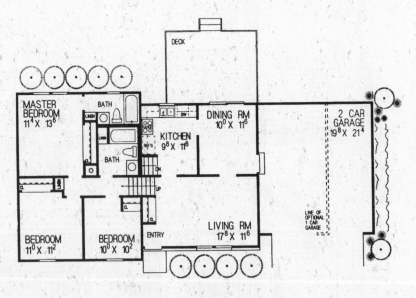

DECK
MASTER BEDROOM 11⁴ X 13⁶
BATH
LINEN
LINEN
BATH
KITCHEN 9⁸ X 11⁶
DINING RM 10⁰ X 11⁶
DW
REF
2 CAR GARAGE 19⁸ X 21⁴
BEDROOM 11⁰ X 11²
BEDROOM 10⁰ X 10²
ENTRY
UP
DN
LIVING RM 17⁸ X 11⁶
LINE OF OPTIONAL 1 CAR GARAGE

Design SHS010129

First Floor: 1,099 square feet
Second Floor: 535 square feet
Total: 1,634 square feet
Width: 44'-8" **Depth:** 41'-4"
Price Schedule: A3

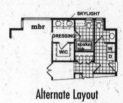

This design offers several different options to make the floor plan exactly as you like it. The exterior is graced by a wrapping veranda, round columns, stone facing with cedar shingled accents and a trio of dormers. Inside, the open plan includes a vaulted great room with a fireplace, a vaulted dining room, a vaulted kitchen and three bedrooms. The kitchen has a pass-through to the dining room and large pantry. The owners bedroom is found on the first floor for privacy. It contains a walk-in closet with a dressing room, a sitting area and a full skylit bath. Family bedrooms are on the second floor.

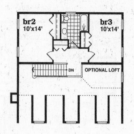

Alternate Layout

Design SHS010128

Square Footage: 1,647
Width: 54'-8" **Depth:** 47'-10"
Price Schedule: A3

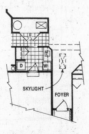

Alternate Layout for Crawlspace

This floor plan is designed for a home that captures a view to the rear of the lot. French doors in the dining room, living room, owners bedroom and breakfast room all lead out to the patio in the back. In the front, a skylit patio is visually zoned from the living room by a plant shelf. Both the living room and dining room have vaulted ceilings and enjoy a warming fireplace set between them. The bedrooms are to the right and include two family bedrooms sharing a full bath. The owners suite is vaulted and has a walk-in closet and private bath with separate tub and shower.

Design SHS010131

Square Footage: 1,652
Width: 78'-6" Depth: 48'-0"
Price Schedule: A3

This long, low ranch home has outdoor living on two porches — one to the front and one to the rear. Vaulted ceilings in the great room, kitchen and owners bedroom add a dimension of extra space. The great room is warmed by a fireplace and is open to the country kitchen with rear-porch access. The fine owners suite also has doors to the rear porch and is graced by a walk-in closet, plus a full bath with a garden tub and dual vanity. The two-car garage contains space for a freezer and extra storage cabinets that are built in.

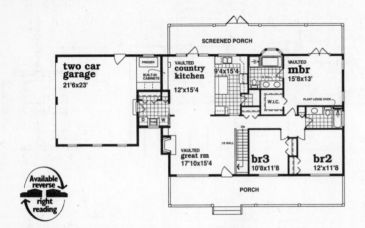

Design SHS010130

Square Footage: 1,666
Width: 60'-6" Depth: 44'-4"
Price Schedule: A4

A courtyard with a planter box leads up a few steps to the double-door entry of this ranch home. The bright, entry opens directly to the living room, which features a corner fireplace and sliding glass doors to the rear yard. The breakfast area has a bay window and is convenient to the U-shaped kitchen with its island work center. The owners bedroom at the other end of the plan features His and Hers wall closets and a private bath with a soaking tub. Two additional bedrooms—one can serve as a den—share a hall bath.

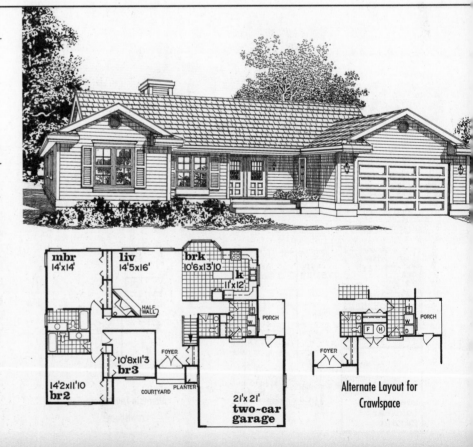

Alternate Layout for Crawlspace

Design SHS010132

Square Footage: 1,662
Width: 47'-0" Depth: 56'-8"
Price Schedule: A4

This elegant design offers horizontal siding with a brick chimney. The focal point of the exterior is the large windowed bay, complemented by a hipped roof. The recessed entry flows into the sunken living room with its fireplace and then on to the formal dining room. The breakfast bay, with greenhouse windows, connects the kitchen and sunken family room. The kitchen is U-shaped for convenience and has abundant counter space. In the owners bedroom, there is another bay window with a cozy window seat, a walk-in closet and a full, private bath with a soaking tub. Additional bedrooms share a full bath.

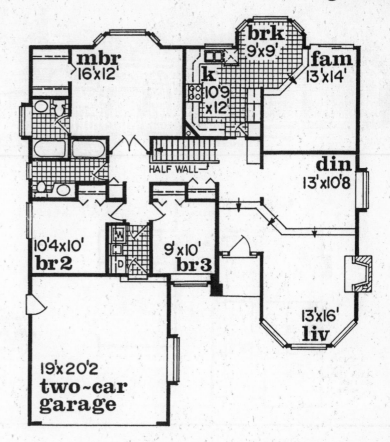

Design SHS010133

Square Footage: 1,689
Width: 58'-0" **Depth:** 52'-6"
Price Schedule: A4

You may not decide to build this design simply because of its delightful covered rear porch, but it certainly will provide its share of enjoyment by taking casual living outdoors. The living room/dining area is highlighted by a fireplace, sliding glass doors to the porch and an open staircase. The efficient kitchen has a handy snack bar and breakfast nook. Notice how effectively the bedrooms are arranged away from the traffic flow of the house. The front bedroom could double as a TV room or study.

Available reverse
right reading

Design SHS010134

Square Footage: 1,678
Width: 46'-8" **Depth:** 56'-8"
Price Schedule: A3

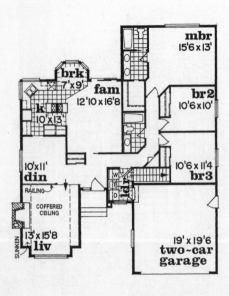

The interior plan of this one-story home is modern and quite comfortable. A sunken living room with a masonry fireplace dominates the front of the plan and is separated from the formal dining room by a low rail. The kitchen, bayed breakfast room and family room work together to create one large, open, casual, gathering space. The kitchen has a convenient center cooking island. Bedrooms sit behind the two-car garage to ensure quiet. The owners suite features a walk-in closet and a private bath with compartmented toilet and tub.

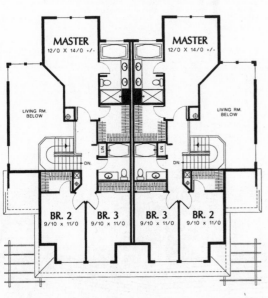

With shingles, stonework, a trellis-covered front walk and twin gables, this fine two-story duplex is sure to please. Inside, the two-story living room greets friends and family alike, offering a fireplace and built-in media center for cozy get-togethers. The C-shaped kitchen features a window over the sink, plenty of counter and cabinet space, and a serving counter into the dining room. A laundry room and a half-bath complete this level. Upstairs, two secondary bedrooms—one with a walk-in closet—share a full hall bath. The owners suite offers a large walk-in closet and a pampering private bath.

MASTER
12/0 X 14/0 +/-

MASTER
12/0 X 14/0 +/-

LIVING RM.
BELOW

LIVING RM.
BELOW

DN.

DN.

BR. 2
9/10 x 11/0

BR. 3
9/10 x 11/0

BR. 3
9/10 x 11/0

BR. 2
9/10 x 11/0

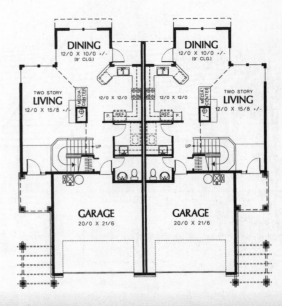

DINING
12/0 X 10/0 +/-
[9' CLG.]

DINING
12/0 X 10/0 +/-
[9' CLG.]

TWO STORY
LIVING
12/0 X 15/8 +/-

MEDIA
CENTER

12/0 X 12/0

12/0 X 12/0

MEDIA
CENTER

TWO STORY
LIVING
12/0 X 15/8 +/-

REF.

REF.

UP

UP

GARAGE
20/0 X 21/6

GARAGE
20/0 X 21/6

Design SHS010135

First Floor: 785 square feet
Second Floor: 902 square feet
Total: 1,687 square feet
Width: 56'-0" **Depth:** 56'-0"
Price Schedule: A3

Design SHS010136

Square Footage: 1,738
Width: 68'-6" Depth: 49'-0"
Price Schedule: A3

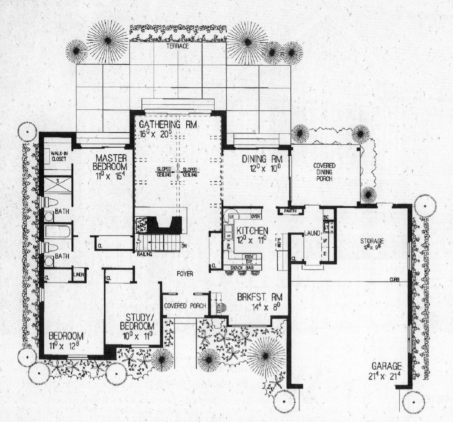

This quaint, shingled cottage offers an unexpected amount of living space in just over 1,700 square feet. The large gathering room with fireplace, dining room with covered porch, and kitchen with breakfast room handle formal parties as easily as they do the casual family get-together. Three bedrooms, one that could also serve as a study, are found in a separate wing of the house. Special note should be taken of all the storage space provided in this home as well as the extra touches that set it apart from many homes of equal size.

FOR PLAN ORDERING INFORMATION SEE PLAN

Design SHS010137

First Floor: 964 square feet
Second Floor: 783 square feet
Total: 1,747 square feet
Width: 48'-0" **Depth:** 32'-0"
Price Schedule: A3

For those interested in both traditional charm and modern convenience, this Cape Cod home fits the bill. Enter the foyer and find a quiet study to the left and a living room with a fireplace to the right. Straight ahead lies the kitchen and breakfast room. The island countertop affords lots of room for meal preparation. The service entry introduces a laundry and powder room. Look for three bedrooms upstairs, including a pampering owners bath with a whirlpool tub, separate shower, double vanity and walk-in closet.

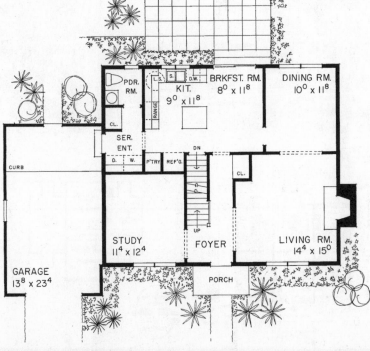

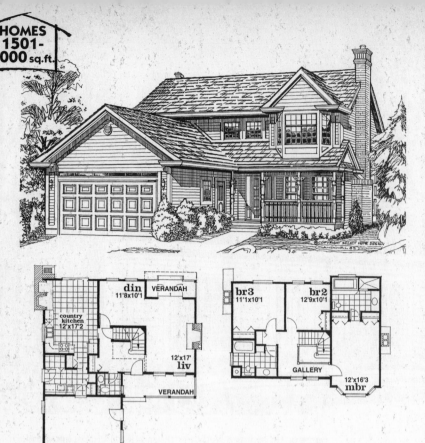

Design SHS010138

First Floor: 879 square feet
Second Floor: 869 square feet
Total: 1,748 square feet
Width: 37'-6" **Depth:** 47'-10"
Price Schedule: A3

Special exterior details—a railed veranda, multi-pane windows and a dormer—lend a country flavor to this three-bedroom home. A central hall at the entry holds a half-bath and a stair to the second floor and also allows passage to the formal living and dining rooms. The living room has a fireplace; the dining room features a private veranda. The country kitchen also has a fireplace and opens to a patio with a built-in barbecue.

Design SHS010139

First Floor: 1,171 square feet
Second Floor: 600 square feet
Total: 1,771 square feet
Width: 50'-0" **Depth:** 44'-0"
Price Schedule: A4

There's nothing that tops gracious Southern hospitality—unless it's offered Southern farmhouse style. The entry hall opens through an archway on the right to a formal dining room. Nearby, the efficient country kitchen shares space with a bay-windowed eating area. The family/great room is warmed by a fireplace. The first-floor owners suite has an abundance of closet space. The second floor holds two family bedrooms that share a full bath.

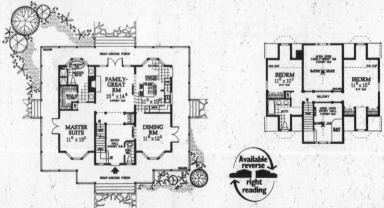

SELECT HOME DESIGNS

FOR PLAN ORDERING INFORMATION SEE PLAN

Design SHS010140

First Floor: 911 square feet

Second Floor: 861 square feet

Total: 1,772 square feet

Width: 38'-0" **Depth:** 52'-0"

Price Schedule: A4

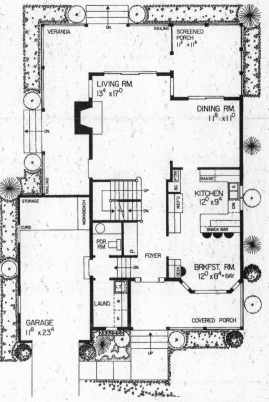

Victorian houses are well known for their orientation on narrow building sites. At only 38 feet wide, this home still offers generous style and comfort. Beautiful arched glass panels, skylights and large double-hung windows allow natural light to fill this home, giving a golden glow to oak and maple hardwood floors and trim. From the covered front porch, the foyer leads to the open living and dining rooms, with an extended-hearth fireplace and access to both the veranda and the screened porch. The U-shaped kitchen conveniently serves both the dining room and the bayed breakfast room. Sleeping quarters on the second floor include an owners suite, plus two family bedrooms that share a full bath.

Design SHS010141

First Floor: 1,032 square feet
Second Floor: 743 square feet
Total: 1,775 square feet
Width: 46'-0" **Depth:** 42'-0"
Price Schedule: A3

Sleek rooflines, classic window details and a covered front porch tastefully combine on the exterior of this three-bedroom home. A bright living room with an adjoining dining room is viewed from the volume entry. Meals will be enjoyed in the bayed breakfast area, which is served by a comfortable kitchen. A raised-hearth fireplace adds warmth to the family room. The second-level hall design provides separation between two secondary bedrooms and the luxurious owners suite with a boxed ceiling. Two closets, a whirlpool bath with a plant sill, and double lavs are featured in the bath/dressing area. Please specify basement or block foundation when ordering.

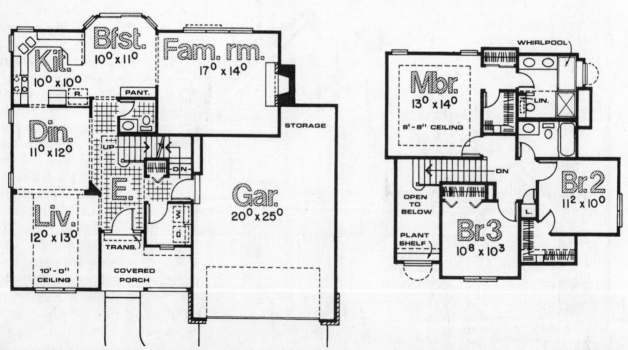

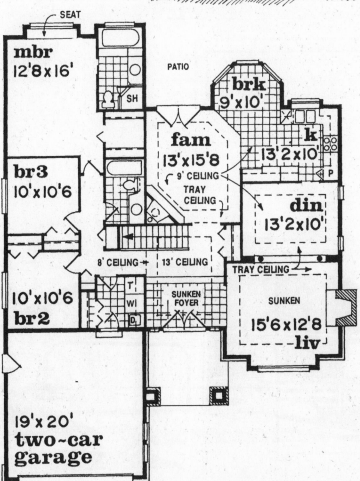

mbr
12'8 x 16'

SEAT

PATIO

SH

br3
10' x 10'6

fam
13' x 15'8

9' CEILING

TRAY
CEILING

brk
9' x 10'

k
13'2 x 10'

din
13'2 x 10'

8' CEILING

13' CEILING

T
WI
D

SUNKEN
FOYER

TRAY CEILING

10' x 10'6
br2

SUNKEN
15'6 x 12'8
liv

19' x 20'
two~car
garage

Design SHS010142

Square Footage: 1,794
Width: 47'-0" Depth: 63'-0"
Price Schedule: A3

Details make the difference in this exquisite one-story home. A bold portico entry opens to a sunken foyer, which boasts a multi-pane transom window over the high tray ceiling. High tray ceilings throughout the design add distinction and increase the sense of spaciousness. Stately decorative columns adorn the sunken living room and provide visual separation between the living room and dining room. The family room, featuring a corner fireplace and French doors to the garden patio, is open to the efficient kitchen and sunny breakfast room with its bay window. The owners suite is filled with amenities: a cozy window seat, a walk-in closet and a bath with a raised whirlpool spa and separate shower. Two family bedrooms share the use of a main bath in the hall. A laundry alcove leads the way to the service entrance to the two-car garage.

The charm of a traditional heritage is apparent in this one-story home with its narrow, horizontal siding, delightful window treatment and high-pitched roof. Inside, the living potential is outstanding. The sleeping wing is self-contained and has four bedrooms and two baths. Formal and informal living areas are well-designed with the living and dining room to the fore, and the family room and the kitchen to the rear.

Design SHS010143

Square Footage: 1,800
Width: 80'-0" **Depth:** 40'-0"
Price Schedule: A4

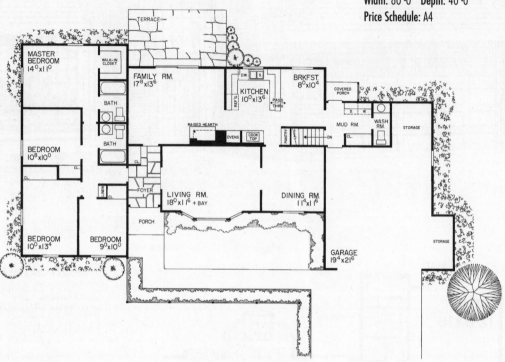

SELECT HOME DESIGNS

FOR PLAN ORDERING INFORMATION SEE PLAN

Design SHS010144

Square Footage: 1,816

Unfinished Lower Level: 1,725 square feet

Width: 58'-4" **Depth:** 48'-0"

Price Schedule: A4

This design works perfectly for a lot that slopes to the rear—you can finish the walkout basement at a later time to include extra living and sleeping space. The main level begins with a skylit foyer, with a planter ledge, stepping up to the spacious living and dining rooms. A pass-through in the dining room separates it from the U-shaped kitchen and attached breakfast nook. A door in the nook leads out to the rear deck. Three bedrooms on the right side of the plan include an owners suite with a bay window, a walk-in closet and a full bath with a whirlpool tub. Family bedrooms share a full hall bath. If you choose, you may also build this home on one level with a crawlspace foundation.

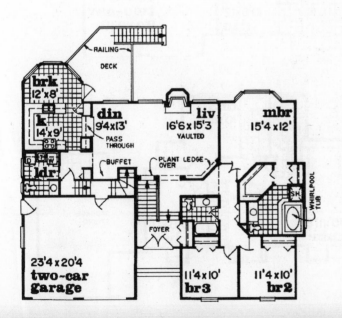

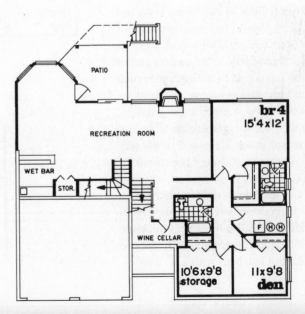

Design SHS010145

First Floor: 996 square feet
Second Floor: 831 square feet
Total: 1,827 square feet
Width; 61'-0" **Depth:** 35'-6"
Price Schedule: A3

A richly gabled roofline defines this fine three-bedroom home. Double doors open to a wide foyer flanked by the formal living and dining rooms. The living room features a fireplace and double-door access to a screened porch. The country kitchen also has access to the screened porch and boasts a center work island, a wood stove, a greenhouse window and space for a breakfast table. The two-car garage is reached via the service entrance through the laundry alcove. Three bedrooms on the second floor include an owners suite with a walk-in closet and private, skylit bath. Bedroom 3 also has a walk-in closet. Both family bedrooms share the use of a full hall bath with a skylight.

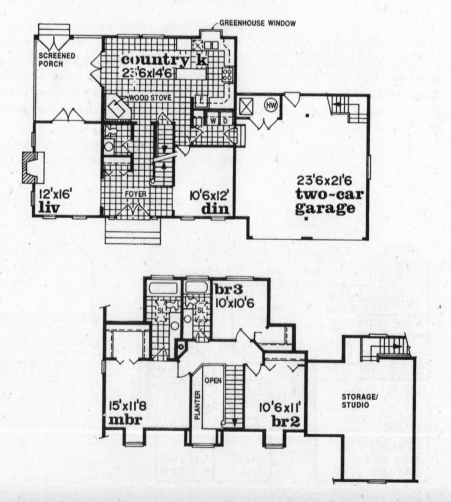

GREENHOUSE WINDOW

SCREENED PORCH

country k
23'6x14'6

WOOD STOVE

W D

HW

12'x16' liv

FOYER

10'6x12' din

23'6x21'6 two~car garage

br3 10'x10'6

SL SL

OPEN

PLANTER

15'x11'8 mbr

10'6x11' br2

STORAGE/ STUDIO

FOR PLAN ORDERING INFORMATION SEE PLAN

Design SHS010146

First Floor: 1,076 square feet
Second Floor: 759 square feet
Total: 1,835 square feet
Width: 38'-0" **Depth:** 48'-6"
Price Schedule: A3

Though this home is perfect for a narrow lot, it is attractive enough for a site of any size or shape. Vaulted ceilings and skylights are the order of the day inside, making the plan seem even larger than it is. A sunken living room with a fireplace opens off the foyer and leads into the formal dining room. An L-shaped kitchen and bayed breakfast nook lie just beyond. The family room is also sunken and has another fireplace. Bedrooms are on the second floor and include an owners suite with a walk-in closet and full bath, and two family bedrooms with a shared bath.

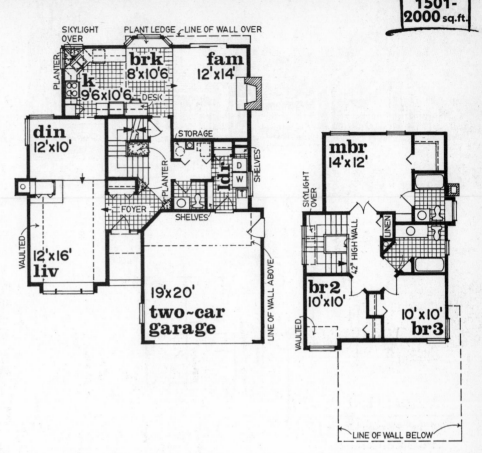

Design SHS010147

Square Footage: 1,835
Width: 70'-4" **Depth:** 51'-8"
Price Schedule: A4

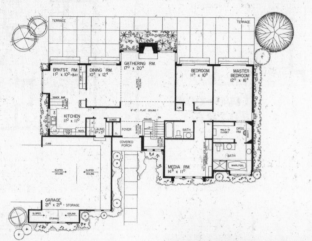

This smart design features a multi-gabled roof and vertical windows. A covered porch leads through a foyer to a gathering room with a fireplace, a sloped ceiling and access to the rear terrace. A modern kitchen with a snack bar features a pass-through to the breakfast room. The dining room is nearby. A media room in the bedroom wing offers a quiet, private area for enjoying music or surfing the Internet. An owners suite includes its own dressing area and a whirlpool tub. A large garage includes an extra storage room.

Design SHS010148

Square Footage: 1,842
Width: 58'-2" **Depth:** 59'-9"
Price Schedule: A3

This grand plan is not only affordable, but is also loaded with amenities. Sloped ceilings dominate the living areas and the owners suite. Notice also the abundance of windows and window walls that allow a sunburst of natural light to warm the home. The media room contains a full wall of built-ins, the gathering room features its own fireplace, and the owners suite pampers with a luxurious whirlpool spa. A garden court in the front and a terrace to the rear enhance outdoor livability. The garage contains a large storage area that could also allow room for a workshop.

SELECT HOME DESIGNS

Design SHS010149

First Floor: 919 square feet
Second Floor: 927 square feet
Total: 1,846 square feet
Width: 44'-0"   **Depth:** 40'-0"
Price Schedule: A4

A wonderful design begins with the wraparound porch of this plan. Explore further and find a two-story entry with a coat closet, a plant shelf and a strategically placed staircase. The island kitchen with a boxed window over the sink is adjacent to a large bay-windowed dinette. The great room includes many windows and a fireplace. A powder bath and laundry room are both conveniently placed on the first floor. Upstairs, the large owners suite contains His and Hers walk-in closets, corner windows and a bath area featuring a double vanity and whirlpool tub. Two pleasant secondary bedrooms have interesting angles, and a third bedroom in the front features a volume ceiling and arched window. Please specify basement, block or slab foundation when ordering.

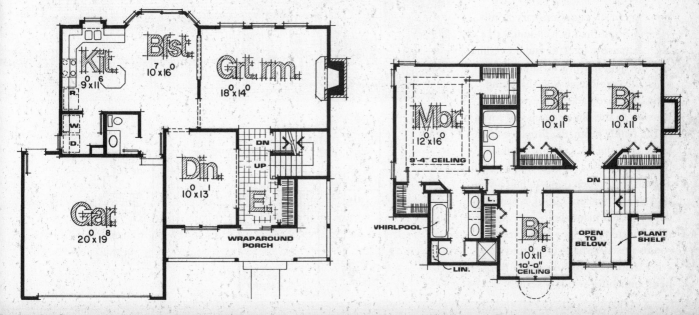

Design SHS010151

First Floor: 1,092 square feet
Second Floor: 757 square feet
Total: 1,849 square feet
Width: 50'-0" Depth: 46'-0"
Price Schedule: A3

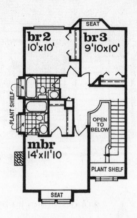

A covered veranda protects the entry of this charming home, and then wraps around to the left side where the spacious living room and dining room are found. The dining room features French-door access to the veranda; the living room is warmed by a fireplace. A covered porch sits beyond the family room. The owners bedroom is on the second floor and has an intimate window seat, walk-in closet and private bath. Bedroom 3 also has a window seat. A hall bath with a soaking tub serves the two family bedrooms.

brk 9'x13'2
fam 15'x12'6
COVERED DECK
k 10'6x11'2
din 12' x 10'
14'x14' **liv**
VERANDAH
21'4 x 21'8 **two-car garage**

br2 10'x10'
br3 9'10x10'
SEAT
PLANT SHELF
OPEN TO BELOW
mbr 14'x11'10
PLANT SHELF
SEAT

Design SHS010150

First Floor: 1,351 square feet
Second Floor: 504 square feet
Total: 1,855 square feet
Width: 44'-0" Depth: 52'-6"
Price Schedule: A3

Here's a contemporary family home that is well-suited to a narrow lot. The vaulted ceiling and full-height window enhance the sense of spaciousness in the living room. The fireplace here extends its warmth to the dining room and foyer. In the family room, the fireplace glow spreads to the kitchen and breakfast bay. Enter the owners bedroom through an arch and French doors to find a window seat, a walk-in closet, a private bath—with a plant shelf—and access to a private patio. Two additional bedrooms upstairs share a bath and a balcony that overlooks the foyer. Both bedrooms offer window seats.

brk 10' x 10'
fam 15' x 12' VAULTED
PATIO
SEAT
mbr 14'8 x 12'
10' x 14' VAULTED
k
ARCH
din 10' x 10'
STOR
HALF WALL
FOYER
PLANT LEDGE
VAULTED
12' x 14' **liv**
SILL
23' x 20' **two-car garage**

SEAT
br 2 10'2 x 10'
OPEN
RAILING
OPEN
PLANT LEDGE
PLANT LEDGE
10' x 10' **br 3**
SEAT

Design SHS010152

First Floor: 1,023 square feet
Second Floor: 837 square feet
Total: 1,860 square feet
Width: 47'-0" **Depth:** 47'-0"
Price Schedule: A3

This home features a grand and livable floor plan. From the two-story foyer, go right to the vaulted living room with a fireplace and the vaulted dining room. The peninsula kitchen blends into a bayed breakfast room and the open family room, which features a fireplace and sliding glass doors to the patio. The upper level contains three bedrooms. The owners suite features a private bath with an arched access, a whirlpool tub, a separate shower and a double vanity. Family bedrooms share a full bath that contains a linen closet.

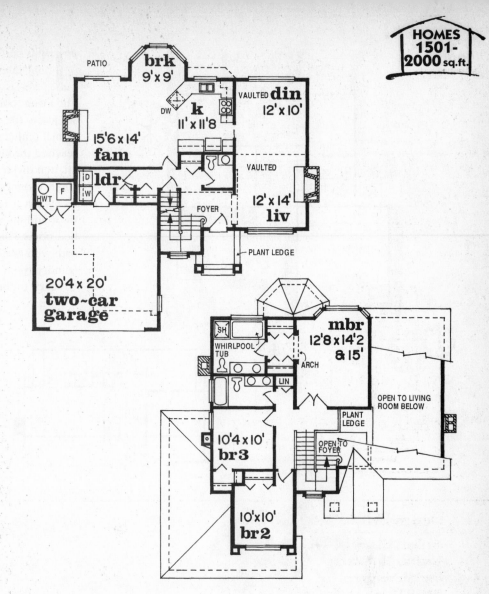

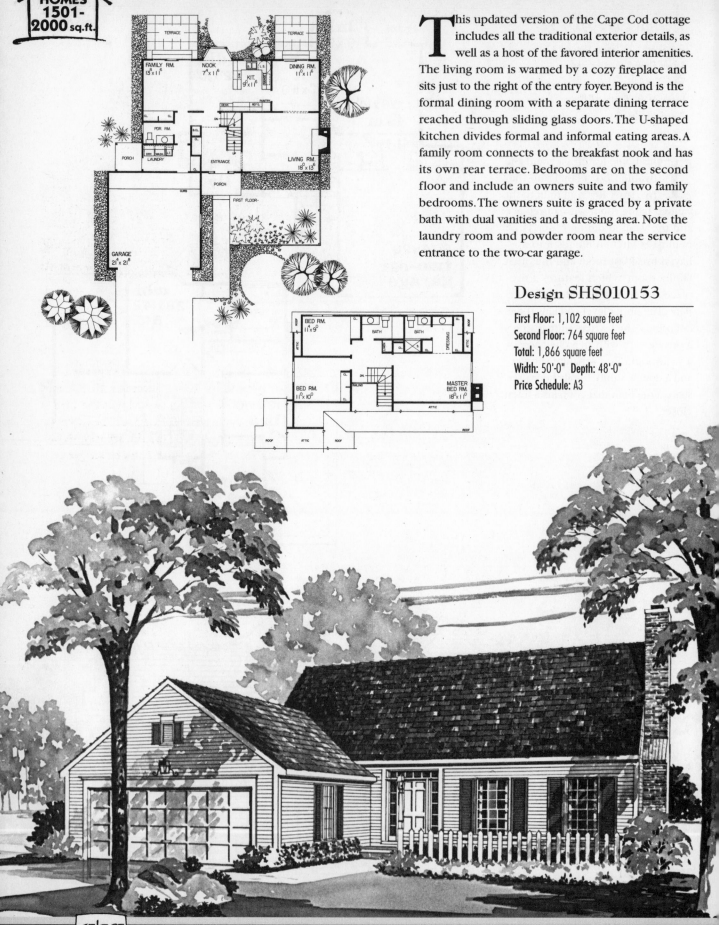

TERRACE

TERRACE

FAMILY RM.
13⁶ x 11⁶

NOOK
7⁶ x 11⁶

DINING RM.
11⁰ x 11⁶

KIT.
9⁰ x 11⁶

DESK

REF/L

PANTRY

DN.

CL.

CL.

PDR. RM.

B.CL.

DRY. WASH. L.S.

CL.

PORCH

LAUNDRY

ENTRANCE

LIVING RM.
18⁰ x 13⁶

CURB

PORCH

FIRST FLOOR.

GARAGE
21⁴ x 21⁸

BED RM.
11⁴ x 9⁰

ROOF

BATH

BATH

DRESSING

ROOF

ATTIC

ATTIC

CL.

CL.

CL.

BED RM.
11⁰ x 10⁰

DN.

RAILING

CL.

MASTER
BED RM.
18⁰ x 11⁶

ATTIC

ROOF

ATTIC

ROOF

ROOF

This updated version of the Cape Cod cottage includes all the traditional exterior details, as well as a host of the favored interior amenities. The living room is warmed by a cozy fireplace and sits just to the right of the entry foyer. Beyond is the formal dining room with a separate dining terrace reached through sliding glass doors. The U-shaped kitchen divides formal and informal eating areas. A family room connects to the breakfast nook and has its own rear terrace. Bedrooms are on the second floor and include an owners suite and two family bedrooms. The owners suite is graced by a private bath with dual vanities and a dressing area. Note the laundry room and powder room near the service entrance to the two-car garage.

Design SHS010153

First Floor: 1,102 square feet
Second Floor: 764 square feet
Total: 1,866 square feet
Width: 50'-0" **Depth:** 48'-0"
Price Schedule: A3

SELECT
HOME DESIGNS

FOR PLAN ORDERING INFORMATION SEE PLAN

HOMES
1501-
2000 sq.ft.

Design SHS010154

Square Footage: 1,880
Width: 88'-0" Depth: 42'-0"
Price Schedule: A3

This wide, wonderful ranch has it all: three bedrooms, a full basement or crawlspace, a formal dining room, and a breakfast room in the country kitchen. All of this revolves around a central great room with a gas fireplace and media wall. The vaulted entry with plant ledges and a stunning window create immediate impact. The owners bedroom features a walk-in closet and private bath with a soaking tub and separate shower. Both the owners bedroom and Bedroom 2 have vaulted ceilings. Entry to the garage contains washer/dryer space and a huge walk-in pantry.

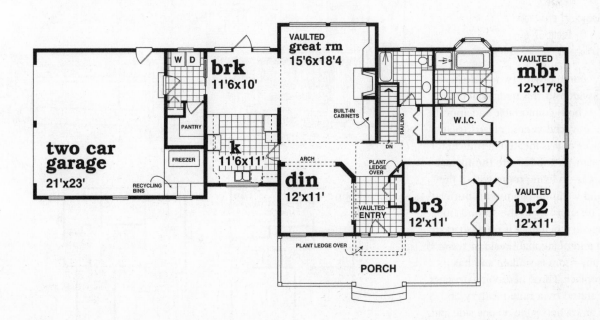

FACTS AT THE BEGINNING OF THIS ISSUE

SELECT
HOME DESIGNS

121

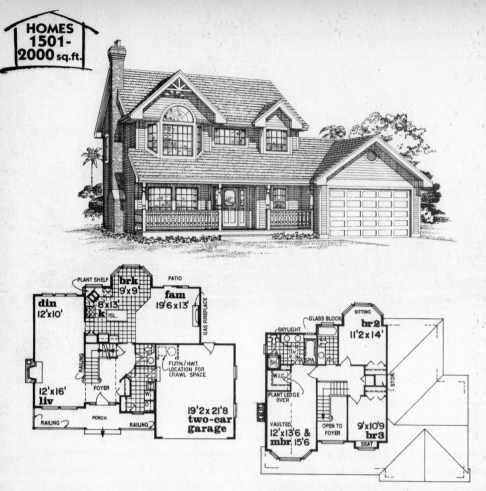

Design SHS010156

First Floor: 1,040 square feet
Second Floor: 840 square feet
Total: 1,880 square feet
Width: 49'-6" **Depth:** 41'-0"
Price Schedule: A3

A covered veranda, prominent bay windows and decorative woodwork adorn this three-bedroom home. The vaulted foyer is brightened by a second-level window. The living room and dining room are on the left; the living room has a cozy fireplace. The gourmet kitchen features an angled sink, corner windows with a plant shelf, an island preparation area and a bay-windowed breakfast nook. The nearby family room has sliding glass doors to the rear and another fireplace. The vaulted owners suite, on the second floor, contains a walk-in closet with a plant ledge and a bay-windowed sitting area.

Design SHS010155

First Floor: 957 square feet
Second Floor: 930 square feet
Total: 1,887 square feet
Bonus Room: 221 square feet
Width: 38'-0" **Depth:** 51'-6"
Price Schedule: A3

Decorated with two circle-head windows, this traditional design is both comfortable and appealing. The covered veranda leads to an entry foyer that is located in the center of the plan. To the left are the formal living areas—a living room with a fireplace and a dining room with buffet space. The stairway to the second floor is at the entry; behind it is the U-shaped kitchen and octagonal breakfast room. The family room is sunken and has its own fireplace. Three bedrooms upstairs are separated by a railed gallery and include an owners suite on one side and family bedrooms on the other.

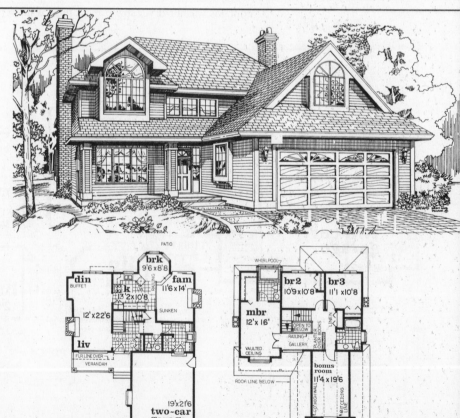

FOR PLAN ORDERING INFORMATION SEE PLAN

PATIO

brk
8'10 x 10'8

fam
15' x 14'

mbr
16' x13'8

WHIRLPOOL TUB

k
10'6 x 12'6

PLANT LEDGE

din
12' x 10'

SH

WALK IN CLOSET

FOYER

ldr
W

F

HW

den
br2
10'2 x 10'10

liv
12' x 15'

PORCH

br3
10'6 x 11'

SKYLIGHT

23' x 23'6
two car
garage

ldr
W
D

Alternate Layout for Basement

Design SHS010157

Square Footage: 1,883
Width: 64'-0" **Depth:** 48'-0"
Price Schedule: A3

The interior relies on a great floor plan. From a skylit, covered porch, the plan begins with a large entry opening to the living room with a fireplace and den—or Bedroom 2—which can be accessed through double doors in the entry or a single door in the hall. Decorative columns line the hall and define the family-room space. A fireplace, flanked by windows, is a focal point in this casual living area. The nearby breakfast room opens to the patio and connects the family room to the U-shaped kitchen. The owners bedroom is huge—and amenity-filled. It also has patio access and features a bath with a whirlpool tub and separate shower. An additional bedroom is served by a full bath. A large laundry room connects the two-car garage to the main house.

FACTS AT THE BEGINNING OF THIS ISSUE

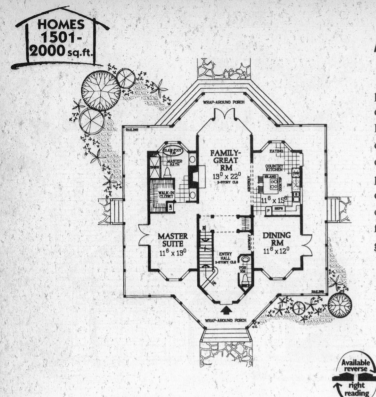

HOMES
1501-
2000 sq.ft.

This Southern country farmhouse seems to reach right out and greet you. The octagonal entry hall is balanced by two bay windows. Inside, Colonial columns and pilasters provide a charming entrance to a family/great room enhanced by a fireplace and three sets of French doors. The L-shaped country kitchen is highlighted by a bay-windowed eating area with a window seat. The spacious first-floor owners suite is complemented by French doors opening onto the porch and a wealth of closet space. A bay window in the bath effectively surrounds an old-fashioned claw-foot tub. The second floor holds two secondary bedrooms and a full bath. Plans for an optional indoor swimming pool/spa and detached garage are included.

Design SHS010158

First Floor: 1,295 square feet
Second Floor: 600 square feet
Total: 1,895 square feet
Width: 50'-0" **Depth:** 55'-3"
Price Schedule: A4

SELECT
HOME DESIGNS

FOR PLAN ORDERING INFORMATION SEE PLAN

Design SHS010159

First Floor: 1,032 square feet

Second Floor: 865 square feet

Total: 1,897 square feet

Width: 46'-0" **Depth:** 42'-0"

Price Schedule: A4

Combining lap siding, distinctive trim detail and brick accents, this elevation will surely capture your imagination! Just off the tiled entry, the volume living room shares an open arrangement with the formal dining room. Meals prepared in the generous kitchen will be enjoyed in the adjoining bayed dinette. The spacious family room has a raised-hearth fireplace. Upstairs, the owners suite contains His and Hers closets, which separate the owners bedroom from the private bath with a double vanity. The whirlpool tub is brightened by an arch-top window. Three secondary bedrooms are served by their own convenient bath and linen closet. Please specify basement or block foundation when ordering.

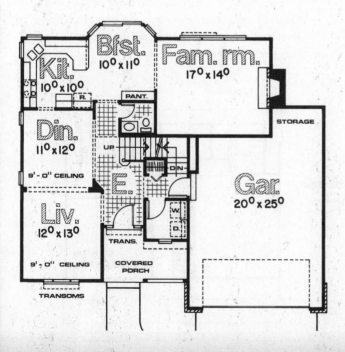

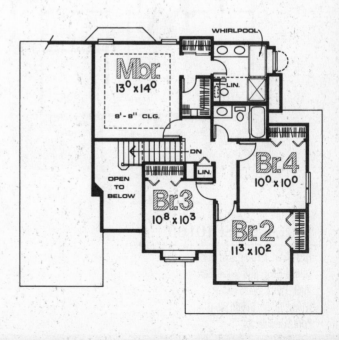

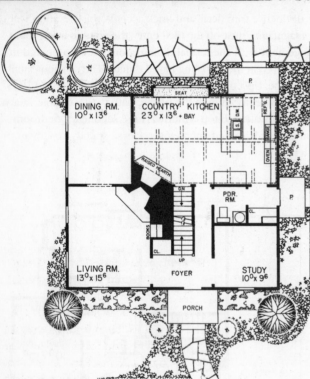

DINING RM.
10⁰ x 13⁶

SEAT

COUNTRY KITCHEN
23⁰ x 13⁶ + BAY

RAISED HEARTH

DN

PDR. RM.

LIVING RM.
13⁰ x 15⁶

FOYER

STUDY
10⁰ x 9⁶

UP

BOOKS

CL.

PORCH

This charming plan is designed to be the perfect starter or retirement home thanks to its ideal blend of comfort and easy style. Inside, it contains a very livable floor plan. An outstanding first floor centers around the huge country kitchen, which includes a beam ceiling, a raised-hearth fireplace, a window seat and backyard access. The living room, with its warming corner fireplace and private study, is located at the front of the plan. Upstairs are three bedrooms and two full baths. Built-in shelves and a linen closet in the upstairs hallway provide excellent storage.

Available reverse
right reading

ROOF

BATH

BATH

BEDROOM
12⁴ x 11⁰

CL.

LINEN

DN

SHLVS

MASTER BEDROOM
13⁰ x 15⁸

WALK-IN CLOSET

CL.

CEILING CLIP

BEDROOM
11⁰ x 12⁰

ROOF

Design SHS010160

First Floor: 1,100 square feet
Second Floor: 808 square feet
Total: 1,908 square feet
Width: 34'-0" **Depth:** 32'-0"
Price Schedule: A4

SELECT
HOME DESIGNS

Design SHS010161

First Floor: 1,038 square feet
Second Floor: 879 square feet
Total: 1,917 square feet
Width: 45'-0" **Depth:** 36'-0"
Price Schedule: A3

Brick facing and a covered front porch adorn this charming two-story traditional home. On the main floor, the living and dining rooms feature decorative columns and tray ceilings. The living room is also warmed by a fireplace. A well-planned kitchen with a pantry and ample counter and cupboard space opens to a comfortable bayed breakfast area. The second floor holds the bedrooms: two family bedrooms with a shared bath and an owners suite with a private bath. Note the two-car garage reached through a service entry with a laundry cove.

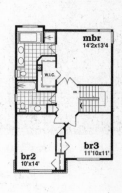

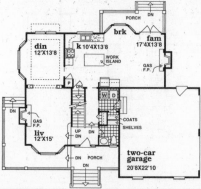

Design SHS010162

First Floor: 1,007 square feet
Second Floor: 917 square feet
Total: 1,924 square feet
Bonus Room: 325 square feet
Width: 53'-0" **Depth:** 44'-0"
Price Schedule: A3

This charming country exterior conceals an elegant interior, starting with formal living and dining rooms, each with a bay window. The gourmet kitchen features a work island and a breakfast area with its own bay window. A fireplace warms the family room, which opens to the rear porch through French doors. Second-floor sleeping quarters include an owners suite with a whirlpool tub and a walk-in closet.

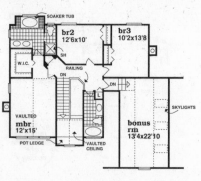

Design SHS010164

First Floor: 1,355 square feet
Second Floor: 582 square feet
Total: 1,937 square feet
Width: 65'-0" **Depth:** 55'-8"
Price Schedule: A3

A portico makes a strong architectural statement and a grand introduction to this country home. To the left of the foyer is the formal dining room, just a step away from the tiled kitchen, which overlooks the great room. The owners suite nestles to the right of the living area, and boasts a lavish walk-through bath with a door to a private area of the deck. Separate vanities, a walk-in closet, a whirlpool tub and a stall shower with a seat highlight the bath. Upstairs, two family bedrooms share a hall bath and a balcony overlook to the great room.

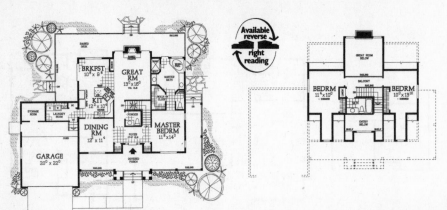

Design SHS010163

First Floor: 1,044 square feet
Second Floor: 894 square feet
Total: 1,938 square feet
Width: 58'-0" **Depth:** 43'-6"
Price Schedule: C1

This charming country traditional home provides a well-lit home office, harbored in a beautiful bay with three windows. The second-floor bay brightens the owners bath, which has a double-bowl vanity, a step-up tub and a dressing area. The living and dining rooms share a two-sided fireplace. The gourmet kitchen has a cooktop island counter and enjoys outdoor views through sliding glass doors in the breakfast area. A sizable bonus room above the two-car garage can be developed into hobby space or a recreation room. This home is designed with a basement foundation.

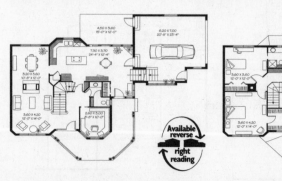

SELECT HOME DESIGNS

FOR PLAN ORDERING INFORMATION SEE PLAN

Design SHS010165

First Floor: 936 square feet
Second Floor: 1,002 square feet
Total: 1,938 square feet
Width: 47'-0" **Depth:** 42'-0"
Price Schedule: A3

A covered railed veranda and decorative woodwork adorn this family home. Dormer windows brighten the vaulted foyer, which opens on the right to the formal living areas: a living room with a bay window and an attached dining room. The kitchen is centralized and holds a cooking island and bayed breakfast nook. An open family room is nearby. It is enhanced by a fireplace and sliding glass doors to the rear yard. Bedrooms are on the second level. The owners suite features a huge walk-in closet and a bath with a soaking tub, a separate shower and dual vanities. Three additional bedrooms share the use of a full bath. The two-car garage has an entry near the half-bath in the foyer.

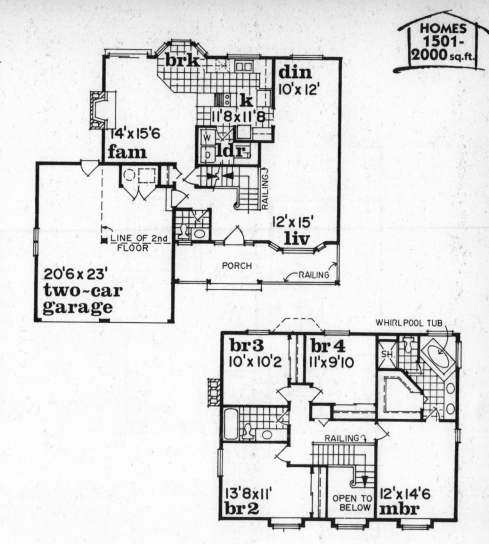

SELECT HOME DESIGNS

Design SHS010166

Square Footage: 1,939
Width: 46'-6" **Depth:** 69'-4"
Price Schedule: A3

spa

whirlpool bath
glass blocks

DECK

brk
10'x11'8

plant ledge

mbr
16'10 x 12'

k
2'6 x12'

oven

ref.

mirror doors

(sunken)
fam
12'2 x 14'

gas
fireplace

din
13'6 x 10'

br2
10' x 11'4

sh

CONV.
ALCOVE

seat

seat

glass blocks

DN.

skylight

lin

FOYER
barrel vault
ceiling

DN

barrel vault ceiling

ldr

W

(sunken)
liv
12'6 x 15'6

gas fireplace

br3
10'x10'2

D

steps

planters
glass blocks

19'2x20'4
**two-car
garage**

window

This unique design begins with a double-door entry into a barrel-vaulted foyer accented by two round-top windows and an arched, glass-block wall. Curved ceilings and open-plan design enhance both the living and dining rooms. The living room is sunken and features a fireplace and box-bay window. The dining room also has a box-bay. Beyond is the U-shaped kitchen, connecting directly to an octagonal breakfast nook. The nook has access to the rear deck and spa beyond. The family room is up just a step or two and is graced by a gas fireplace and conversation alcove with built-in seats. The owners bedroom also has access to the rear deck via a luxurious bath with a spa tub, separate shower and compartmented toilet. Two additional bedrooms share a full bath that has twin vanities.

FOR PLAN ORDERING INFORMATION SEE PLAN

Design SHS010168

First Floor: 968 square feet
Second Floor: 982 square feet
Total: 1,950 square feet
Width: 40'-0" **Depth:** 46'-0"
Price Schedule: A3

This traditional home offers lovely formal rooms for entertaining. The living room has a centered fireplace and access to the front covered porch. A gourmet kitchen with a cooktop island counter serves the dining room. French doors open the morning nook to the outdoors, while a second fireplace warms the family room. Upstairs, the owners suite has a corner walk-in closet, a double-bowl lavatory and an oversized shower. Three secondary bedrooms are connected by a stair hall.

Available reverse
right reading

Design SHS010167

First Floor: 1,160 square feet
Second Floor: 797 square feet
Total: 1,957 square feet
Width: 54'-8" **Depth:** 42'-0"
Price Schedule: A3

This home appears much larger than it actually is. Half-round elements repeat over the entry and over the gable at the garage roof. The interior is filled with thoughtful appointments. The living room has a vaulted ceiling and fireplace, plus sliding glass doors to a rear deck. The country kitchen contains a work island, planning desk and large pantry. Attached is space for eating or gathering with access to the rear patio. A service area connects the home to the two-car garage and features a half-bath and laundry room. Upstairs are three bedrooms, or two bedrooms and a den. The owners suite has a vaulted ceiling, a walk-in closet and a full bath with a corner tub.

SELECT
HOME DESIGNS

Design SHS010169

First Floor: 1,132 square feet
Second Floor: 864 square feet
Total: 1,996 square feet
Width: 65'-6" **Depth:** 31'-0"
Price Schedule: A3

This traditional farmhouse has great outdoor livability in a covered veranda and a rear sun deck. The foyer leads to a sunken living room, which offers a fireplace, and the adjoining dining room. A U-shaped kitchen features a pass-through snack bar to the breakfast room. The family room is also sunken and has a fireplace and double-door access to the rear yard. Bedrooms on the second floor include an owners suite with a private bath and three family bedrooms sharing a full bath. Two of the family bedrooms have walk-in closets, as does the owners bedroom. To accommodate narrow lots, this design may be easily adapted to 32 feet wide by building without the family room, utility room and garage.

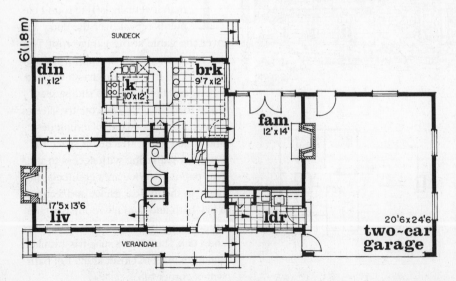

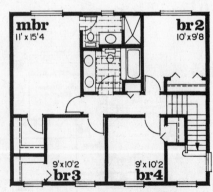

Design SHS010170

First Floor: 1,074 square feet
Second Floor: 916 square feet
Total: 1,990 square feet
Width: 52'-0" **Depth:** 56'-4"
Price Schedule: A3

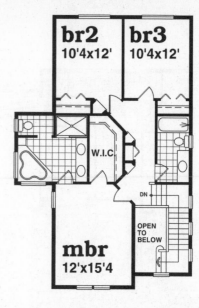

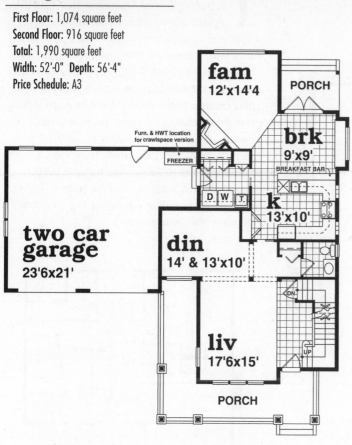

Country charm lends exceptional appeal to this three-bedroom design. Tapered columns dress the wraparound porch—a great spot to enjoy summer breezes. Inside, open formal rooms are defined by lovely decorative columns. A tiled U-shaped kitchen has a breakfast area with French doors to the rear porch. The family room enjoys a corner fireplace and wide windows. Upstairs, a spacious owners suite has an angled whirlpool tub.

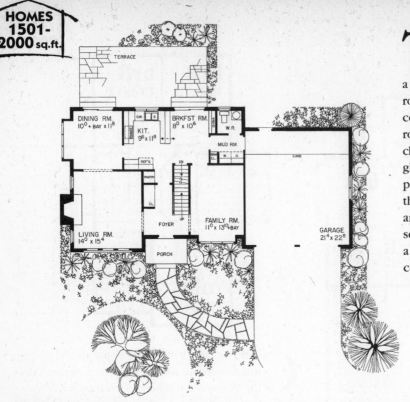

TERRACE

DINING RM.
10⁰ + BAY x 11⁸

D.W. S

BRKFST RM.
8⁰ x 10⁶

KIT.
9⁶ x 11⁸

RANGE

W.R.

MUD RM.

W. D.

CURB

REFG.

DN

PANTRY

CL.

FOYER

UP

FAMILY RM.
11⁰ x 13⁰ + BAY

GARAGE
21⁴ x 22⁸

LIVING RM.
14⁰ x 15⁴

PORCH

The exterior of this English Tudor-style home reflects the craftsmanship that lifts this design above others. Flanking the foyer is a spacious family room and a comfortable living room with a fireplace. The U-shaped kitchen is conveniently located between the formal dining room and the breakfast room that has a built-in china cabinet. Both of these rooms feature sliding glass doors that open onto the rear terrace. A powder room and a mudroom are located near the two-car garage. Two family bedrooms, a bath and an owners bedroom are located on the second floor. A walk-in closet, a built-in vanity, a private bath and an adjoining nursery/study complete the owners suite.

BEDROOM
15⁰ x 12⁰

BATH

LINEN

BATH

SHLVS.

WALK-IN CLOSET

VANITY

HALL

DN

CL.

CL.

CL.

CL.

NURSERY/ STUDY
8⁴ x 9⁴

CL.

MASTER BEDROOM
11⁰ x 16⁸

BEDROOM
12⁰ x 12⁴

CL.

Design SHS010171

First Floor: 999 square feet

Second Floor: 997 square feet

Total: 1,996 square feet

Width: 60'-0" Depth: 28'-10"

Price Schedule: A3

SELECT
HOME DESIGNS

FOR PLAN ORDERING INFORMATION SEE PLAN

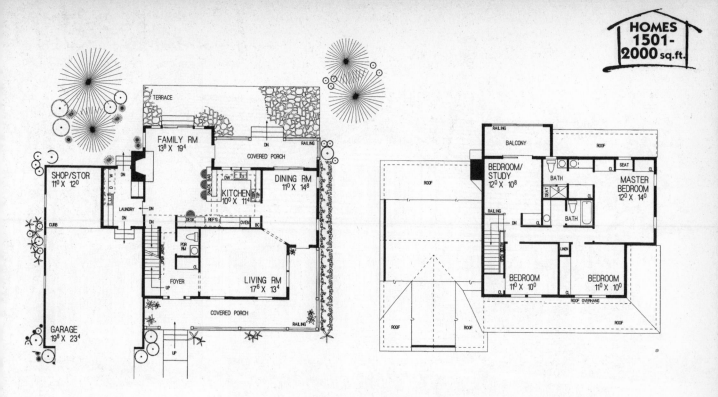

Design SHS010172

First Floor: 1,096 square feet
Second Floor: 900 square feet
Total: 1,996 square feet
Width: 56'-0" **Depth:** 44'-0"
Price Schedule: A3

Covered porches to the front and rear are the first signal that this is a fine example of Folk Victorian styling. Complementing the exterior is a grand plan for family living. A formal living room and an attached dining room provide space for entertaining guests. The large family room with its fireplace is the perfect spot for everyday gatherings. Both areas have access to outdoor spaces. Four bedrooms occupy the second floor. The owners suite features two lavatories, a window seat and three closets. One of the family bedrooms has its own private balcony and could be used as a study. Note the open staircase and convenient linen storage.

HOMES 1501-2000 sq.ft.

Design SHS010173

First Floor: 1,111 square feet
Second Floor: 886 square feet
Total: 1,997 square feet
Width: 34'-1" **Depth:** 50'-0"
Price Schedule: A3

Don't be fooled by a small-looking exterior. This plan offers three bedrooms and plenty of living space. Notice that the screened porch leads to a rear terrace with access to the breakfast room. A living room/dining room combination adds spaciousness to the floor plan. Other welcome amenities include boxed windows in the breakfast room and dining room, a fireplace in the living room, a planning desk and pass-through snack bar in the kitchen, a whirlpool tub in the owners bath and an open two-story foyer. The thoughtfully placed flower box, beyond the kitchen window above the sink, adds a homespun touch to this already-comfortable design.

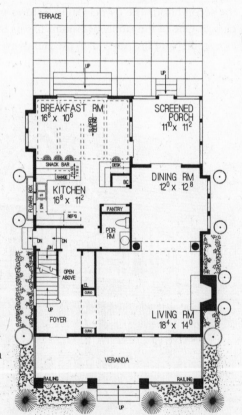

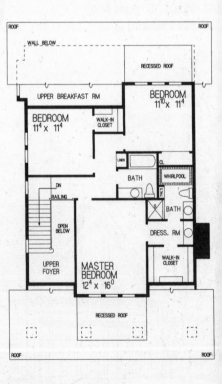

SELECT HOME DESIGNS

FOR PLAN ORDERING INFORMATION SEE PLAN

Design SHS010174

Square Footage: 1,999
Width: 60'-0" **Depth:** 55'-0"
Price Schedule: A3

Small families will appreciate the layout of this traditional ranch. The foyer opens to the gathering room with its fireplace and sloped ceiling. The dining room opens to the gathering room for entertaining ease and offers sliding glass doors to a rear terrace. The breakfast room also provides access to a covered porch for dining outdoors. The media room to the left of the home offers a bay window and a wet bar, or it can double as a third bedroom.

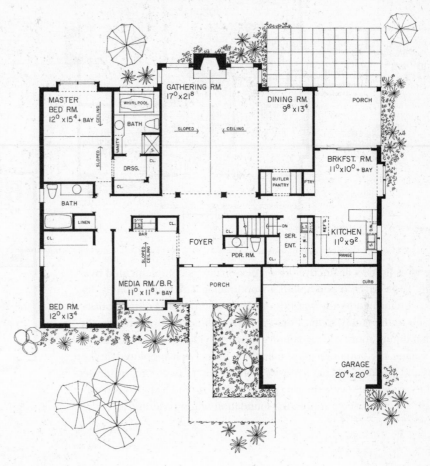

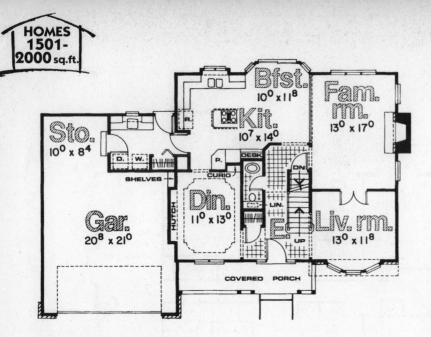

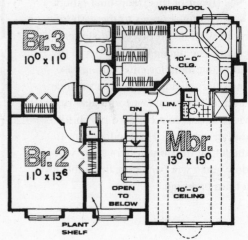

Design SHS010175

First Floor: 1,093 square feet
Second Floor: 905 square feet
Total: 1,998 square feet
Width: 55'-4" **Depth:** 37'-8"
Price Schedule: A3

This home's distinctive design personality is complemented by a large covered porch with a wood railing. The living room is distinguished by the warmth of a bay window and French doors leading to the family room. A built-in curio cabinet adds interest to the formal dining room. A large laundry room provides practical access to the garage, the outdoors and the kitchen. In the well-appointed kitchen, an island cooktop will save you steps. The owners bedroom on the second floor delights with special ceiling treatment and a spacious bath. Please specify basement or block foundation when ordering.

FOR PLAN ORDERING INFORMATION SEE PLAN

Design SHS010176

First Floor: 1,336 square feet
Second Floor: 931 square feet
Total: 2,267 square feet
Width: 39'-0" **Depth:** 42'-0"
Price Schedule: A4

With horizontal wood siding and cedar shake shingle accents, this quaint farmhouse features a covered front porch that opens through double doors to the central foyer. A living room with a fireplace is on the right; the formal dining room is on the left. Behind the living room, a den with cozy dimensions awaits for a home office or quiet reading space. The family room is found to the rear of the first floor, near the breakfast nook and kitchen. Double doors in the nook open to a rear deck. Bedrooms on the second floor include an owners suite with a deck, walk-in closet and fine bath. Family bedrooms share a full bath that separates them.

HOMES 2001-2500 sq.ft.

Design SHS010178

First Floor: 1,391 square feet
Second Floor: 611 square feet
Total: 2,002 square feet
Width: 64'-0" **Depth:** 44'-0"
Price Schedule: C1

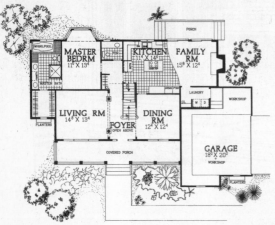

Muntin windows, shutters and flower boxes add exterior appeal to this well-designed family farmhouse. In the living room, a long expanse of windows set the pace. Informal living takes off in the open kitchen and family room. An island cooktop will be a favorite feature, as will be the fireplace. Sleeping accommodations are defined by the owners bedroom, where a bay window provides a perfect sitting nook. The owners bath has a large, walk-in closet; a vanity; twin lavatories; a stall shower and a whirlpool tub. Three bedrooms reside upstairs.

Design SHS010177

First Floor: 1,026 square feet
Second Floor: 994 square feet
Total: 2,020 square feet
Bonus Room: 377 square feet
Width: 58'-0" **Depth:** 32'-0"
Price Schedule: A4

This inviting country home is enhanced by a full-width covered front porch, a fieldstone exterior and a trio of dormers on the second floor. Double doors open to a foyer flanked by a living room and a dining room. A U-shaped kitchen adjoins a breakfast room with sliding glass doors to the patio. Second-floor space includes two family bedrooms with a shared bath and an owners suite that features a full bath and walk-in closet. A large bonus room adds living space on the second floor.

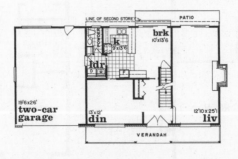

FOR PLAN ORDERING INFORMATION SEE PLAN

Design SHS010180

First Floor: 1,134 square feet
Second Floor: 874 square feet
Total: 2,008 square feet
Width: 61'-4" **Depth:** 38'-0"
Price Schedule: A4

This board-and-batten farmhouse design carries down-home country charm with a dash of uptown New England flavor. Warm weather will invite friends and family out to the large, front covered porch to enjoy the outdoors. Just off the front entrance is a spacious living room that opens to the formal dining room, which enjoys a bay window and easy service from the U-shaped kitchen. The family room offers casual living space warmed by a raised-hearth fireplace and extended by double-door access to the rear terrace. The second floor houses two family bedrooms, which share a full bath, and a generous owners suite with a walk-in closet and a private bath.

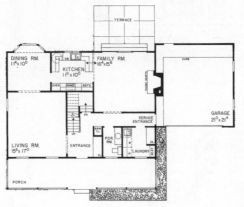

Design SHS010179

First Floor: 1,062 square feet
Second Floor: 949 square feet
Total: 2,011 square feet
Width: 52'-0" **Depth:** 38'-0"
Price Schedule: A4

Dormer windows and a delightful covered porch highlight the facade of this farmhouse plan. The interior caters to family living with formal areas on the left and open, casual areas to the rear. Both the family room and the living room sport fireplaces; the family room has sliding glass doors to the rear yard. A breakfast bay offers casual dining space near the island kitchen. Four bedrooms are on the second floor. They include three family bedrooms and an owners suite with a private bath and walk-in closet. Bedroom 4 boasts a window seat.

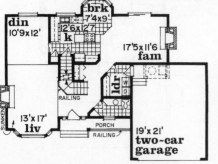

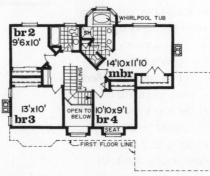

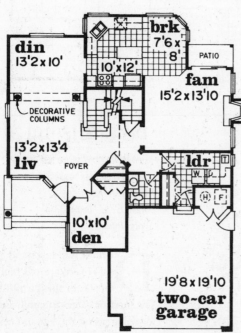

din
13'2 x 10'

brk
7'6 x 8'

PATIO

10'x12'

DECORATIVE COLUMNS

fam
15'2 x 13'10

13'2 x 13'4
liv

FOYER

ldr
W

10'x10'
den

19'8 x 19'10
two-car garage

Design SHS010181

First Floor: 1,237 square feet
Second Floor: 794 square feet
Total: 2,031 square feet
Width: 40'-0" **Depth:** 53'-8"
Price Schedule: A4

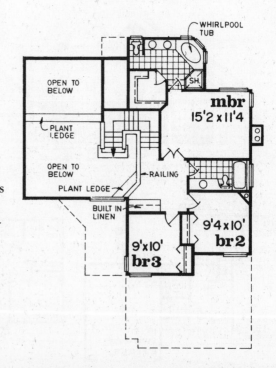

WHIRLPOOL TUB

OPEN TO BELOW

PLANT LEDGE

SH.

mbr
15'2 x 11'4

OPEN TO BELOW

RAILING

PLANT LEDGE

BUILT IN LINEN

9'x10'
br3

9'4 x 10'
br2

A weather-protected entry with decorative columns introduces this innovative design. The foyer spills into an open-plan living and dining room. A pair of columns and a planter-bridge visually zone the two rooms. A fireplace and sliding glass doors to the rear patio highlight the family room, which is separated from the formal living and dining areas by the island kitchen and light-filled breakfast room. The laundry room and a powder room are nearby. A den opens through double doors just off the foyer. The second floor is home to the owners bedroom and two family bedrooms. The owners suite features a walk-in closet and a bath with a whirlpool tub and separate shower. Two family bedrooms share a full bath.

Design SHS010182

First Floor: 1,056 square feet
Second Floor: 987 square feet
Total: 2,043 square feet
Width: 46'-6" **Depth:** 54'-6"
Price Schedule: A4

Victorian detailing and a wrap-around covered porch grace this three-bedroom farm-house. An archway introduces the octagonal living room and its adjoining dining room. Sliding glass doors in the dining room lead to the porch; the living room enjoys a fireplace. A pocket door separates the kitchen and bayed breakfast nook from the dining room. Workspace in the kitchen is L-shaped for convenience. The family room is open to this area and features sliding glass doors to the rear yard and a fireplace. Reach the two-car garage through a service entrance near the laundry room. Bedrooms are upstairs. The owners suite has a bay window, a walk-in closet and a private bath with a corner whirlpool tub and a double vanity. Two family bedrooms include one nestled in a windowed bay.

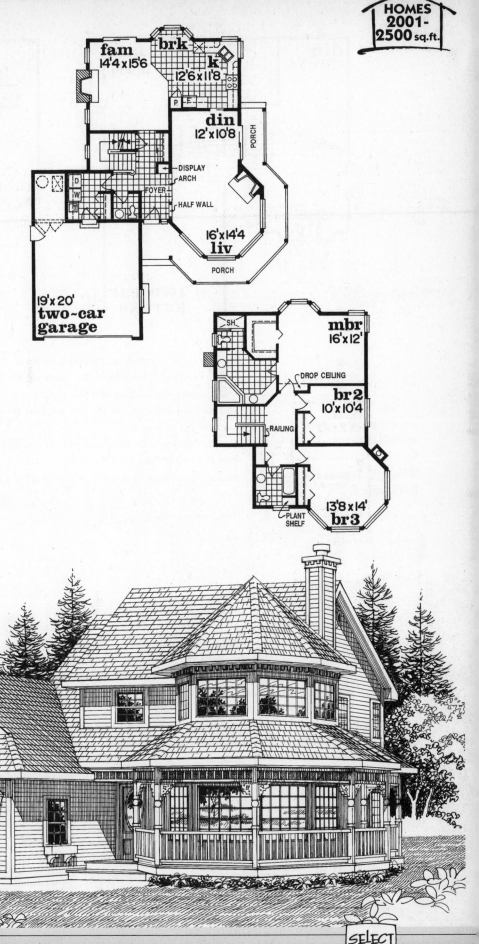

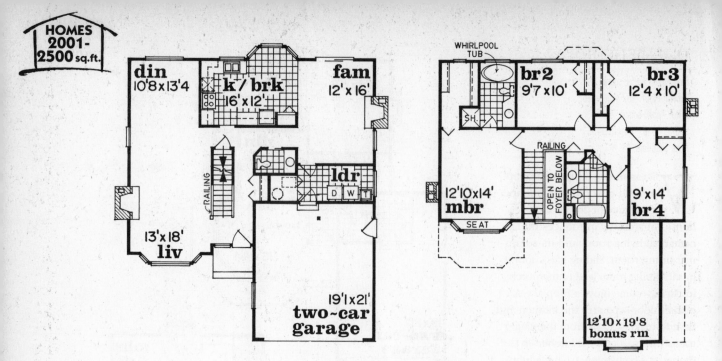

din
10'8 x 13'4

k / brk
16' x 12'

fam
12' x 16'

RAILING

ldr
D W

13' x 18'
liv

19'1 x 21'
two~car
garage

WHIRLPOOL TUB

br2
9'7 x 10'

br3
12'4 x 10'

SH.

RAILING

OPEN TO FOYER BELOW

12'10 x 14'
mbr
SEAT

9' x 14'
br4

12'10 x 19'8
bonus rm

Design SHS010183

First Floor: 1,106 square feet
Second Floor: 960 square feet
Total: 2,066 square feet
Bonus Room: 267 square feet
Width: 40'-0" **Depth:** 46'-6"
Price Schedule: A4

Y ou get more than you bargain for in this lovely design—bonus space on the second floor allows for future development of an additional bedroom or a game room. The first floor offers a classic, center-hall design with formal living and dining rooms on the left and a family room open to the breakfast nook and kitchen in the rear. Both the family and living rooms feature fireplaces. The family room also has sliding-glass-door access to the rear yard. Four bedrooms are found on the second floor. The three family bedrooms share the use of a hall bath. The owners suite contains a charming window seat, a walk-in closet and a bath with a whirlpool tub.

Design SHS010184

Square Footage: 2,034
Width: 75'-0" **Depth:** 47'-5"
Price Schedule: A4

Small families that require room to entertain large gatherings will appreciate this home. From the front covered porch to the entertainment terrace that extends across the rear of the house, this plan allows traffic to flow and gather. A tiled foyer leads into the breakfast room and the gathering room. The angled kitchen, with a snack bar that's open to the gathering room, cleverly connects the dining area and breakfast room. The owners suite, located away from the family-living area, includes a compartmented bath with a garden tub, a dressing area and two walk-in closets.

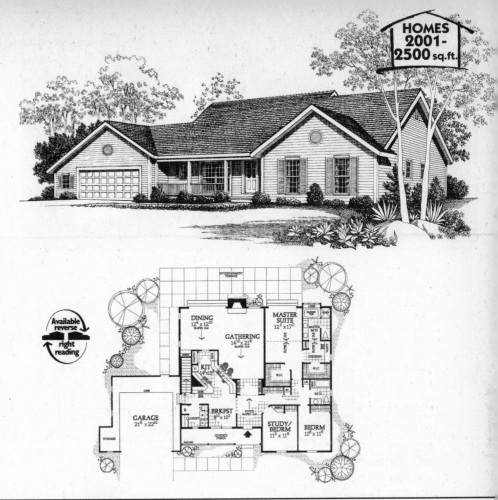

Design SHS010185

First Floor: 1,404 square feet
Second Floor: 640 square feet
Total: 2,044 square feet
Bonus Room: 695 square feet
Width: 68'-6" **Depth:** 36'-0"
Price Schedule: A4

A rustic plan with just the right classic touches, this home is made for country living. The covered porch shelters an entry that opens to a two-story foyer that's flanked by the owners bedroom and the living room. The living room shares a three-sided fireplace with the dining room and features columns and a half-wall at its entry. The owners suite opens through double doors and offers a walk-in closet and a full bath with a whirlpool tub. The second floor has two family bedrooms, a full bath and a large bonus space that can be finished later as additional bedrooms or hobby space.

HOMES
2001-
2500 sq.ft.

Design SHS010186

First Floor: 1,185 square feet
Second Floor: 880 square feet
Total: 2,065 square feet
Width: 50'-0" Depth: 43'-6"
Price Schedule: C1

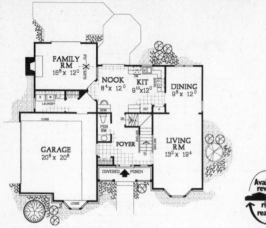

A stately brick exterior, interesting rooflines and classic window treatment—including a two-story bay window—will set this traditional home apart from the other homes in your neighborhood. Inside, amenities fill the plan, beginning with a half-bath and coat closet conveniently located in the front foyer. This open space leads to the corner living room with the first of three bay windows, to the two-car garage with another bay window or to the gourmet kitchen with a pantry, a desk, a breakfast nook and plenty of counter space. The family room at the rear of the home, with its cozy fireplace and backyard access, is the perfect place to relax after dinner.

Design SHS010187

First Floor: 1,045 square feet
Second Floor: 1,023 square feet
Total: 2,068 square feet
Unfinished Basement: 1,035 square feet
Width: 45'-8" Depth: 37'-10"
Price Schedule: A4

This is the perfect plan for narrow or difficult lots—it features a shallow depth and compact width. Its appeal, however, is great with varied rooflines, horizontal siding, brick accents and a covered entry. The interior floor plan includes many extras: fireplaces in both the living and family rooms, tray ceilings in the living and dining rooms, a half-bath at the entry, a bayed breakfast nook and buffet space in the dining room. Four bedrooms, including a luxurious owners suite, are on the second floor. Unfinished space in the basement allows for future expansion.

FOR PLAN ORDERING INFORMATION SEE PLAN

This transitional design carries the best of both worlds—popular details of both traditional and contemporary architecture. The high rooflines allow for dramatic full-height windows and vaulted ceilings in the formal areas. A den, just off the foyer, is a well-appreciated haven of quiet. The casual areas are open and include the hearth-warmed family room, bayed breakfast nook and island kitchen. A laundry alcove leads to the two-car garage with extra storage space. Three bedrooms occupy the second floor. They include two family bedrooms—one with a vaulted ceiling—and an owners suite with two walk-in closets and a full bath with a separate shower and tub. Note the half-bath just beyond the den.

Design SHS010188

First Floor: 1,204 square feet
Second Floor: 867 square feet
Total: 2,071 square feet
Width: 56'-0" **Depth:** 43'-4"
Price Schedule: A4

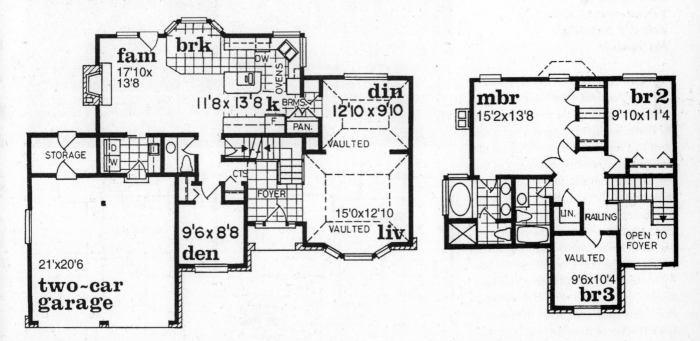

Design SHS010189

First Floor: 1,113 square feet
Second Floor: 965 square feet
Total: 2,078 square feet
Width: 46'-0" **Depth:** 41'-5"
Price Schedule: C1

Elegant detail, a charming veranda and a tall brick chimney make a pleasing facade on this four-bedroom, two-story Victorian home. Yesterday's simpler lifestyle is reflected throughout this plan. From the large bayed parlor with its sloped ceiling to the sunken gathering room with a fireplace, there's plenty to appreciate about the floor plan. The L-shaped kitchen with an attached breakfast room has plenty of storage space and easily serves the dining room through a discreet doorway. Upstairs sleeping quarters include an owners suite with a private dressing area and whirlpool bath, and three family bedrooms arranged to share a hall bath.

Design SHS010190

First Floor: 1,146 square feet
Second Floor: 943 square feet
Total: 2,089 square feet
Bonus Room: 494 square feet
Width: 56'-0" **Depth:** 38'-0"
Price Schedule: C2

Two covered porches will entice you outside, while inside a special sun room on the first floor brings the outdoors in. The foyer opens on the right to a comfortable family room that may be used as a home office. On the left, the living area is warmed by the sun room and a cozy, corner fireplace. A formal dining area lies adjacent to an efficient kitchen with a central island and breakfast nook overlooking the back porch. The second level offers two bedrooms served by a full bath. A spacious owners suite with a walk-in closet and luxurious bath completes the second floor. This home has a daylight basement.

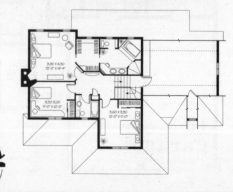

SELECT HOME DESIGNS

Design SHS010191

Square Footage: 2,076
Width: 64'-8" **Depth:** 54'-7"
Price Schedule: C1

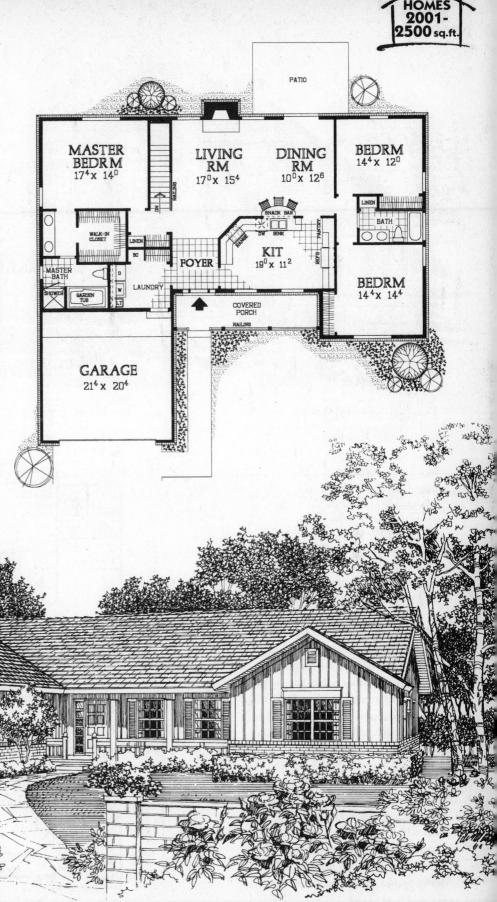

Multi-pane windows, mock shutters and a covered front porch exhibit the charm of this home's facade. Inside, the foyer is flanked by a spacious, efficient kitchen to the right and a large, convenient laundry room to the left. Directly ahead is the living room, which is graced by a warming fireplace. To the right of the living room is the formal dining room; both rooms share a snack bar and direct access to the kitchen. Sleeping quarters are split, with two family bedrooms and a full bath on the right side of the plan and the deluxe owners suite on the left. The owners bath offers such luxuries as a walk-in closet, twin vanities, a garden tub and a separate shower.

PATIO

MASTER BEDRM
17⁴ x 14⁰

LIVING RM
17⁰ x 15⁴

DINING RM
10⁰ x 12⁶

BEDRM
14⁴ x 12⁰

WALK-IN CLOSET

LINEN

LINEN

BATH

FOYER

KIT
19⁰ x 11²

SNACK BAR

PANTRY

MASTER BATH

SHOWER

GARDEN TUB

LAUNDRY

BEDRM
14⁴ x 14⁴

COVERED PORCH

RAILING

GARAGE
21⁴ x 20⁴

Design SHS010192

First Floor: 1,445 square feet

Second Floor: 652 square feet

Total: 2,097 square feet

Width: 56'-8" **Depth:** 48'-4"

Price Schedule: A4

A portico entry, graceful arches and brick detailing provide appeal and a low-maintenance exterior for this design. A half-circle transom over the entry lights the two-story foyer, while a plant shelf lines the hallway to the sunken family room. This living space holds a vaulted ceiling, masonry fireplace and French-door access to the railed patio. The nearby kitchen has a center prep island, built-in desk overlooking the family room and extensive pantries in the breakfast area. The formal dining room has a tray ceiling and access to the foyer and the central hall. The owners suite is on the first level for privacy and convenience. It features a walk-in closet and lavish bath with twin vanities, whirlpool tub and separate shower. Three family bedrooms, two of which feature built-in desks, are on the second floor.

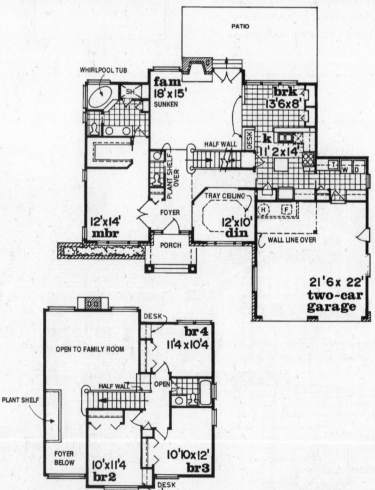

SELECT HOME DESIGNS

Design SHS010194

First Floor: 1,098 square feet
Second Floor: 996 square feet
Total: 2,094 square feet
Width: 62'-6" **Depth:** 40'-0"
Price Schedule: A4

This deluxe farmhouse is decorated with a covered railed veranda and shuttered windows. Flanking the foyer are a den with a double-door entry and the living room/dining room combination with a fireplace. The L-shaped kitchen can be reached from either the central hall or from an entry at the dining room. An island work counter and planning desk add to the kitchen's efficiency. A light-filled breakfast room serves casual meals.

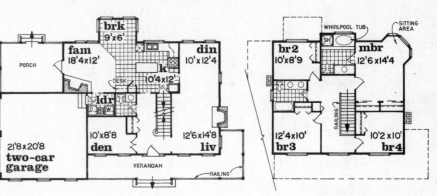

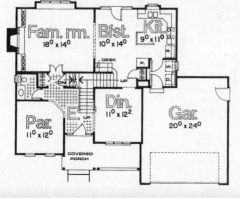

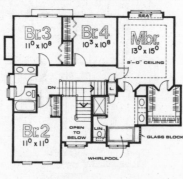

Design SHS010193

First Floor: 1,082 square feet
Second Floor: 1,021 square feet
Total: 2,103 square feet
Width: 50'-0" **Depth:** 40'-0"
Price Schedule: C1

A covered porch invites you into this country-style home. Handsome bookcases frame the fireplace in the spacious family room. Double doors off the entry provide the family room with added privacy. The kitchen features an island, a lazy Susan and easy access to a walk-in laundry. The owners bedroom features a boxed ceiling and separate entries into a walk-in closet and a pampering bath. The upstairs hall bath is compartmented, allowing maximum usage for today's busy family. Please specify basement, block or slab foundation when ordering.

HOMES 2001-2500 sq.ft.

Design SHS010196

Square Footage: 2,129
Width: 70'-0" Depth: 66'-8"
Price Schedule: A4

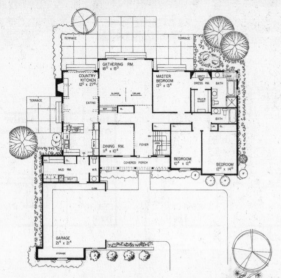

P ride of ownership will be for-ever yours as the occupant of this Early American home. The covered front porch provides a shelter for the inviting paneled front door with its flanking side window lights. The U-shaped work center is efficient. It is but a step from the mudroom area with its laundry equipment, closets, cupboards, counter space and powder room. There are two dining areas — an informal eating space and a formal, separate dining room. The more formal gathering room is spacious with a sloping ceiling and two sets of sliding glass doors to the rear terrace.

Design SHS010195

First Floor: 1,425 square feet
Second Floor: 704 square feet
Total: 2,129 square feet
Width: 55'-4" **Depth:** 52'-4"
Price Schedule: C1

T his charming Tudor adaptation features a complete second-floor owners suite with a balcony overlooking the living room, plus a studio and a private bath. The first floor contains a convenient kitchen with a pass-through to the breakfast room. A formal dining room just is steps away. An adjacent rear living room enjoys its own fireplace. Other features include a rear media room or optional third bedroom. A downstairs bedroom enjoys an excellent front view.

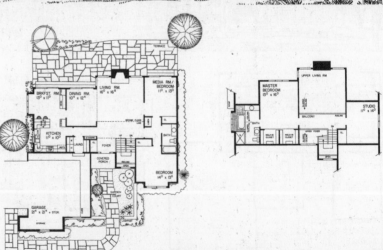

FOR PLAN ORDERING INFORMATION SEE PLAN

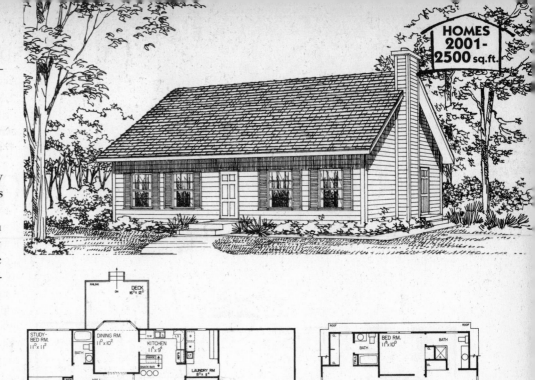

Design SHS010198

First Floor: 1,312 square feet
Second Floor: 795 square feet
Total: 2,107 square feet
Width: 68'-0" **Depth:** 30'-0"
Price Schedule: A4

The design of this 1½-story Cape Cod home provides plenty of room for all your family's needs. The kitchen extends as one large room over the snack bar into an expansive family room. A bayed formal dining room, a living room, a study/bedroom and a full bath complete this floor. Upstairs, two family bedrooms share a full bath, while the owners suite features its own private bath. The house may be enhanced by the addition of a fireplace, a bay window, a two-car garage, a laundry room and a rear deck.

Design SHS010197

First Floor: 1,100 square feet
Second Floor: 1,016 square feet
Total: 2,116 square feet
Width: 47'-0" **Depth:** 41'-0"
Price Schedule: A4

With stylish details borrowed from Craftsman, Victorian and farmhouse styles, this design is elegant without being pretentious. The entry opens to a two-story foyer that holds a half-bath, coat closet and stairs to the second floor. The living and dining rooms are on the right. The dining room has a buffet alcove. A family room is in the opposite corner and features patio access. Both the family room and the living room have fireplaces.

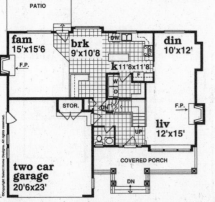

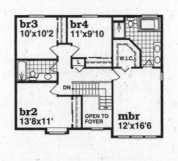

Design SHS010199

First Floor: 1,050 square feet
Second Floor: 1,085 square feet
Total: 2,135 square feet
Width: 50'-8" Depth: 39'-4"
Price Schedule: A4

This lovely country design features a stunning wrapping porch and plenty of windows to provide the interior with natural light. The living room boasts a centered fireplace, which helps to define this spacious open area. A nine-foot ceiling on the first floor adds a sense of spaciousness and light. The casual family room leads outdoors to a rear porch. Upstairs, four bedrooms cluster around a central hall. The owners suite features a walk-in closet and a deluxe bath with an oval tub and a separate shower. This home is designed with a basement foundation.

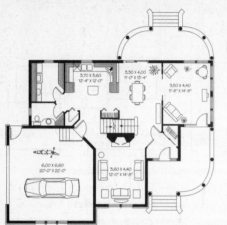

Available reverse | right reading

Design SHS010200

First Floor: 1,092 square feet
Second Floor: 1,050 square feet
Total: 2,142 square feet
Width: 47'-0" Depth: 48'-0"
Price Schedule: A4

This charming home comes highly recommended. It begins with a quaint front porch opening to a raised foyer. On the left side of the plan are a living room with a tray ceiling and fireplace, and a dining room with buffet space. The kitchen, breakfast nook and family room combine for one great gathering space. The owners suite boasts a vaulted ceiling, a large walk-in closet and a lavish full bath with twin vanities and a whirlpool spa. Three additional bedrooms share a full bath that features a skylight and a soaking tub.

FOR PLAN ORDERING INFORMATION SEE PLAN

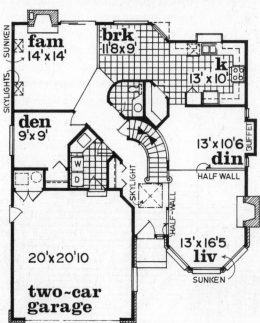

fam
14' x 14'

SUNKEN

brk
11'8 x 9'

k
13' x 10'

SKYLIGHTS

den
9' x 9'

W
D

SKYLIGHT

HALF-WALL

13' x 10'6
din

BUFFET

HALF WALL

20' x 20'10

13' 16'5
liv

SUNKEN

**two~car
garage**

Design SHS010201

First Floor: 1,227 square feet

Second Floor: 938 square feet

Total: 2,165 square feet

Width: 40'-8" Depth: 49'-4"

Price Schedule: A4

Two octagonal windows and a dramatic volume roof complement the traditional nature of this two-story home. A sweeping, curved staircase dominates the skylit foyer and leads to three bedrooms and a bonus room on the second floor. The owners suite is grand with a built-in vanity, a walk-in closet and a full bath with a whirlpool tub. Use the bonus space for an additional bedroom or a game room. The first floor holds a sunken living room that features a fireplace and is defined by half-walls. The dining room has buffet space. The family room is to the rear and features skylights and a fireplace. A U-shaped kitchen easily serves both the formal dining room and the breakfast nook. A cozy den is tucked away between the garage and the family room.

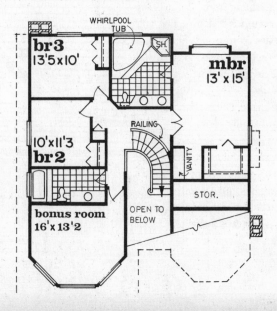

WHIRLPOOL
TUB

SH

br3
13'5 x 10'

mbr
13' x 15'

RAILING

VANITY

10' x 11'3
br2

STOR.

OPEN TO
BELOW

bonus room
16' x 13'2

GARAGE
21⁰ x 22⁶

COVERED
PORCH

GREAT
RM
16² x 17⁴

MASTER
SUITE
14⁰ x 15¹⁰

SITTING

LAUNDRY
RM

BREAKFAST
RM

Available
reverse

right
reading

KIT
11⁰ x 12⁶

FOYER

WALK-IN
CLOSET

DINING
11⁸ x 14⁶

MASTER
BATH

COVERED
PORCH

BEDRM
11² x 12⁰

BATH

BEDRM
11² x 12⁰

OPEN
TO
BELOW

Design SHS010202

First Floor: 1,655 square feet
Second Floor: 515 square feet
Total: 2,170 square feet
Width: 68'-6" **Depth:** 66'-5"
Price Schedule: C1

An arched clerestory, multi-pane windows and a balustrade porch splash this classic country exterior with an extraordinary new spirit. Inside, the two-story foyer is flanked by the sunny, formal dining room and an elegant stairway. The great room offers a fireplace with a tiled hearth, a built-in media center and a snack bar that it shares with the large island kitchen and breakfast room. Ceramic tiles dress up the L-shaped kitchen, which boasts a built-in desk, extra closet space and double ovens. The first-floor owners suite is appointed with a sitting area and enjoys private access to the rear covered porch, while the private bath boasts an angled whirlpool tub and twin lavatories. Upstairs, two secondary bedrooms—each with its own balcony—share a full bath that contains ample linen storage.

Design SHS010203

Square Footage: 2,172
Width: 76'-0" Depth: 46'-0"
Price Schedule: C1

This one-story with grand rooflines holds a most convenient floor plan. The great room with a fireplace to the rear complements a front-facing living room. The formal dining room with its tray ceiling sits just across the hall from the living room and is also easily accessible to the kitchen. An island, pantry, breakfast room and patio are highlights in the kitchen. A bedroom at this end of the house works fine as an office or guest bedroom since a full bath is close by. Two additional bedrooms are to the right of the plan: an owners suite with a grand bath and one additional secondary bedroom. A three-car garage provides extra storage space.

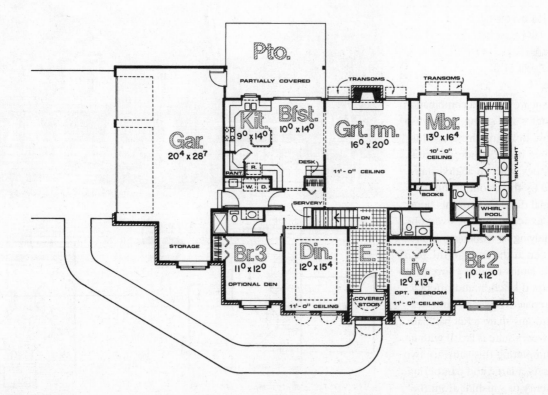

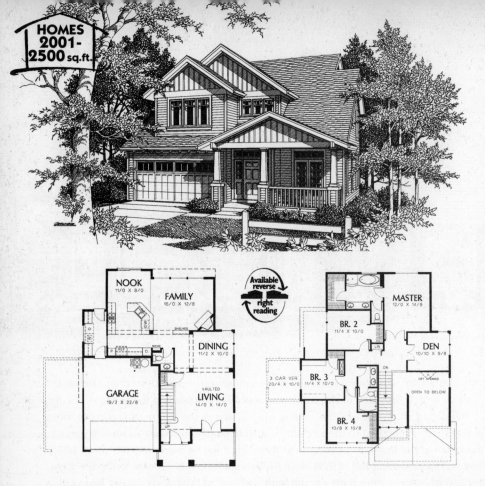

Design SHS010205

First Floor: 1,072 square feet
Second Floor: 1,108 square feet
Total: 2,180 square feet
Width: 40'-0" Depth: 48'-6"
Price Schedule: A4

A covered porch introduces this two-story home and complements the horizontal wood siding with vertical siding trim. Inside, an open floor plan reigns. The vaulted living room is to the front, where double doors open to the porch. Columns separate the living room from the formal dining room and the family room from the main hall. A corner fireplace and built-in shelves adorn the family room. The nook has sliding glass doors to the rear yard and is open to the kitchen. Three family bedrooms, an owners suite and a den are on the second floor. Note the walk-in closet and sumptuous bath in the owners suite.

Design SHS010204

First Floor: 1,158 square feet
Second Floor: 1,044 square feet
Total: 2,202 square feet
Width: 54'-0" Depth: 51'-0"
Price Schedule: A4

Strong square pillars, a combination of shingles and siding, and stylish window detailing dress up this fine Craftsman home. Inside, graceful detail continues, with an angled staircase echoed by the layout of the parlor and formal dining room. This home is designed to accommodate everyone. For quiet studying or working at home, there's the den at the front of the plan. The spacious family room is convenient to the L-shaped kitchen and offers a warming fireplace. Upstairs, three secondary bedrooms share a full hall bath, while the owners suite is lavish with its luxuries. Completing this suite are two walk-in closets, a large and pampering bath and plenty of sunshine from the corner windows.

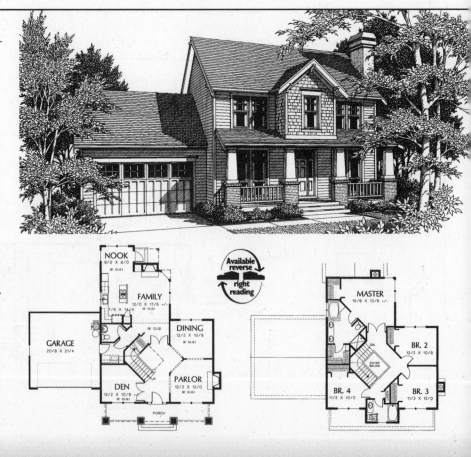

A Palladian window, fish-scale shingles and turret-style bays set off this country-style Victorian exterior. Muntin windows and a quintessential wraparound porch dress up an understated theme and introduce an unrestrained floor plan with plenty of bays and niches. An impressive tile entry opens to the formal rooms, which nestle to the left side of the plan and enjoy natural light from an abundance of windows. The turret houses a secluded study on the first floor and provides a sunny bay window for a family bedroom upstairs. The second-floor owners suite boasts its own fireplace, a dressing area with a walk-in closet, and a lavish bath with a garden tub and twin vanities. The two-car garage offers space for a workshop or extra storage, and leads to a service entrance to the walk-through utility room.

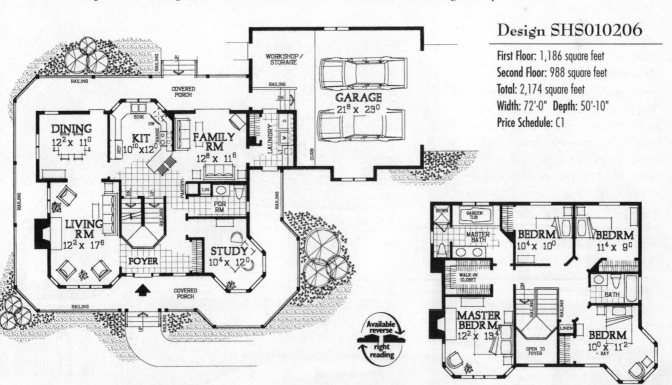

Design SHS010206

First Floor: 1,186 square feet
Second Floor: 988 square feet
Total: 2,174 square feet
Width: 72'-0" Depth: 50'-10"
Price Schedule: C1

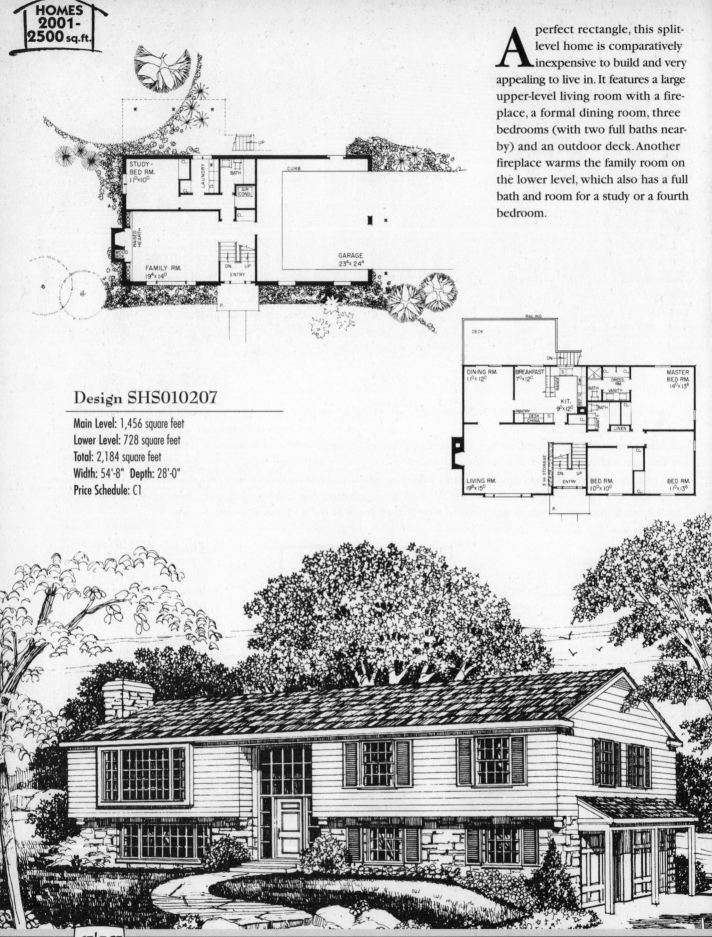

A perfect rectangle, this split-level home is comparatively inexpensive to build and very appealing to live in. It features a large upper-level living room with a fire-place, a formal dining room, three bedrooms (with two full baths near-by) and an outdoor deck. Another fireplace warms the family room on the lower level, which also has a full bath and room for a study or a fourth bedroom.

STUDY-BED RM. 11⁰x10⁰

CL.

LAUNDRY

BATH

AIR COND.

CURB

CL.

RAISED HEARTH

WOOD BOX

FAMILY RM. 19⁴x14⁰

DN.

UP

ENTRY

GARAGE 23⁴x24⁴

UP

Design SHS010207

Main Level: 1,456 square feet
Lower Level: 728 square feet
Total: 2,184 square feet
Width: 54'-8" **Depth:** 28'-0"
Price Schedule: C1

RAILING

DECK

DN.

DINING RM. 11⁰x12⁰

BREAKFAST 7⁰x12⁰

RANGE

S

BATH

CL.

CL.

DRESS. RM.

VANITY

MASTER BED RM. 14⁰x13⁶

KIT. 9⁰x12⁰

REF.

DW.

BATH

CL.

PANTRY

DESK

CHINA

C.

VANITY

LINEN

LIVING RM. 19⁸x15⁰

3' HI STORAGE

DN.

UP

ENTRY

BED RM. 10⁰x10⁰

CL.

BED RM. 11⁰x13⁶

CL.

P.

FOR PLAN ORDERING INFORMATION SEE PLAN

Design SHS010208

First Floor: 1,500 square feet

Second Floor: 690 square feet

Total: 2,190 square feet

Width: 80'-0" **Depth:** 32'-0"

Price Schedule: C1

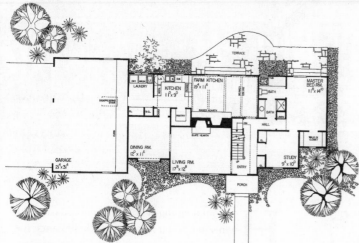

From the large living room with a fireplace and an adjacent dining room to the farm kitchen with an additional fireplace, this plan offers full livability. A front study might be used as a guest bedroom. Upstairs there are two bedrooms and a sitting room plus a full bath to accommodate the needs of family members.

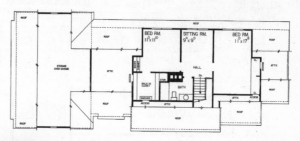

Design SHS010209

Square Footage: 2,203

Width: 77'-2" **Depth:** 46'-6"

Price Schedule: C1

Nothing completes a traditional-style home quite as well as a country kitchen with a fireplace and built-in wood box. Notice also the second fireplace (with a raised hearth) and the sloped ceiling in the living room. The nearby dining room has an attached porch and separate dining terrace. Aside from two family bedrooms with a shared full bath, there is also a marvelous owners suite with rear-terrace access, a walk-in closet, a whirlpool tub and double vanities. A handy washroom is near the laundry, just off the two-car garage.

Available reverse right reading

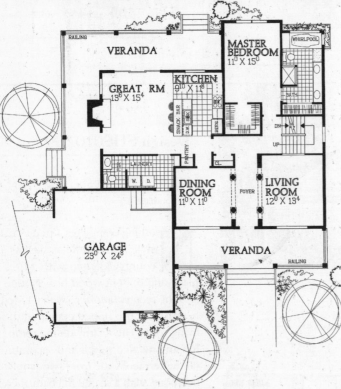

Horizontal siding with corner boards, muntin windows and a raised veranda enhance the appeal of this country home. Twin carriage lamps flank the sheltered entrance. Inside, the central foyer delights with its two sets of columns at the openings to the formal living and dining rooms. In the L-shaped kitchen, an adjacent snack bar offers everyday ease. Open to the kitchen, the great room boasts a centered fireplace, a high ceiling and access to the veranda. Sleeping accommodations start off with the owners bedroom; a connecting bath will be a favorite spot. Upstairs, three family bedrooms share a full bath that includes twin lavatories.

Design SHS010210

First Floor: 1,395 square feet

Second Floor: 813 square feet

Total: 2,208 square feet

Width: 53'-8" Depth: 57'-0"

Price Schedule: A4

SELECT
HOME DESIGNS

FOR PLAN ORDERING INFORMATION SEE PLAN

Design SHS010211

First Floor: 1,136 square feet
Second Floor: 1,083 square feet
Total: 2,219 square feet
Width: 25'-8" **Depth:** 54'-9"
Price Schedule: A4

This inviting narrow-lot design borrows classic details from a bygone era—a covered veranda in the front, a gabled roof and fish-scale detailing. Ideal for city lots, this design features four bedrooms, including an owners suite with a walk-in closet and a private bath with a separate tub and shower and double vanities. One of the three family bedrooms is graced by box windows. The entry opens to a living room/dining room combination with a fireplace.

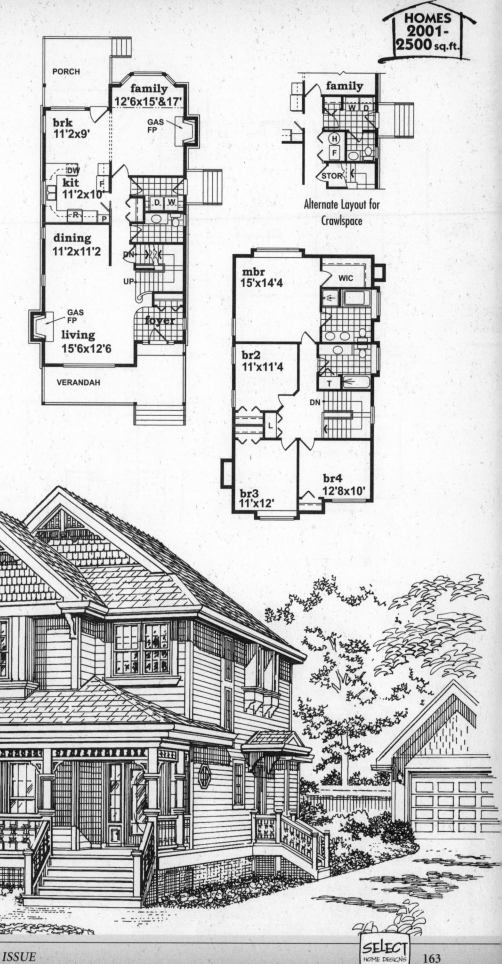

PORCH

family
12'6x15'&17'

GAS FP

brk
11'2x9'

DW

kit
11'2x10'

F

R

P

D. W.

dining
11'2x11'2

DN

UP

GAS FP

living
15'6x12'6

foyer

VERANDAH

family

W D

H F

STOR

Alternate Layout for Crawlspace

mbr
15'x14'4

WIC

br2
11'x11'4

T

DN

L

br3
11'x12'

br4
12'8x10'

SELECT HOME DESIGNS

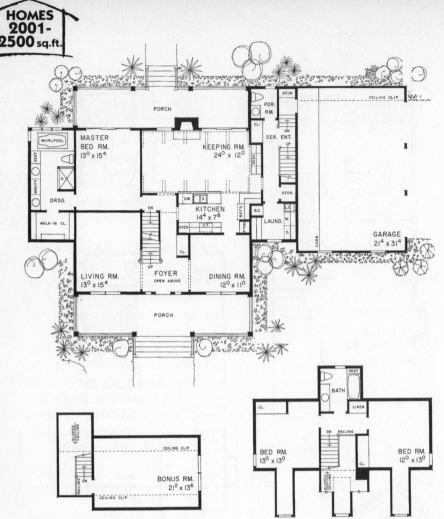

PORCH

MASTER
BED RM.
13⁰ x 15⁴

WHIRLPOOL

SEAT

VANITY

DRSG.

WALK-IN CL.

KEEPING RM.
24⁰ x 12⁰

PDR. RM.

STOR.

CL.

CEILING CLIP

SER. ENT.

DN

UP

KITCHEN
14⁴ x 7⁸

D.W.

S.

OVEN

C.T.

STOR.

CL.

DN

UP

B.C.

LAUND.

CURB

GARAGE
21⁴ x 31⁴

LIVING RM.
13⁰ x 15⁴

FOYER
OPEN ABOVE

DINING RM.
12⁰ x 11⁰

PORCH

SLOPED CEILING

RAILING ON

CEILING CLIP

BONUS RM.
21² x 13⁶

CEILING CLIP

SEAT

BATH

CL.

LINEN

BED RM.
13⁰ x 13⁰

DN

RAILING

CL.

BED RM.
12⁰ x 13⁰

SLOPED CEILING

Design SHS010212

First Floor: 1,635 square feet
Second Floor: 586 square feet
Total: 2,221 square feet
Bonus Room: 321 square feet
Width: 76'-0" **Depth:** 48'-0"
Price Schedule: C2

Don't be fooled by the humbled appearance of this farmhouse. All the amenities abound. A grand front entrance opens into living and dining rooms. The family will surely enjoy the ambience of the keeping room with its fireplace and beam ceiling. A service entry, with a laundry room nearby, separates the garage from the main house. An over-the-garage bonus room allows for room to grow or a nice study. Two quaint bedrooms and a full bath make up the second floor.

SELECT
HOME DESIGNS

FOR PLAN ORDERING INFORMATION SEE PLAN

Design SHS010214

First Floor: 1,140 square feet

Second Floor: 1,096 square feet

Total: 2,236 square feet

Bonus Room: 414 square feet

Width: 60'-8" Depth: 35'-4"

Price Schedule: A4

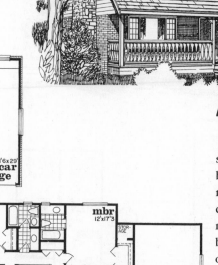

This classic floor plan features a double-door entry to a center hall, flanked by living areas. The sunken living room is on the left and boasts a fireplace; the den is on the right and has double-door access. A dining room sits between the living room and the U-shaped kitchen. Four bedrooms and a large bonus room are on the second floor. The owners bedroom has a walk-in closet with extra storage space and a full bath. Family bedrooms share a full hall bath.

Design SHS010213

First Floor: 1,092 square feet

Second Floor: 1,147 square feet

Total: 2,239 square feet

Width: 47'-0" Depth: 48'-0"

Price Schedule: A4

Shingle siding and a covered front porch add style to this farmhouse design. The interior is arranged thoughtfully and with an eye to varied lifestyles. Formal areas are on the left: a living room with a tray ceiling and fireplace, and a formal dining room. The second floor has four bedrooms—one of them an owners suite. The owners bedroom has a vaulted ceiling and walk-in closet and features a luxury bath with separate tub and shower. Family bedrooms share a full bath.

HOMES 2001-2500 sq.ft.

Design SHS010216

First Floor: 1,602 square feet
Second Floor: 654 square feet
Total: 2,256 square feet
Width: 54'-0" **Depth:** 50'-0"
Price Schedule: C1

From the beautiful bay window in the dining room to the French doors connecting the formal living room to the family room with a fireplace, this home delivers a wealth of amenities. An open dinette is adjacent to the kitchen that features a snack bar and a pantry. The owners suite features a boxed ceiling and a skylit owners dressing/bath area with a decorator plant ledge, a double vanity and a windowed whirlpool tub. Upstairs, Bedroom 2 echoes the bay window from the dining room. Three second-floor bedrooms share a compartmented bath that has two lavatories. Please specify basement or block foundation when ordering.

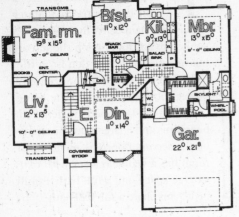

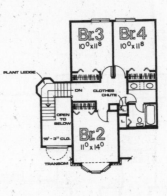

Design SHS010215

First Floor: 1,353 square feet
Second Floor: 899 square feet
Total: 2,252 square feet
Bonus Room: 183 square feet
Width: 38'-0" **Depth:** 59'-0"
Price Schedule: A4

This three-bedroom plan has bonus space and offers horizontal siding with brick. Note the fireplace and window seat in the living room. The nearby L-shaped kitchen, with a center cooking island, adjoins a sunny breakfast room and large family room. A private den could serve as guest space if needed. On the second floor are three bedrooms and bonus space to develop into a fourth bedroom if needed. The owners suite has a coffered ceiling and a bath with a raised tub and shower.

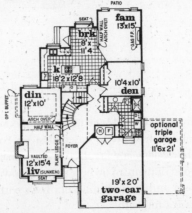

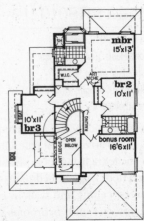

SELECT HOME DESIGNS

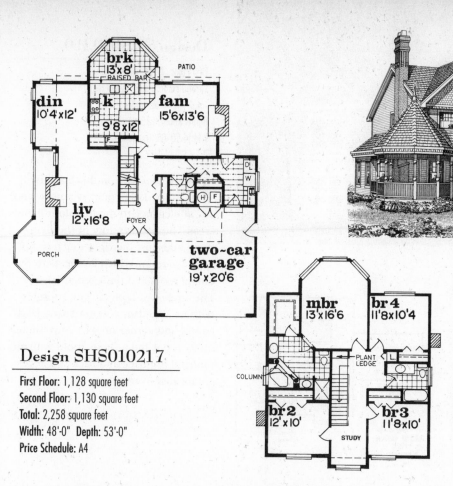

Design SHS010217

First Floor: 1,128 square feet

Second Floor: 1,130 square feet

Total: 2,258 square feet

Width: 48'-0" **Depth:** 53'-0"

Price Schedule: A4

A gazebo porch, topped with a turret roof, and nostalgic wood detailing grace this four-bedroom Victorian design. Double front doors open to a spacious living room and adjoining dining room. The living room has a warming fireplace. The kitchen, with a center prep island and raised eating bar, serves a sunny breakfast bay and the family room. The owners suite features a bay window, walk-in closet and bath with a corner whirlpool tub that's adorned with columns. Three family bedrooms share a full bath.

Design SHS010218

First Floor: 1,196 square feet

Second Floor: 1,069 square feet

Total: 2,265 square feet

Bonus Room: 430 square feet

Width: 57'-0" **Depth:** 32'-0"

Price Schedule: A4

This home offers shuttered windows and a covered porch. The center foyer opens to a tray ceiling in both the living room and dining room. The dining room also offers a window seat in a box window, while the living room features a fireplace. Across the foyer, a den provides a place for quiet study. The kitchen and breakfast bay include a built-in desk and a corner pantry. Upstairs, two family bedrooms share a skylit bath and balcony overlook to the foyer. The owners bedroom has a walk-in closet and a private skylit bath. A bonus room offers additional space for future expansion.

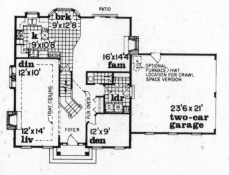

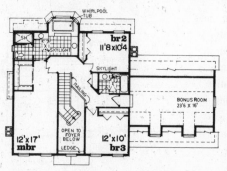

Design SHS010219

First Floor: 1,185 square feet
Second Floor: 1,086 square feet
Total: 2,271 square feet
Bonus Room: 193 square feet
Width: 50'-0" **Depth:** 43'-10"
Price Schedule: C1

Bay windows on this brick two-story design offer symmetry and elegance to the first-floor living areas. The bay window in the living room adds just the right touch to this spacious room, which connects to the dining room and the kitchen beyond. The kitchen will please any gourmet with its abundant counter space, large pantry and corner nook. A convenient utility room and a family room with an optional fireplace and backyard access are located nearby.

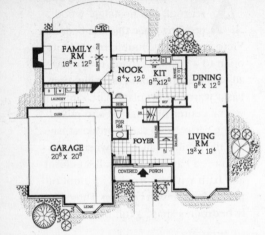

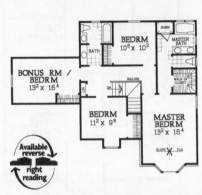

Design SHS010220

First Floor: 1,160 square feet
Second Floor: 1,111 square feet
Total: 2,271 square feet
Width: 42'-0" **Depth:** 42'-0"
Price Schedule: C1

Amenities fill this two-story country home, beginning with a porch that offers entry to the first floor. Formal living and dining rooms border the central foyer, each with windowed views to the front property. At the rear of the first floor is an open family area with a U-shaped kitchen, a bayed breakfast or morning area and a large family room with a fireplace and access to the rear porch. Upstairs, three family bedrooms share a centrally located utility room and a full hall bath with dual sinks. The owners bedroom features a bath with separate sinks and a walk-in closet. An additional half-bath on the first floor completes this exquisite design.

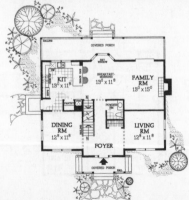

FOR PLAN ORDERING INFORMATION SEE PLAN

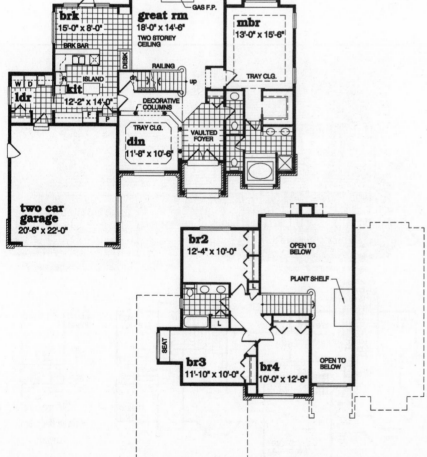

brk
15'-0" x 8'-0"

great rm
18'-0" x 14'-6"
TWO STOREY
CEILING

GAS F.P.

mbr
13'-0" x 15'-6"

BRK BAR

ISLAND

RAILING

TRAY CLG.

kit
12'-2" x 14'-0"

DESK

dn   up

W D

ldr

DECORATIVE
COLUMNS

TRAY CLG.

VAULTED
FOYER

din
11'-8" x 10'-6"

F P

**two car
garage**
20'-6" x 22'-0"

br2
12'-4" x 10'-0"

OPEN TO
BELOW

PLANT SHELF

br3
11'-10" x 10'-0"

L

SEAT

br4
10'-0" x 12'-6"

OPEN TO
BELOW

Design SHS010221

First Floor: 1,542 square feet
Second Floor: 739 square feet
Total: 2,281 square feet
Width: 56'-8" **Depth:** 48'-8"
Price Schedule: A4

A traditional brick facade, with soaring rooflines, gives this two-story family home an air of distinction. The vaulted entry is flanked by an elegant formal dining room with a tray ceiling and decorative columns to the left, and the owners suite to the right. The gourmet kitchen with a center island leads to a great room with an imposing fireplace. The elegant main-floor owners suite features a large walk-in closet and a bath with a whirlpool tub and separate shower. Family bedrooms are on the second floor—one is appointed with a window seat. All three of these bedrooms share the use of a full bath.

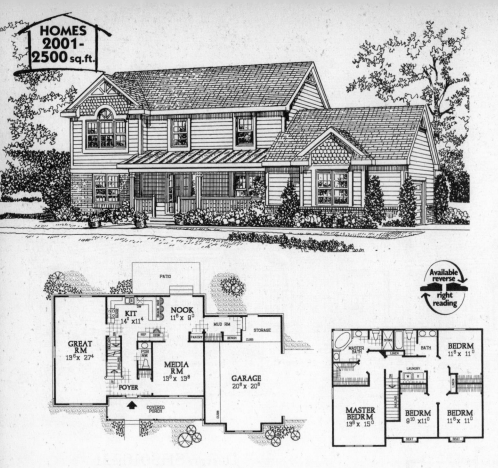

Available reverse
right reading

Design SHS010223

First Floor: 1,179 square feet
Second Floor: 1,120 square feet
Total: 2,299 square feet
Width: 61'-8" **Depth:** 35'-8"
Price Schedule: C1

A covered porch and multi-pane windows draw attention to this four-bedroom farmhouse. From the porch, the foyer leads to the media room or straight ahead, past the powder room, to the kitchen. The breakfast nook, with a snack bar, opens to the rear patio. A mudroom off the nook accesses the garage through a storage area. Laundry facilities are on the second floor, where three family bedrooms—two of them with window seats—share a bath that offers a double-bowl vanity. The owners suite provides a walk-in closet and a private bath that has a corner tub and separate vanities.

Design SHS010222

First Floor: 1,180 square feet
Second Floor: 1,121 square feet
Total: 2,301 square feet
Width: 48'-0" **Depth:** 52'-6"
Price Schedule: A4

A turret roof, prominent bay window and a wraparound veranda identify this four-bedroom design as classic Victorian. The plans include two second-level layouts—one with four bedrooms or one with three bedrooms and a vaulted ceiling over the family room. Both include a lavish owners suite with an octagonal tray ceiling in the sitting room, a walk-in closet and a private bath with a columned whirlpool spa and separate shower. The first floor holds a formal living room with windows overlooking the veranda, a formal dining room and a family room with a fireplace.

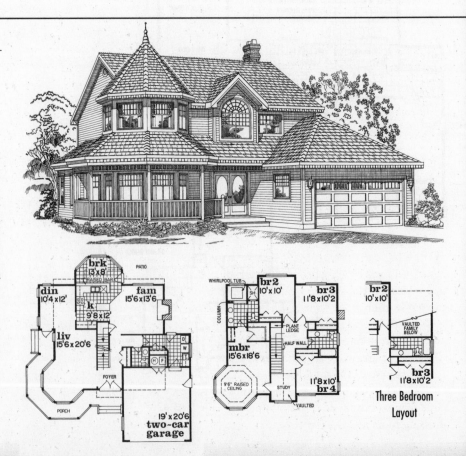

Three Bedroom Layout

FOR PLAN ORDERING INFORMATION SEE PLAN

Design SHS010225

First Floor: 1,346 square feet

Second Floor: 961 square feet

Total: 2,307 square feet

Bonus Room: 186 square feet

Width: 61'-4" **Depth:** 43'-0"

Price Schedule: A4

This elegant home begins with stucco siding, corner quoins and a dramatic two-story entry flooded with natural light. Living and dining rooms flank a raised central foyer; the family room lies directly ahead. A cozy den on the left makes a great guest room. A rear deck is reached through doors in both the breakfast bay and the family room. The second floor holds an owners suite with a private bath and walk-in closet, and two family bedrooms with a shared bath. A large bonus room can be used as an additional bedroom or as a game room.

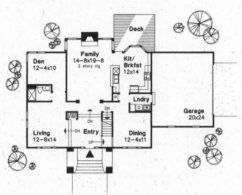

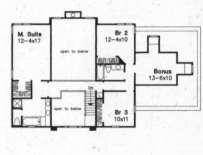

Perfect for a narrow lot, this shingle-and-stone Nantucket Cape design caters to the casual lifestyle. The side entrance gives direct access to the wonderfully open living areas: a gathering room with a fireplace and an abundance of windows; an island kitchen with an angled, pass-through snack bar; and a dining area with sliding glass doors to a covered eating area. Note also the large terrace that further extends the living potential. Also on this floor is the large owners suite with a compartmented bath, private dressing room and walk-in closet.

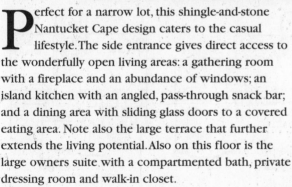

Design SHS010224

First Floor: 1,387 square feet

Second Floor: 929 square feet

Total: 2,316 square feet

Width: 30'-0" **Depth:** 51'-8"

Price Schedule: A4

Design SHS010227

First Floor: 1,297 square feet
Second Floor: 1,027 square feet
Total: 2,324 square feet
Width: 39'-0" Depth: 50'-0"
Price Schedule: A3

With Mediterranean good looks, this home is built with a sunny stucco exterior and brightened by large window areas and open spaces. The main entry leads to formal areas on the left—a living room and dining room—and then back to the sunken family room. Glass blocks separate the family room from the breakfast nook. The island kitchen is just beyond. Finishing the first floor are a powder room and a hidden-away den. Four bedrooms reside on the second floor. Three of these are for family and guests, while the owners suite is preserved as a private retreat. Note the walk-in closet and lovely ensuite area with separate tub and shower.

Design SHS010226

First Floor: 1,360 square feet
Second Floor: 966 square feet
Total: 2,326 square feet
Bonus Room: 56'-8" Depth: 47'-4"
Bonus Room: 198 square feet
Price Schedule: A4

This impressive home is accented by brick detailing and dominant arched windows. Inside, the living and dining rooms boast coffered ceilings; the living room has a bay window. A large family room, with sliding glass doors and a fireplace, is joined in the rear of the plan by a breakfast bay and island kitchen. A cozy den opens just off the foyer. Second-floor bedrooms include an owners suite with two walk-in closets and a bath with a whirlpool tub set in a bay window. Family bedrooms share a full bath. A large bonus room has a vaulted ceiling.

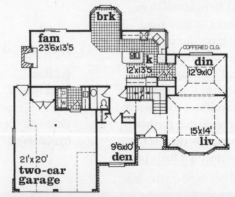

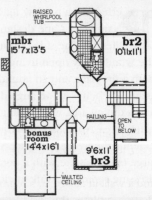

FOR PLAN ORDERING INFORMATION SEE PLAN

Design SHS010229

First Floor: 1,235 square feet
Second Floor: 1,084 square feet
Total: 2,319 square feet
Width: 40'-0" **Depth:** 50'-0"
Price Schedule: A3

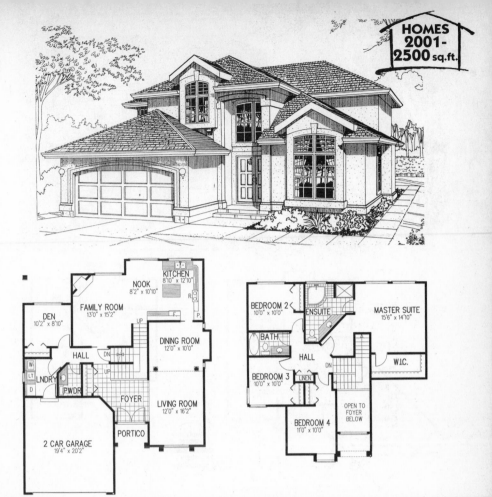

An elegant entry with double doors and a transom in the two-story foyer are the perfect introduction to this fine design. Formal rooms are separated by columns and sit on the right side of the entry hall. The family room, nook and island kitchen align at the back of the plan for one open area of casual living. A den is tucked away behind the two-car garage for privacy. A laundry room connects the garage to the main house and, thus, serves as a mudroom. Four bedrooms are found on the second floor. The three family bedrooms share a full bath. The owners suite, however, is a private retreat with a walk-in closet and a full bath that features a separate tub and shower.

The heart of this stately brick home is found at the rear of the plan, where a large area made up of the kitchen, breakfast or morning area, and family room provide the perfect atmosphere for casual living. A formal dining room, conveniently accessible to the kitchen, and a formal living room, both with sunny bay windows, are located at the front of the home. Upstairs, three family bedrooms share a centrally located utility room and a full hall bath. The owners bedroom features a box-bay window seat and a bath with separate sinks and a walk-in closet. An additional half-bath on the first floor completes this exquisite design.

Design SHS010228

First Floor: 1,192 square feet
Second Floor: 1,127 square feet
Total: 2,319 square feet
Width: 42'-8" **Depth:** 37'-4"
Price Schedule: C1

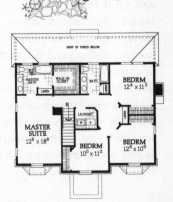

Design SHS010230

First Floor: 1,205 square feet
Second Floor: 1,123 square feet
Total: 2,328 square feet
Width: 57'-2" **Depth:** 58'-7"
Price Schedule: A4

A covered porch, multi-pane windows and shingle-with-stone siding combine to give this bungalow plenty of curb appeal. Inside, the foyer is flanked by the formal living room and an angled staircase. The formal dining room adjoins the living room, and the kitchen is accessible through double doors. A large family room is graced by a fireplace and opens off a cozy eating nook. The second level presents many attractive angles. The owners suite has a spacious walk-in closet and a sumptuous bath complete with a garden tub and separate shower. Three family bedrooms share a full hall bath.

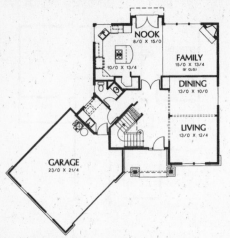

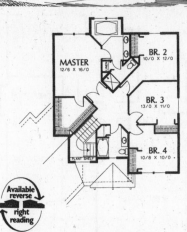

Design SHS010231

First Floor: 1,463 square feet
Second Floor: 872 square feet
Total: 2,335 square feet
Width: 44'-0" **Depth:** 58'-10"
Price Schedule: A4

The interior plan begins with a vaulted foyer hosting a sweeping curved staircase, and then spilling into a sunken living room with a masonry fireplace, a vaulted ceiling and a full, floor-to-ceiling, half-round window. The kitchen features a pantry, center cooking island, built-in desk and sunny breakfast bay. A den with a walk-in closet and nearby bath can easily double as guest space. The owners suite on the second floor boasts a drop ceiling, bay-windowed sitting area, spacious wall closet and lavish owners bath. Family bedrooms share a full bath.

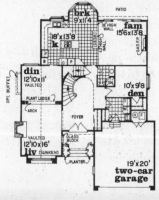

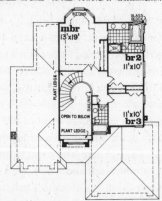

Design SHS010232

First Floor: 1,366 square feet

Second Floor: 969 square feet

Total: 2,335 square feet

Attic: 969 square feet

Width: 59'-6" **Depth:** 46'-0"

Price Schedule: C1

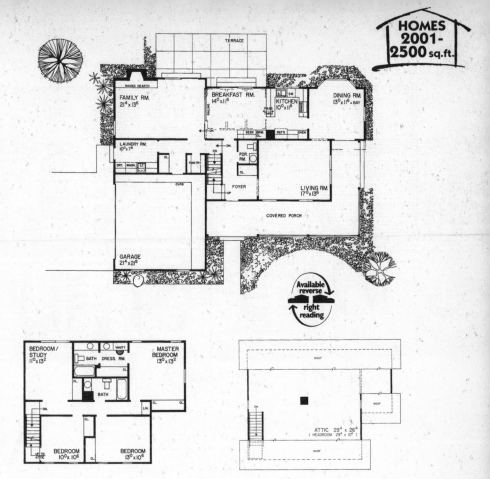

Here's a great farmhouse adaptation with all the most up-to-date features. There is the quiet corner living room, which has an opening to the sizable dining room. This room will enjoy plenty of natural light from the delightful bay window overlooking the rear yard and is conveniently located near the efficient U-shaped kitchen. The kitchen features many built-ins and a pass-through to the beam-ceilinged nook. Sliding glass doors to the terrace are found in both the family room and nook. The service entrance to the garage is flanked by a clothes closet and a large, walk-in pantry. Recreational activities and hobbies can be pursued in the basement area. Four bedrooms and two baths are located on the second floor. The owners bedroom has a dressing room and double vanity.

SELECT
HOME·DESIGNS

Design SHS010233

First Floor: 1,617 square feet
Second Floor: 725 square feet
Total: 2,342 square feet
Width: 62'-0" **Depth:** 41'-0"
Price Schedule: C1

With end gables, and five front gables, this design becomes an updated house of seven gables. Meanwhile, brick veneer, the use of horizontal siding, radial head windows and interesting roof planes add an extra measure of charm. The attached, side-opening, two-car garage is a delightfully integral part of the appealing exterior. Designed for a growing family with a modest building budget, the floor plan incorporates four bedrooms and both formal and informal living areas. The central foyer, with its open staircase to the second floor, looks up to the balcony. The spacious family room has a high ceiling and a dramatic view of the balcony. In the U-shaped kitchen, a snack bar caters to quick, on-the-run meals.

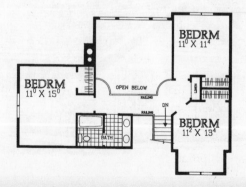

Design SHS010235

First Floor: 1,441 square feet
Second Floor: 918 square feet
Total: 2,359 square feet
Width: 66'-4" Depth: 46'-4"
Price Schedule: C1

Corner quoins, louver vents and arches add a special touch of elegance to the brick facade of this traditional home. The two-story foyer leads to a corner living room. Beyond the convenient powder room is a formal dining room, spacious family room and amenity-filled kitchen. The kitchen features a snack bar and a counter-laden kitchen with a walk-in pantry. A decoratively arched curios niche provides entry to the first-floor owners bedroom. Three additional bedrooms with ample closet space are available on the second floor. They share a full bath, a multi-media loft and a large, conveniently located utility room.

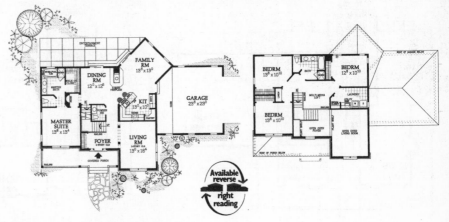

An octagonal tower, a wraparound porch and rich amenities combine to give this house lots of appeal. The tower is occupied by a sunny den on the first floor and a delightful bedroom on the second floor. A large, efficient kitchen easily serves both the formal dining room and the cheerful nook. Upstairs, two secondary bedrooms share a full hall bath, while the owners bedroom revels in its luxurious private bath.

Design SHS010234

First Floor: 1,337 square feet
Second Floor: 1,025 square feet
Total: 2,362 square feet
Width: 50'-6" Depth: 72'-6"
Price Schedule: A4

HOMES 2001- 2500 sq.ft.

Design SHS010236

First Floor: 1,193 square feet
Second Floor: 1,188 square feet
Total: 2,381 square feet
Width: 62'-0" **Depth:** 47'-0"
Price Schedule: A4

Graced by a wraparound veranda, multi-pane shutters and decorative wood trim, this four-bedroom design is as attractive as it is comfortable. Large bay windows and high ceilings throughout the first level further enhance the charm. The living room, with its masonry fireplace, extends to the bay-windowed dining area. The kitchen features an eating or serving bar and a center preparation island, which make easy work of mealtimes.

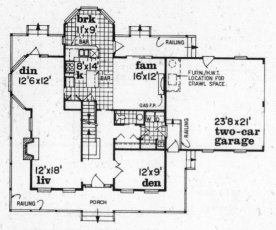

Design SHS010237

First Floor: 1,321 square feet
Second Floor: 1,070 square feet
Total: 2,391 square feet
Width: 63'-2" **Depth:** 50'-8"
Price Schedule: A4

Touches of Victoriana add a whisper of the grace of yesteryear to this captivating home. Choose brick or wood siding as the exterior finish, as you like. The foyer separates a den from the formal living and dining rooms. The living room has a cozy fireplace; the den overlooks the rear sun deck. The hearth room and breakfast room form one large gathering area, served handily by an island kitchen. A door from the hearth room leads out to a covered porch and the sun deck beyond. Four bedrooms occupy the four corners of the second floor. Bedroom 4 and the owners suite have walk-in closets.

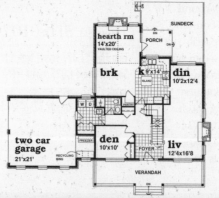

SELECT HOME DESIGNS

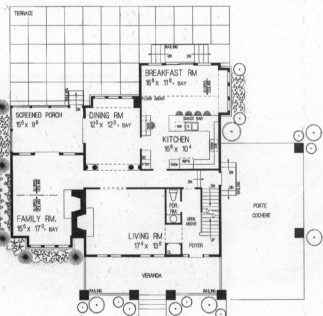

ozy living abounds in this comfortable two-story bungalow. Enter the foyer and find a spacious living room with a fireplace to the left. Straight ahead is a U-shaped kitchen with a snack bar, a planning desk and easy access to the formal dining room. The bayed family room features a fireplace and entry to a screened porch. Upstairs, secondary bedrooms offer ample closet space and direct access to a shared bath. The owners suite contains a large walk-in closet, double-bowl vanity and compartmented shower and toilet.

Design SHS010238

First Floor: 1,482 square feet

Second Floor: 885 square feet

Total: 2,367 square feet

Width: 64'-0" **Depth:** 50'-0"

Price Schedule: C2

HOMES 2001-2500 sq.ft.

Design SHS010240

First Floor: 1,447 square feet
Second Floor: 958 square feet
Total: 2,405 square feet
Width: 66'-4" **Depth:** 48'-0"
Price Schedule: C1

The asymmetrical front facade of this three-bedroom, traditional-style home offers great curb appeal. The two-story foyer provides access to all rooms, including the formal living room and dining room. The large, U-shaped kitchen features a walk-in pantry, an island worktop and a snack bar to the morning nook with its terrace access. The family room is complete with a three-sided fireplace. Upstairs, the owners bedroom features a large bath with a walk-in closet and a special whirlpool tub with a seat. Two family bedrooms share a full hall bath and a multi-media loft area.

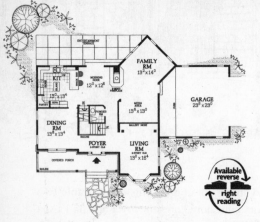

Design SHS010239

First Floor: 1,375 square feet
Second Floor: 1,016 square feet
Total: 2,391 square feet
Width: 62'-7" **Depth:** 54'-0"
Price Schedule: C1

Covered porches, front and back, are a fine preview to the livable nature of this Victorian design. Living areas are defined in a family room with a fireplace, formal living and dining rooms and a kitchen with a breakfast room. An ample laundry room, a garage with a storage area, and a powder room round out the first floor. Three second-floor bedrooms are joined by a study and two full baths. The owners suite on this floor has two closets, including an ample walk-in, as well as a relaxing bath with a tile-rimmed whirlpool tub and a separate shower with a seat.

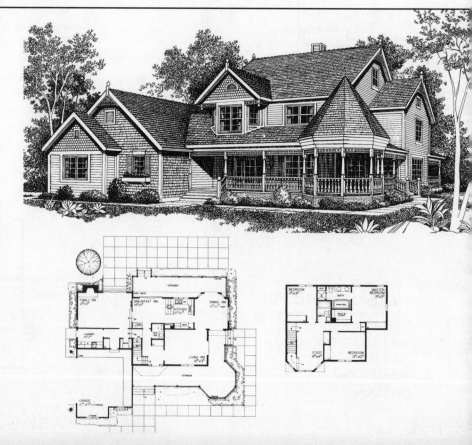

Available reverse right reading

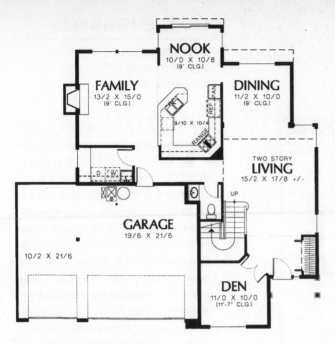

NOOK
10/0 X 10/8
(9' CLG.)

FAMILY
13/2 X 15/0
(9' CLG.)

DINING
11/2 X 10/0
(9' CLG.)

REF. PAN.

9/10 X 10/4

RANGE

TWO STORY
LIVING
15/2 X 17/8 +/-

D W

GARAGE
19/6 X 21/6

10/2 X 21/6

UP

DEN
11/0 X 10/0
(11'-7" CLG.)

A two-story living room greets family and friends upon entry to this fine four-bedroom Craftsman home. A cozy den is isolated toward the front of the home, assuring privacy. The angled kitchen reigns in the center of the home, with easy access to the formal dining room, sunny nook and spacious family room. A fireplace in the family room promises warmth and welcome.

Design SHS010241

First Floor: 1,255 square feet
Second Floor: 1,141 square feet
Total: 2,396 square feet
Width: 40'-0" Depth: 50'-0"
Price Schedule: A4

Available
reverse
right
reading

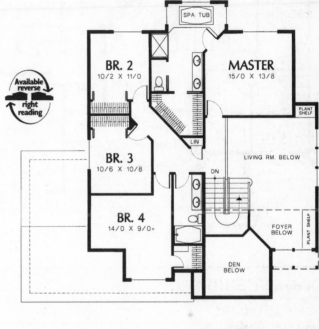

SPA TUB

BR. 2
10/2 X 11/0

MASTER
15/0 X 13/8

PLANT
SHELF

LIN

LIVING RM. BELOW

BR. 3
10/6 X 10/8

DN

BR. 4
14/0 X 9/0+

PLANT SHELF

FOYER
BELOW

DEN
BELOW

HOMES
2001-
2500 sq.ft.

Design SHS010242

Square Footage: 2,415
Width: 74'-0" **Depth:** 54'-0"
Price Schedule: A4

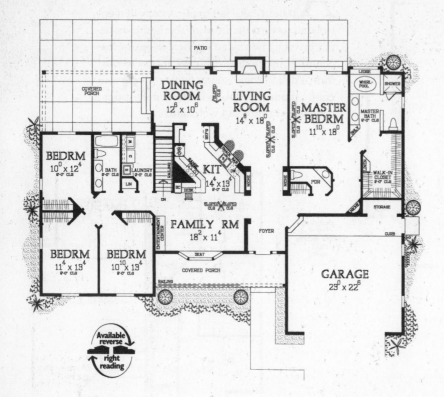

PATIO

COVERED PORCH

DINING ROOM
12⁶ x 10⁶

LIVING ROOM
14⁸ x 18⁰

MASTER BEDRM
11¹⁰ x 18⁰

WHIRL-POOL   SHOWER   LEDGE

MASTER BATH
9'-0" CLG

BEDRM
10⁰ x 12⁴
8'-0" CLG

BATH
8'-0" CLG

LAUNDRY
8'-0" CLG

LIN

DN

KIT
14⁴ x 13⁴

SLOPED CLG   SLOPED CLG

NICHE

NICHE

PDR

WALK-IN CLOSET
9'-0" CLG

STORAGE

CURB

BEDRM
11⁴ x 13⁴
8'-0" CLG

BEDRM
10¹⁰ x 13⁴
8'-0" CLG

FAMILY RM
18² x 11⁴

ENTERTAINMENT CENTER

SEAT

COVERED PORCH

RAILING

FOYER

GARAGE
23⁰ x 22⁶

Available reverse right reading

A covered porch, shutters and a centered dormer with an arched window dress up this country home with blue-ribbon style. To the left of the foyer, the family room features a built-in entertainment center and a bay window that provides a window seat overlooking the front yard. Nearby, the kitchen—angled for interest—contains a walk-in pantry and a snack bar that opens onto the adjacent living room and dining room. From here, access is provided to the rear covered porch, supplying a spacious area for outdoor dining. Split planning places the restful owners suite to the rear for privacy. Amenities include a large walk-in closet and a soothing bath with a whirlpool tub, separate shower and double-bowl vanity. Three secondary bedrooms share a full bath and easy access to the laundry room.

SELECT HOME DESIGNS

FOR PLAN ORDERING INFORMATION SEE PLAN

Design SHS010244

Square Footage: 2,418
Width: 76'-8" Depth: 60'-8"
Price Schedule: A4

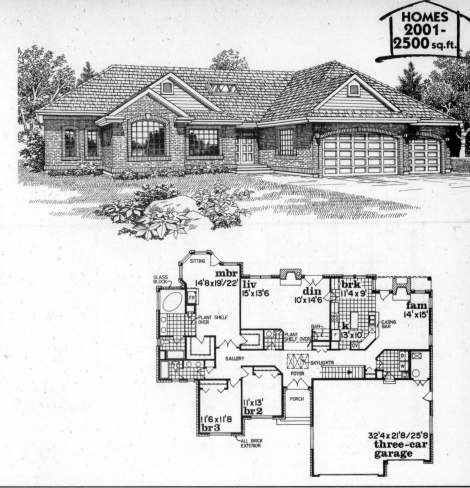

This sprawling ranch has a floor plan designed to capture a view to the rear of the lot. The skylit foyer introduces the living and dining rooms; a plant ledge visually separates the entry from these rooms. A wet bar, fireplace and French doors adorn the dining room. The efficient kitchen, with a long center preparation island, built-in desk and snack bar, is open to both the breakfast room and the family room. A lavish bath adorns the owners suite. It contains a whirlpool spa under a glass block wall, a double vanity and separate shower. The family bedrooms share a main bath that features a twin vanity and soaking tub.

Design SHS010243

Square Footage: 2,419
Width: 85'-2" Depth: 46'-8"
Price Schedule: A4

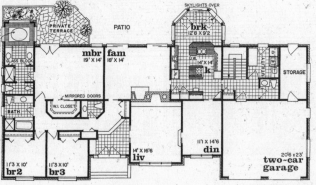

Long and low, with brick siding and multi-pane shuttered windows, this ranch home is the picture of elegance. Enter through double doors to a sunken foyer and sunken living room with a fireplace. The dining room is beyond the living room and a step up. The family room, to the rear of the plan, features a fireplace and sliding glass doors to the rear patio. The kitchen provides a cooktop island and counter and cabinet space to suit any gourmet. The owners bedroom enjoys a private terrace and bath with two vanities, a whirlpool tub and a separate shower. Two family bedrooms are to the front of the plan.

Design SHS010245

Square Footage: 2,424
Width: 68'-0" Depth: 64'-0"
Price Schedule: A4

MASTER SUITE
13⁰ X 14⁴

WOOD DECK

MORNING RM
9² X 12⁶
12'-0" CEILING

RAILING
DN

BATH

BEDRM
9⁶ X 11¹⁰
8'-0" CEILING

KIT
13⁶ X 14²
9'-0" CEILING

FAMILY RM
15⁸ X 14²
VAULTED CEILING

MASTER BATH

WHIRLPOOL

OFFICE/ DEN
12⁰ X 10¹⁰
9'-0" CEILING

BEDROOM
11⁸ X 11⁰
8'-0" CEILING

LAUNDRY

DINING RM
12⁴ X 13⁰
COFFERED CEILING

LIVING RM
11¹⁰ X 14⁶
SLOPED CEILING

FOYER

CURB

STORAGE/ WORKSHOP

GARAGE
26² X 19⁸

COVERED PORCH

RAILING

This unique one-story plan seems tailor-made for a small family or for empty-nesters. Formal areas are situated well for entertaining—living room to the right and formal dining room to the left. A large family room is found to the rear. It has access to a rear wood deck and is warmed in the cold months by a welcome hearth. The U-shaped kitchen features an attached morning room for casual meals. It is near the laundry and a washroom. Bedrooms are split. The owners suite sits to the right of the plan and has a walk-in closet and fine bath. A nearby den has a private porch. Two family bedrooms on the other side of the home share a bath.

FOR PLAN ORDERING INFORMATION SEE PLAN

Floor plan labels

Second floor (right):
- MASTER SUITE 13'0" X 16'6"
- OPEN TO BELOW
- BEDROOM 4 10'0" X 11'0"
- ENSUITE
- WIC
- HALL
- LINEN
- BATH
- OPEN TO BELOW
- PLANT LEDGE
- BEDROOM 2 9'10" X 11'6"
- BEDROOM 3 9'10" X 11'6"

First floor (left):
- NOOK 12'10" X 9'6"
- PATIO
- OPEN TO ABOVE
- FAMILY ROOM 16'0" X 14'10"
- DEN 10'0" X 9'6"
- ISLAND
- KITCHEN 12'10" X 19'0"
- DINING ROOM 9'10" X 12'0"
- HALL
- LDRY
- PWDR
- STORAGE
- LIVING ROOM 12'4" X 13'6"
- OPEN TO ABOVE
- FOYER
- 2 CAR GARAGE 20'0" X 20'8"/19'8"
- VERANDAH
- DN

Craftsman details add wonderful features to this mid-sized family home. The front veranda is complemented by a patio at the rear. Enter the home via the front entry or from the two-car garage, which connects to the main living areas at a service entry with laundry facilities. Formal rooms are to the front: a living room with a fireplace and a dining room with hutch space. The family room is two stories tall and features another fireplace and access to the rear patio. The breakfast nook and island kitchen are nearby for convenience. A den is tucked away beside the family room for an out-of-the-way retreat. Bedrooms are on the second floor: three family bedrooms and an owners suite. Special features in the owners suite include a walk-in closet and bath with separate tub and shower.

Design SHS010246

First Floor: 1,307 square feet
Second Floor: 1,116 square feet
Total: 2,423 square feet
Width: 40'-0" **Depth:** 49'-9"
Price Schedule: A3

Design SHS010247

First Floor: 1,261 square feet
Second Floor: 1,185 square feet
Total: 2,446 square feet
Width: 60'-0" Depth: 44'-0"
Price Schedule: A4

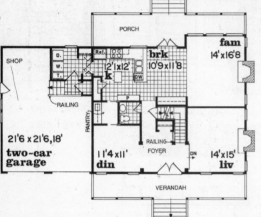

Covered porches to front and rear make this a very comfortable farmhouse. Double doors open to the foyer, which is flanked by the formal dining room and sunken living room. A butler's pantry, complete with a wet bar, separates the dining room from the L-shaped island kitchen. A sunny breakfast room adjoins the kitchen on one side and the family room with a fireplace on the other. The owners suite is on the second level and offers a walk-in closet and a full bath. Three family bedrooms share a full bath that features a dressing room with a double vanity.

Design SHS010248

First Floor: 1,333 square feet
Second Floor: 1,129 square feet
Total: 2,462 square feet
Width: 69'-8" Depth: 49'-0"
Price Schedule: A4

A large wraparound porch graces the exterior of this home and gives it great outdoor livability. The raised foyer leads to a hearth-warmed living room and to the bay-windowed dining room beyond. French doors open from the breakfast and dining rooms to the spacious porch. The family room has built-ins surrounding another hearth. The front study is adorned with a beam ceiling and also features built-ins. Three family bedrooms and an owners suite are found on the second floor. The owners suite features a walk-in closet and private bath.

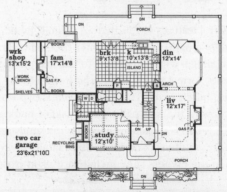

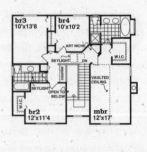

Design SHS010249

First Floor: 1,292 square feet
Second Floor: 1,189 square feet
Total: 2,481 square feet
Bonus Room: 343 square feet
Width: 60'-0" Depth: 41'-6"
Price Schedule: A4

This country home retains just enough classic details to make it elegant, yet still a country-style design. The covered front porch, with round columns, and the five dormer windows add touches of grace. The entry foyer is lit by a second-story dormer and leads to a living room with a fireplace on the left and a study on the right. If you choose, the study may become a formal dining room. The family room at the back is graced by a decorative beam ceiling and shares a fireplace with the hearth room, where a French door leads out to the deck. The U-shaped kitchen features a center island. All four bedrooms are on the second floor, along with a bonus room of 343 square feet to finish as you choose. The owners suite has a private bath, while family bedrooms share a full bath. A built-in desk in the center serves family students.

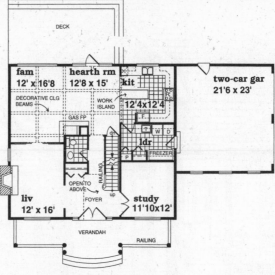

Alternate Formal Dining Room

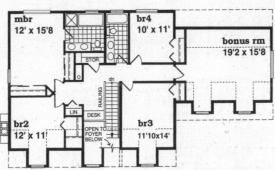

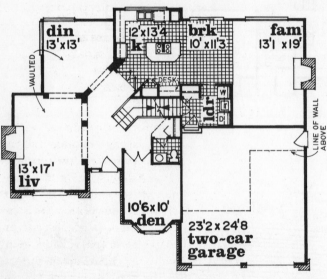

din
13'x13'

12'x13'4
k

brk
10'x11'3

fam
13'1 x 19'

VAULTED

DESK

ldr

13'x17'
liv

LINE OF WALL ABOVE

10'6 x 10'
den

23'2 x 24'8
two-car
garage

Design SHS010250

First Floor: 1,484 square feet
Second Floor: 1,010 square feet
Total: 2,494 square feet
Width: 55'-8" **Depth:** 47'-8"
Price Schedule: A4

A full-height turret bay adds elegance to the facade of this home. The interior is graced with lofty vaulted ceilings throughout the living and dining room areas. An open kitchen with an island cooktop features an attached breakfast nook with sliding glass doors to the rear yard. The hearth-warmed family room is open to this area. A bay-windowed den opens through double doors just off the entry. The second floor holds two family bedrooms and an owners suite with double walk-in closets and a private bath with a whirlpool tub and double vanities. A large storage area on the second floor provides additional unfinished space. Note the laundry area in a service entrance that leads to the two-car garage.

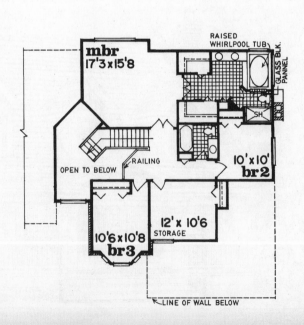

RAISED WHIRLPOOL TUB

GLASS BLK. PANNEL

mbr
17'3 x 15'8

OPEN TO BELOW

RAILING

SH

10' x 10'
br 2

10'6 x 10'8
br 3

12' x 10'6
STORAGE

LINE OF WALL BELOW

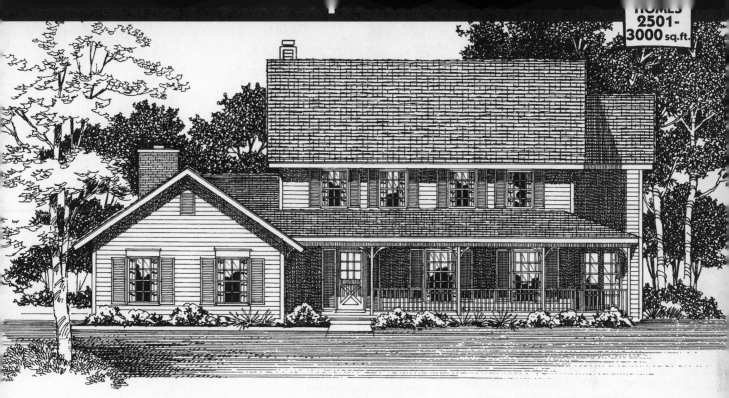

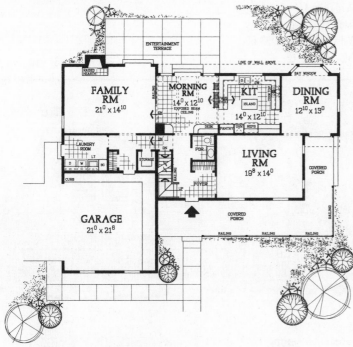

Design SHS010251

First Floor: 1,595 square feet
Second Floor: 1,112 square feet
Total: 2,707 square feet
Width: 63'-6" **Depth:** 48'-0"
Price Schedule: C2

Horizontal clapboard siding, varying roof planes and finely detailed window treatments set a delightful tone for this farmhouse favorite. A tiled foyer leads past a convenient powder room to a spacious central morning room with an exposed-beam ceiling and a wide door to the entertainment terrace. The U-shaped island kitchen serves the formal dining room, which enjoys a bay window and leads to an expansive living room. Upstairs, a gallery hall connects the owners suite, three family bedrooms and a hall bath.

Available reverse right reading

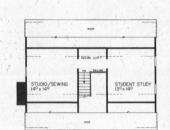

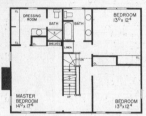

The facade of this three-story, pitch-roofed house has a symmetrical placement of windows and a restrained but elegant central entrance. The central hall, or foyer, expands midway through the house to a family kitchen. Off the foyer are two rooms—a living room with a fireplace and a study. Three bedrooms are housed on the second floor, including a deluxe owners suite with a pampering bath. The windowed, third-floor attic can be used as a study and a studio.

Design SHS010252

First Floor: 1,023 square feet
Second Floor: 1,008 square feet
Third Floor: 476 square feet
Total: 2,507 square feet
Width: 49'-8" **Depth:** 32'-0"
Price Schedule: C2

Design SHS010253

First Floor: 1,324 square feet
Second Floor: 1,192 square feet
Total: 2,516 square feet
Width: 67'-6" **Depth:** 47'-6"
Price Schedule: C1

A turret, wood detailing and a wraparound veranda indicate that this is a Victorian home. The double-door entry opens to a foyer with a lovely curved staircase. The living room has a fireplace, and the formal dining room has a buffet alcove and access to the veranda. The family room has a fireplace and sliding glass doors to the rear yard. A tray ceiling highlights the owners suite.

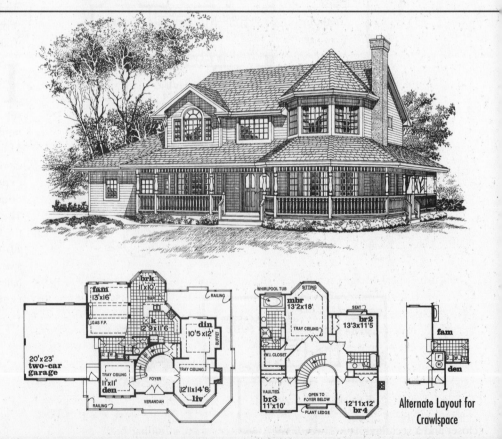

Alternate Layout for Crawlspace

A.J. YOUNG
FUQUAY VARINA, N.C.

PATIO

KIT 10² x14⁴

NOOK 8¹⁰ x 14⁴

FAMILY RM 14⁴ x 12⁰

DINING 13⁰ x 9⁰

LIVING 13⁰ x 14²

PANTRY

SHELF

FOYER

LAUNDRY

PDR RM

WALK-IN CLOSET

DESK

COVERED PORCH

STUDY 12⁴ x 10²

GARAGE 22⁰ x 22⁶

CURB

BEDRM 10⁸ x 10⁶

BEDRM 10⁸ x 10²

BATH

OPEN TO BELOW

SLOPING CEILING

LINEN

RAILING

WALK-IN CLOSET

DESK

BEDRM 13⁰ x 10²

OPEN TO BELOW

RAILING

PLANT SHELF

MASTER BEDRM 14⁶ x 12⁶

SHWR

SEAT

MASTER BATH

VANITY

GARDEN TUB

Available reverse → right reading

Curb appeal is a given with this two-story, brick, traditional home. Four gables provide the facade with elegant symmetry, while decorative segmental arches complement the three arched windows that fill each room with sunlight. The entry foyer leads to all rooms on both the first and second floors. While a quiet study, or possible guest room, is tucked away at the front of the home, the remaining first-floor rooms—combination living/dining rooms, open kitchen, breakfast nook and family room—flow from one to the other for easy living. The U-shaped kitchen offers plenty of counter space, while the family room features French doors to the rear yard and a warming fireplace. On the upper level, the owners bedroom includes a large walk-in closet and a secluded bath. Three family bedrooms share a full hall bath.

Design SHS010254

First Floor: 1,356 square feet
Second Floor: 1,162 square feet
Total: 2,518 square feet
Width: 58'-8" **Depth:** 44'-6"
Price Schedule: C2

Design SHS010256

First Floor: 1,722 square feet
Second Floor: 812 square feet
Total: 2,534 square feet
Width: 84'-6" **Depth:** 40'-6"
Price Schedule: C1

A home in the country, this design offers delightful details on its exterior: a trio of dormers, shuttered windows and a covered front porch. The vaulted foyer is brightened by a second-story dormer and is flanked by the living and dining rooms. A corner fireplace warms the living room. The gourmet kitchen offers a center prep island, a convenient butler's pantry and an attached breakfast room with sliding glass door access to the rear garden. A vaulted family room with a fireplace is separated from the breakfast room by a half-wall. The owners bedroom remains on the first floor for privacy. Three family bedrooms share two skylit baths on the second floor. Bedroom 3 has a vaulted ceiling.

Design SHS010255

First Floor: 1,324 square feet
Second Floor: 1,206 square feet
Total: 2,530 square feet
Width: 69'-6" **Depth:** 48'-4"
Price Schedule: C1

This design may be finished in brick or horizontal siding with a wrapping veranda. Details for both options are included in the plans. The same, roomy floor plan serves both exteriors. From the wide foyer, the plan stretches to a living/dining room combination with a tray ceiling, a fireplace and French doors to the covered porch at the back. On the opposite side of the foyer is a den with bay window. Amenities in the kitchen include a spacious angled counter and work island. Four bedrooms are situated on the second floor. The owners suite features a vaulted bath with a whirlpool tub and double sinks. The three family bedrooms share a bath with a compartmented tub and vanity.

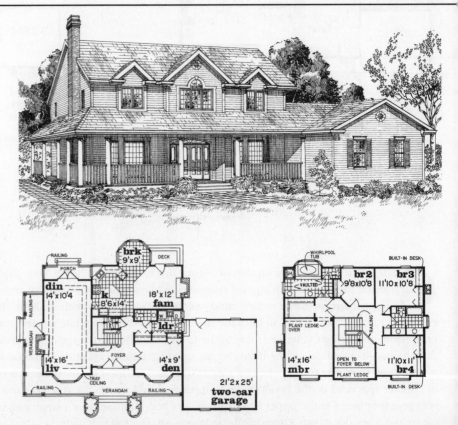

FOR PLAN ORDERING INFORMATION SEE PLAN

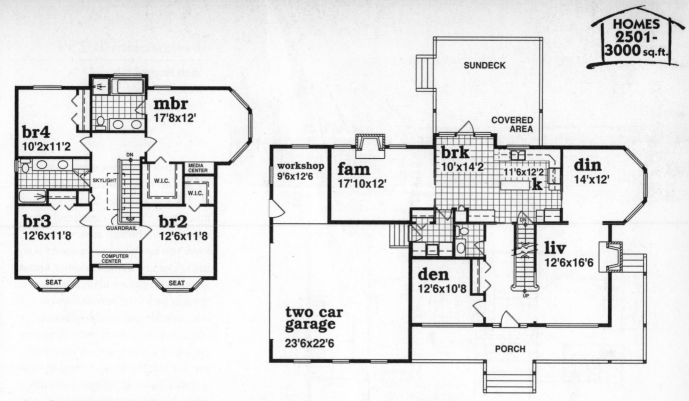

Second Floor:

br4
10'2x11'2

mbr
17'8x12'

DN

SKYLIGHT

MEDIA CENTER

W.I.C.

W.I.C.

br3
12'6x11'8

GUARDRAIL

COMPUTER CENTER

br2
12'6x11'8

SEAT

SEAT

First Floor:

SUNDECK

COVERED AREA

workshop
9'6x12'6

fam
17'10x12'

brk
10'x14'2

11'6x12'2

k

din
14'x12'

DN

two car garage
23'6x22'6

den
12'6x10'8

UP

liv
12'6x16'6

PORCH

Country elegance combined with a well-planned interior make this a perfect family home. Nine-foot ceilings throughout the first level provide an enhanced feeling of spaciousness for living areas. The kitchen and breakfast nook serve as the hub of the first-floor plan. On the right are the living room and formal dining room; the family room resides on the left. Fireplaces warm both the living room and the family room. A private den is found just off the entry. The second floor holds three family bedrooms and an owners suite with a private bath. A large workshop area is found in the garage.

Design SHS010257

First Floor: 1,317 square feet
Second Floor: 1,216 square feet
Total: 2,533 square feet
Width: 65'-0" Depth: 44'-0"
Price Schedule: C1

Design SHS010259

Square Footage: 2,547
Width: 74'-8" Depth: 56'-8"
Price Schedule: C1

A brick exterior, with traditional arch details and elegant rooflines, defines this stately ranch home. Formal dining and living rooms open through arches from the foyer. The family room, separated from the kitchen by a snack counter, features a corner fireplace and double doors to the rear patio. The private owners suite is separated from family bedrooms and offers a walk-in closet and a luxurious bath with a whirlpool spa, oversized shower, twin vanity and compartmented toilet. Three additional bedrooms allow design flexibility—use one as a guest room, den or home office.

COVERED PATIO

br 4
13'6 x 11'

brk
14' x 10'

COVERED PATIO

SH
DESK

mbr
20' x 15'

fam
15' x 20'

k
14' x 10'

EATING BAR

OV

br 3
10' x 10'

PANTRY

F

ldr
W
D

ARCHES

PLANT SHELF OVER

ARCHES

ETCHED GLASS

12'6 x 11'6
din

11'4 x10'
br 2

16' x 13'
liv

21' x 22'
two-car garage

Design SHS010258

Square Footage: 2,549
Width: 88'-8" Depth: 53'-6"
Price Schedule: C2

C overed porches to the front and rear will be the envy of the neighborhood when this house is built. The interior plan meets family needs perfectly in well-zoned areas: a sleeping wing with four bedrooms and two baths, a living zone with formal and informal gathering space, and a work zone with a U-shaped kitchen and laundry/powder room. The two-car garage has a huge storage area.

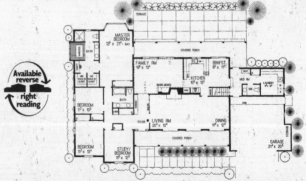

Available reverse

right reading

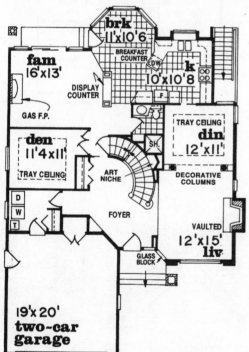

brk
11'x10'6
BREAKFAST COUNTER

fam
16'x13'

DW

k
10'x10'8

F

DISPLAY COUNTER

GAS F.P.

TRAY CEILING
din
12'x11

den
11'4x11

TRAY CEILING

SH.

D W T

ART NICHE

DECORATIVE COLUMNS

FOYER

VAULTED
12'x15'
liv

GLASS BLOCK

19'x20'
two~car garage

Design SHS010260

First Floor: 1,383 square feet
Second Floor: 1,156 square feet
Total: 2,539 square feet
Width: 40'-0" **Depth:** 59'-0"
Price Schedule: C1

This well-planned stucco home is suited for a narrow lot. Its interior begins with a two-story foyer that displays a sweeping, curved staircase, an art niche and a plant ledge. The vaulted ceiling in the living room is enhanced by a full-height window and a fireplace. Columns separate the living and dining rooms; the dining room has a tray ceiling. The step-saving kitchen is adjacent to a carousel breakfast room with a French door to the rear yard. A gas fireplace warms the family room, which features a room-divider display counter and sliding glass doors. A den with a tray ceiling rounds out the first floor. The owners suite also has a tray ceiling and a window seat. Its bath has a raised whirlpool tub and separate shower. Three family bedrooms share a full bath.

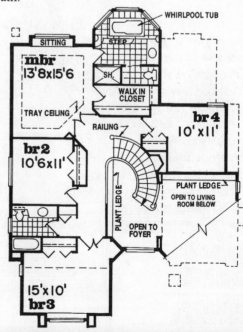

WHIRLPOOL TUB

SITTING

STEP

SH

mbr
13'8x15'6

WALK IN CLOSET

TRAY CEILING

RAILING

br4
10'x11'

br2
10'6x11'

PLANT LEDGE

PLANT LEDGE
OPEN TO LIVING ROOM BELOW

OPEN TO FOYER

15'x10'
br3

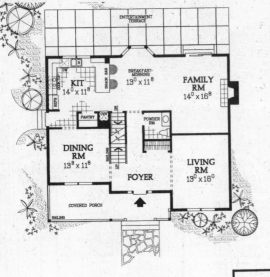

As a house that you will call home, this plan has an abundance of amenities for a large or growing family. The covered porch welcomes you and protects you from inclement weather. The spacious foyer is flanked by a large formal living room and a formal dining room and leads to a bay-windowed breakfast room. Nearby is an efficient kitchen with a snack bar and a family room enhanced by a fireplace and access to the rear terrace. Upstairs, three secondary bedrooms share a full bath with a double-bowl vanity. The spacious owners suite has its own private bath and a walk-in closet. The laundry room with a utility sink is also located on the second floor for convenience.

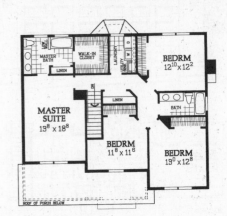

Alternate Layout for Garage

Design SHS010261

First Floor: 1,300 square feet

Second Floor: 1,251 square feet

Total: 2,551 square feet

Width: 44'-0" **Depth:** 38'-0"

Price Schedule: C1

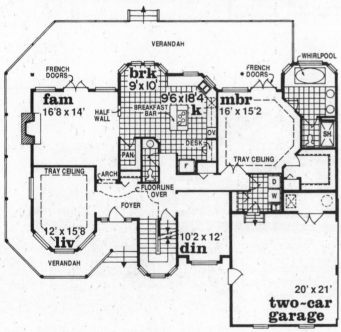

VERANDAH

brk 9'x10'

fam 16'8 x 14'

FRENCH DOORS

BREAKFAST BAR

9'6 x 18'4 **k**

FRENCH DOORS

mbr 16' x 15'2

WHIRLPOOL

half wall

DESK

PAN

F

OV

TRAY CEILING

SH.

TRAY CEILING

ARCH

FLOORLINE OVER

FOYER

D W

12' x 15'8 **liv**

VERANDAH

10'2 x 12' **din**

20' x 21' **two-car garage**

Design SHS010262

First Floor: 1,783 square feet
Second Floor: 768 square feet
Total: 2,551 square feet
Bonus Room: 456 square feet
Width: 64'-6" **Depth:** 50'-0"
Price Schedule: C1

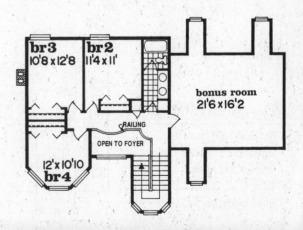

br3 10'8 x 12'8

br2 11'4 x 11'

bonus room 21'6 x 16'2

RAILING

OPEN TO FOYER

12' x 10'10 **br4**

Spindles and wood detailing add to the exterior of this Victorian home. A wrapping veranda introduces the entry and opens to a vaulted foyer lit by a transom window. The living room has a tray ceiling and is just across the hall from the dining room with its box-bay window. An arched entry leads to the spacious family room. Note the fireplace and French-door access to the veranda. A gourmet kitchen, with an adjoining bayed breakfast nook, includes a walk-in pantry, a built-in desk and a center cooking island with a breakfast bar. The owners bedroom also has a tray ceiling and includes private access to the veranda, a walk-in closet and a lavish bath with a whirlpool tub. Family bedrooms are on the second floor along with a bonus room.

HOMES 2501-3000 sq.ft.

Design SHS010263

First Floor: 1,452 square feet
Second Floor: 1,100 square feet
Total: 2,552 square feet
Bonus Room: 687 square feet
Width: 62'-0" **Depth:** 48'-0"
Price Schedule: C3

Enter the foyer and you'll be greeted by double doors opening to a den on the left and a spacious living room with a fireplace on the right. The dining room is separated from the living room by a plant bridge and pair of columns. The full-sized family room features a three-sided fireplace and a corner media center, plus access to the rear yard. A staircase from the family room leads to bonus space over the garage. Four bedrooms on the second floor cluster around a center hall. The owners suite and one family bedroom have walk-in closets.

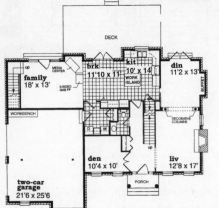

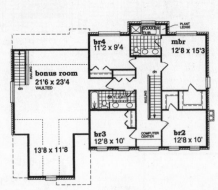

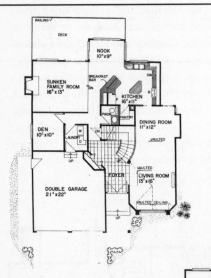

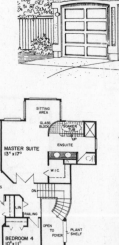

Design SHS010264

First Floor: 1,389 square feet
Second Floor: 1,170 square feet
Total: 2,559 square feet
Width: 42'-0" **Depth:** 53'-0"
Price Schedule: A4

A recessed, covered entry with a column leads the way into the interior spaces of this stucco beauty. The two-story foyer connects to formal spaces on the right side of the plan, which, in turn, lead to the island kitchen, nook and sunken family room. A fireplace warms the family room, which also opens to the rear deck. Family bedrooms are on the second floor and include three bedroom suites sharing a full bath. The owners suite opens through double doors and has a sitting area separated from the bath by glass blocks. The bath contains a spa-style tub, separate shower, double sinks and compartmented toilet.

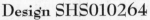

SELECT HOME DESIGNS

Design SHS010265

First Floor: 1,290 square feet
Second Floor: 1,270 square feet
Total: 2,560 square feet
Width: 65'-0" **Depth:** 53'-4"
Price Schedule: C1

With both farmhouse flavor and Victorian details, this plan features a wraparound veranda and a large bayed area on the first and second floors. The living room is nestled in one of these bays and has a tray ceiling, a masonry fireplace and French-door access to the veranda. A pair of columns separates the living and dining rooms. Note the tray ceiling in the dining room. The kitchen has a handy center work island and is open to both the breakfast bay and the family room. A fireplace is enjoyed from all angles. The owners suite is tucked into the bay on the second floor. Its amenities include a fireplace, a walk-in closet and a private bath with a whirlpool tub. Three family bedrooms share a full bath.

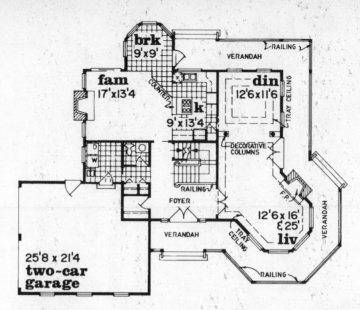

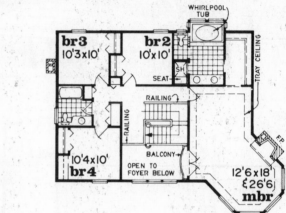

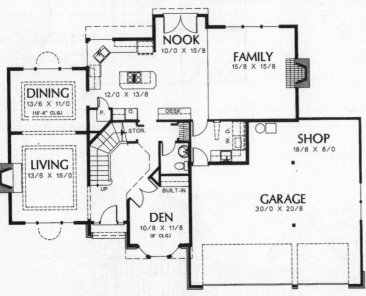

NOOK
10/0 X 15/8

FAMILY
15/8 X 15/8

DINING
13/6 X 11/0
(13'-8" CLG.)

12/0 X 13/8

DESK

SHOP
18/8 X 8/0

P.

O.

STOR.

W. D.

LIVING
13/6 X 15/0

UP

BUILT-IN

GARAGE
30/0 X 20/8

DEN
10/8 X 11/8
(9' CLG.)

Design SHS010266

First Floor: 1,465 square feet
Second Floor: 1,103 square feet
Total: 2,568 square feet
Bonus Room: 303 square feet
Width: 63'-0" **Depth:** 48'-0"
Price Schedule: C1

Available
reverse
right
reading

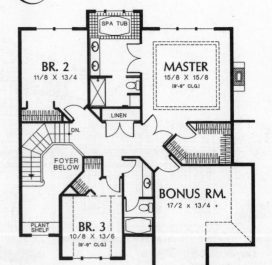

SPA TUB

BR. 2
11/8 X 13/4

MASTER
15/8 X 15/8
(9'-9" CLG.)

LINEN

DN.

FOYER
BELOW

BONUS RM.
17/2 x 13/4 +

PLANT
SHELF

BR. 3
10/8 X 13/6
(9'-9" CLG.)

With a plan that boasts excellent traffic patterns, this home will accommodate the modern family well. Formal dining and living rooms remain to one side of the house and create an elegant atmosphere for entertaining. Highlights of the front den include a bay window and built-in bookshelves. The gourmet kitchen opens into a nook and a family room. Two second-floor family bedrooms share a large hall bath along with a bonus room that's perfect for a game room. The spacious owners suite has a walk-in closet and luxurious spa bath.

Design SHS010267

First Floor: 1,291 square feet
Second Floor: 1,291 square feet
Total: 2,582 square feet
Width: 64'-6" **Depth:** 47'-0"
Price Schedule: C1

Traditional with an essence of farmhouse flavor, this four-bedroom home begins with a wraparound covered porch. The floor plan revolves around a central hall with a formal living room and dining room on the left and private den on the right. The casual family room sits to the rear and is open to a bayed breakfast room and an L-shaped kitchen with an island work center. Both the family room and the living room are warmed by hearths. Two rear porches are reached through doors in the family room and the bayed dining room. The owners suite on the second level has a bayed sitting room and a bath with a whirlpool tub and separate shower. Three family bedrooms share a full bath. Note the window seat on the second-floor landing.

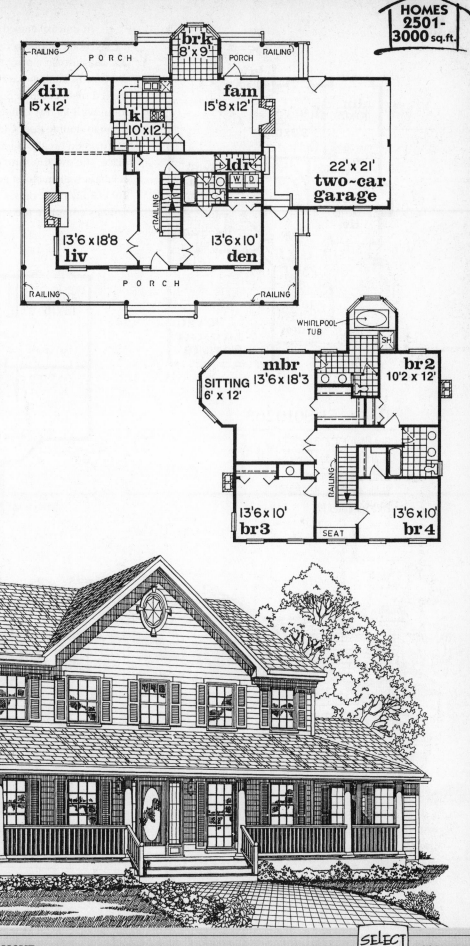

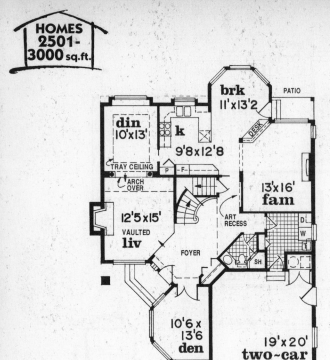

din 10'x13'

k 9'8x12'8

brk 11'x13'2

PATIO

DESK

TRAY CEILING

ARCH OVER

P F

12'5x15'

VAULTED **liv**

ART RECESS

FOYER

13'x16' **fam**

D.L.

W

SH.

10'6 x 13'6 **den**

19'x20' **two-car garage**

An unusual angled entry adds interest to the facade of this home. It opens to a vaulted foyer with a sweeping, curved staircase; a plant ledge lines the railed gallery overlooking the foyer. A sunken, vaulted living room lies to the left. Arches framed by decorative pillars separate it from the formal dining room with its tray ceiling. A cozy den is on the right, accessed through double doors. In the back are a U-shaped kitchen with an attached breakfast bay and an open family room with a fireplace. The owners suite on the second floor is graced by a tray ceiling, a walk-in closet and a private bath with a whirlpool tub. Two family bedrooms, a media room and a full bath with dual vanities complete the second floor.

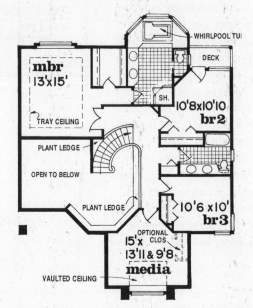

mbr 13'x15'

TRAY CEILING

PLANT LEDGE

OPEN TO BELOW

PLANT LEDGE

WHIRLPOOL TUB

DECK

SH.

10'8x10'10 **br2**

10'6 x10' **br3**

15'x 13'11 & 9'8 **media**

OPTIONAL CLOS.

VAULTED CEILING

Design SHS010268

First Floor: 1,416 square feet

Second Floor: 1,206 square feet

Total: 2,622 square feet

Width: 40'-0" **Depth:** 57'-6"

Price Schedule: C1

FOR PLAN ORDERING INFORMATION SEE PLAN

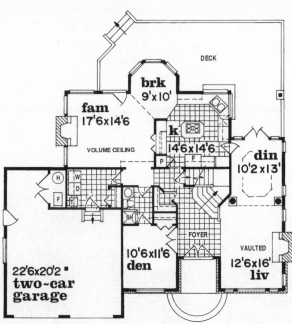

DECK

brk
9'x10'

fam
17'6x14'6

VOLUME CEILING

k
14'6x14'6

din
10'2x13'

FOYER

VAULTED

10'6x11'6
den

12'6x16'
liv

22'6x20'2
two-car garage

Design SHS010269

First Floor: 1,464 square feet
Second Floor: 1,154 square feet
Total: 2,618 square feet
Width: 56'-0" **Depth:** 50'-0"
Price Schedule: C1

High vaulted ceilings and floor-to-ceiling windows enhance the spaciousness of this home. Decorative columns separate the living room from the tray-ceilinged dining room. French doors beyond open to the rear deck. A gourmet kitchen offers a center preparation island, a pantry pass-through to the family room and a breakfast bay. The family room is spacious and boasts a fireplace and vaulted ceiling open to the second-level hallway. The den has a wall closet and private access to a full bath and can be used as extra guest space if needed. The owners suite is on the second floor and holds a bay-windowed sitting area, a walk-in closet and a bath with a whirlpool tub and separate shower. Family bedrooms are at the other end of the hall and share a full bath.

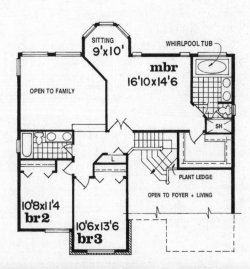

SITTING
9'x10'

WHIRLPOOL TUB

mbr
16'10x14'6

OPEN TO FAMILY

PLANT LEDGE

OPEN TO FOYER + LIVING

10'8x11'4
br2

10'6x13'6
br3

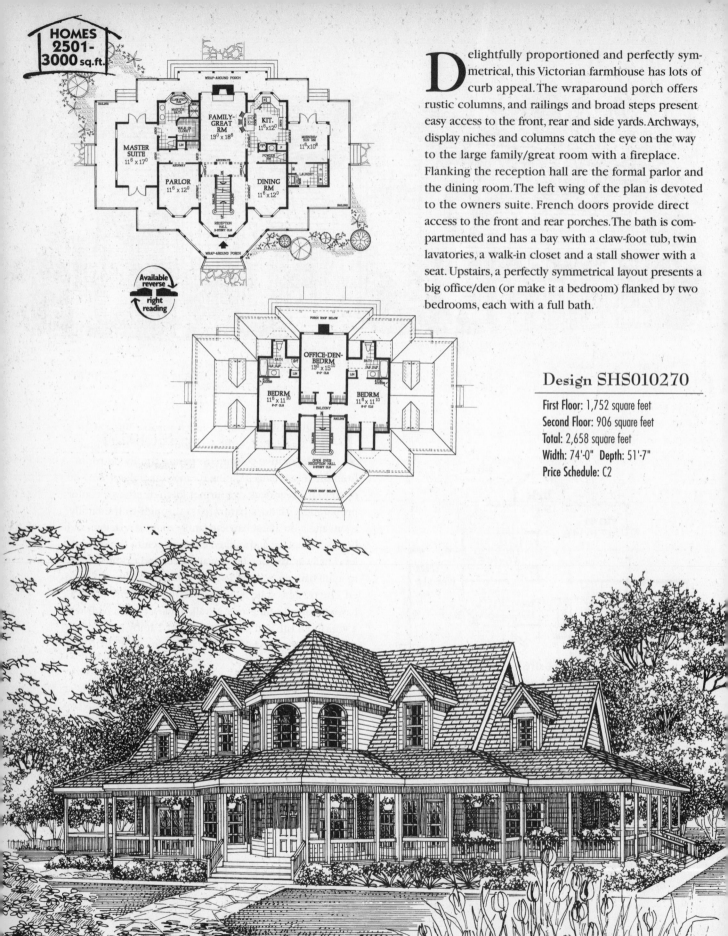

WRAP-AROUND PORCH

MASTER
SUITE
11⁸ x 17⁰

CLAW-FOOT
TUB
MASTER
BATH
WALK-IN
CLOSET
LIN

FAMILY-
GREAT
RM
13⁰ x 18⁶

KIT.
11⁸ x 12⁰

MORNING
11⁶ x 10⁸

PARLOR
11⁸ x 12⁰

ARCHWAY

ARCHWAY

DINING
RM
11⁸ x 12⁰

POWDER
RM

LAUNDRY

RECEPTION
HALL
2-STORY CLG

WRAP-AROUND PORCH

RAILING

RAILING

Available
reverse
right
reading

PORCH ROOF BELOW

BATH

OFFICE-DEN-
BEDRM
13⁰ x 15¹⁰
9'-0" CLG

BATH

LIN

LIN

BEDRM
11⁸ x 11¹⁰
9'-0" CLG

BEDRM
11⁸ x 11¹⁰
9'-0" CLG

BALCONY

RAILING

OPEN OVER
RECEPTION HALL
2-STORY CLG

PORCH ROOF BELOW

Delightfully proportioned and perfectly symmetrical, this Victorian farmhouse has lots of curb appeal. The wraparound porch offers rustic columns, and railings and broad steps present easy access to the front, rear and side yards. Archways, display niches and columns catch the eye on the way to the large family/great room with a fireplace. Flanking the reception hall are the formal parlor and the dining room. The left wing of the plan is devoted to the owners suite. French doors provide direct access to the front and rear porches. The bath is compartmented and has a bay with a claw-foot tub, twin lavatories, a walk-in closet and a stall shower with a seat. Upstairs, a perfectly symmetrical layout presents a big office/den (or make it a bedroom) flanked by two bedrooms, each with a full bath.

Design SHS010270

First Floor: 1,752 square feet
Second Floor: 906 square feet
Total: 2,658 square feet
Width: 74'-0" **Depth:** 51'-7"
Price Schedule: C2

SELECT
HOME DESIGNS

FOR PLAN ORDERING INFORMATION SEE PLAN

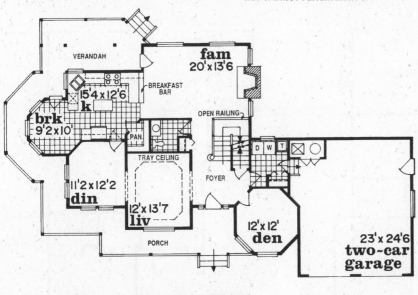

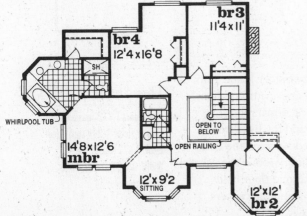

Design SHS010271

First Floor: 1,362 square feet
Second Floor: 1,270 square feet
Total: 2,632 square feet
Width: 79'-0" **Depth:** 44'-0"
Price Schedule: C1

Rich with Victorian details—scalloped shingles, a wrap-around veranda and turrets—this beautiful facade conceals a modern floor plan. Archways announce a distinctive living room with a lovely tray ceiling and help define the dining room. An octagonal den across the foyer is a private spot for reading or studying. The U-shaped island kitchen holds an octagonal breakfast bay and a pass-through breakfast bar to the family room.

SELECT HOME DESIGNS

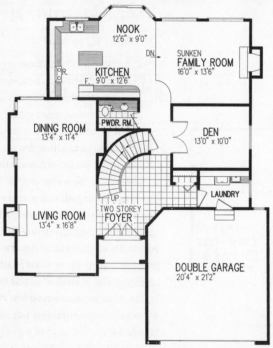

NOOK
12'6" x 9'0"

DN.

SUNKEN
FAMILY ROOM
16'0" x 13'6"

KITCHEN
9'0" x 12'6"

F.

R.

DINING ROOM
13'4" x 11'4"

PWDR. RM.

DEN
13'0" x 10'0"

UP
TWO STOREY
FOYER

LAUNDRY

LIVING ROOM
13'4" x 16'8"

DOUBLE GARAGE
20'4" x 21'2"

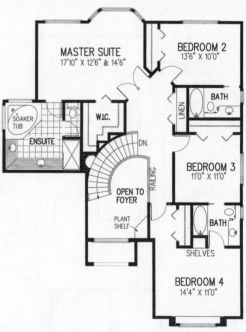

MASTER SUITE
17'10" X 12'6" & 14'6"

BEDROOM 2
13'6" X 10'0"

LINEN

BATH

SOAKER
TUB

W.I.C.

ENSUITE

DN.

OPEN TO
FOYER

RAILING

BEDROOM 3
11'0" X 11'0"

PLANT
SHELF

BATH

SHELVES

BEDROOM 4
14'4" X 11'0"

Grand classic details complement the stucco facade of this two-story home. Faux columns accent each corner area and the entry looms two stories with a transom window above for radiant light. A classic floor plan includes formal rooms on the left and casual space to the rear. Both the sunken family room and the living room have fireplaces. The den opens through double doors and is situated between the two-car garage and the family room. The garage connects at a handy laundry room. The galley-style kitchen is made even more convenient by an island. The second floor holds four bedrooms. Bedroom 3 and 4 share a full bath, while Bedroom 2 and the owners suite have private baths. The owners suite also enjoys a walk-in closet.

Design SHS010272

First Floor: 1,372 square feet
Second Floor: 1,299 square feet
Total: 2,671 square feet
Width: 43'-0" **Depth:** 54'-6"
Price Schedule: A4

Design SHS010273

Square Footage: 2,657
Width: 68'-0" Depth: 71'-6"
Price Schedule: C1

Elegant arched windows, a portico entry and low-maintenance stucco distinguish this California design. The interior is well-appointed and thoughtfully planned. Flanking the foyer are the formal living and dining rooms, defined by decorative columns and plant shelves. The living room boasts a tray ceiling and a fireplace. A sunken family room sits in the center of the plan and is graced by double doors to the patio, a fireplace, a vaulted ceiling and a skylight. Two steps up is the U-shaped kitchen with an island and attached breakfast room, separated by a snack-bar counter. Family bedrooms and a full bath are on the left side of the plan. The owners suite and a den with a full bath are located on the right. The owners suite contains access to the patio and a bath with a whirlpool tub, double-bowl vanity and separate shower. An alternate bedroom layout is included in the plans.

Floor plan labels:

GLASS BLOCK
SH.
WHIRLPOOL TUB
PATIO
mbr
20'8 x18'6 12'
VAULTED
SUNKEN
PLANT SHELF OVER
DESK
brk
14'x9'
BAR
br2
11'4x10'2
fam
17'8x20'
SUNKEN
14'x12'
k
SKYLIGHT
VAULTED
VEST.
36' HIGH WALL
10'4x11'2
br3
ldr
W
GALLERY
PLANT SHELF OVER
12'x10'
den
H F.
PLANT SHELF OVER
VAULTED FOYER
VAULTED
12'x12'
din
PORCH
TRAY CEILING
12'x14'2
liv
25'4x25'6
two-car
garage

Alternate Bedroom Layout

br2
10'4x10'
10'4x10'
br3
ldr
W
D

Design SHS010274

First Floor: 1,620 square feet
Second Floor: 1,064 square feet
Total: 2,684 square feet
Bonus Room: 296 square feet
Width: 54'-4"   **Depth:** 64'-4"
Price Schedule: C1

Designed in horizontal siding with solid-brick accents, this traditional home stands the test of time. A sweeping horseshoe-shaped staircase dominates the two-story foyer. The octagonal living room has a masonry fireplace. The nearby dining room is accessed through double doors and connects to the modified U-shaped kitchen with its attached breakfast nook. A family room has another fireplace. Away from daily traffic, the den opens off the foyer through double doors. Three bedrooms occupy the second floor: an owners suite and two family bedrooms. A bonus room with a private staircase provides space for an additional bedroom or a hobby room.

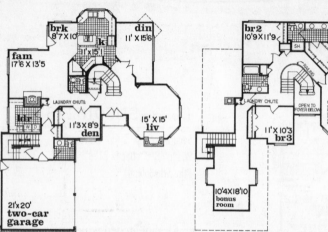

Design SHS010275

First Floor: 1,416 square feet
Second Floor: 1,277 square feet
Total: 2,693 square feet
Width: 71'-0"   **Depth:** 48'-0"
Price Schedule: C1

This distinctive country design features a polygonal tower surrounded by a wraparound porch. The center-hall entry introduces formal living areas—a living room with a hearth-warmed sitting room—and a casual family room with a fireplace and a nearby island kitchen that features an attached breakfast nook. A den is privately tucked into a corner off the entry.

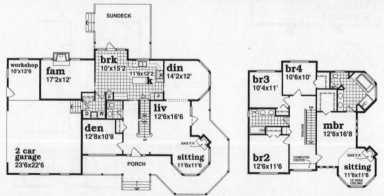

Design SHS010276

First Floor: 1,794 square feet
Second Floor: 887 square feet
Total: 2,681 square feet
Width: 90'-0" **Depth:** 37'-4"
Price Schedule: C1

HOMES
2501-
3000 sq.ft.

Home-grown comfort is the key to the appeal of this traditionally Tudor-styled home. From the kitchen with an attached family room to the living room with a fireplace and an attached formal dining room, this plan has it all. Notice the first-floor owners bedroom with a whirlpool tub and an adjacent study. On the second floor are three more bedrooms with ample closet space and a full bath.

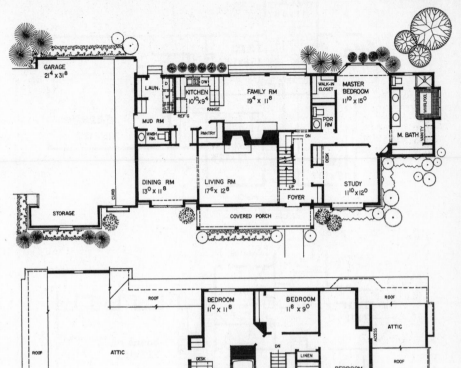

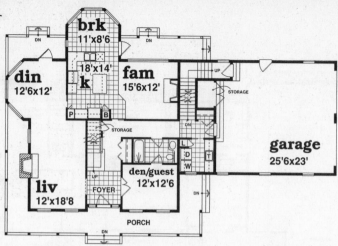

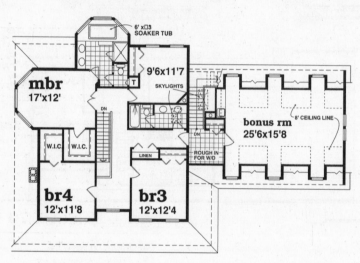

Design SHS010277

First Floor: 1,422 square feet
Second Floor: 1,273 square feet
Total: 2,695 square feet
Bonus Room: 340 square feet
Width: 72'-0" Depth: 47'-8"
Price Schedule: C1

With a veranda that almost completely surrounds the first floor, this house is made for indoor/outdoor living. The veranda can be accessed at three different points in the plan: the main entry, the octagonal dining room and the bayed breakfast room. Both the living room and the family room are warmed by hearths; the den has access to a full bath so it can easily double as a guest room. The main stairway in the center is complemented by an additional stairway near the laundry that leads up to the bedrooms or to a handy bonus room that can be developed later. Four bedrooms are found on the second floor—one an owners suite with a lavish bath. Both the owners bedroom and Bedroom 4 have walk-in closets. The two-car garage contains a large storage area.

Design SHS010278

First Floor: 1,532 square feet
Second Floor: 1,168 square feet
Total: 2,700 square feet
Width: 64'-0" **Depth:** 53'-2"
Price Schedule: C3

This stately two-story home makes a grand first impression with its columned front entry and varying roof planes. Inside, the gracious foyer opens to a study on the left and a living room and dining room on the right. The spacious kitchen includes a work island and an open breakfast area. An expansive family room is just a step down from the kitchen and features a sloped ceiling and a raised hearth. From here, a rear deck opens up to provide superb outdoor livability. On the upper level, four bedrooms include an owners bedroom suite with a walk-in closet, a built-in vanity and a private whirlpool bath.

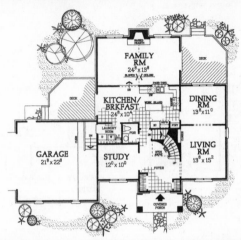

Design SHS010279

First Floor: 1,531 square feet
Second Floor: 1,215 square feet
Total: 2,746 square feet
Width: 56'-6" **Depth:** 55'-6"
Price Schedule: C1

Curves, keystone arches, a bay window and a stone-accented wall all make up the facade of this distinctive home. A tiled front entry features a winding staircase to the second floor, where there are four bedrooms. Family bedrooms share a full bath, while the owners suite holds a private bath with a raised whirlpool tub, separate shower and dual vanities. The first floor has formal and informal spaces: a living room with a fireplace, an attached dining room, a family room with a corner fireplace, a breakfast bay and an island kitchen.

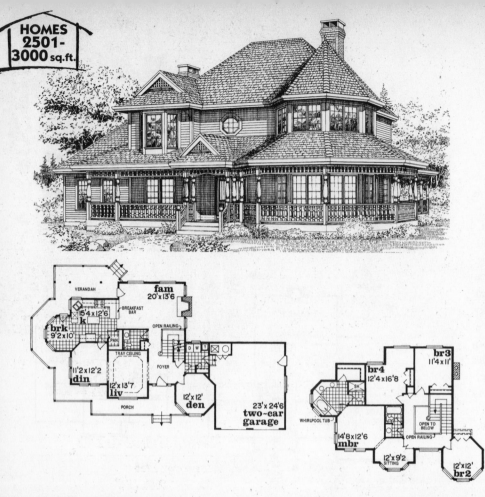

Design SHS010280

First Floor: 1,462 square feet
Second Floor: 1,288 square feet
Total: 2,750 square feet
Width: 70'-8" **Depth:** 54'-0"
Price Schedule: C1

A touch of Victoriana enhances the facade of this home: a turret roof over a wrap-around porch with turned wood spindles. Special attractions on the first floor include a tray ceiling in the octagonal living room, fireplaces in the country kitchen and the living room, a coffered ceiling in the family room and double-door access to the cozy den. The owners suite boasts a coffered ceiling, walk-in closet and whirlpool tub.

Design SHS010281

First Floor: 1,639 square feet
Second Floor: 1,158 square feet
Total: 2,797 square feet
Width: 80'-0" **Depth:** 44'-0"
Price Schedule: C1

This grand farmhouse design is anything but ordinary. Its lovely details—a Palladian window, a covered veranda and shutters—put it a cut above the rest. The interior features classic floor planning with a vaulted center-hall foyer and staircase to the second floor. Formal areas—a living room and a dining room—are on the right, while a cozy den and the large family room are on the left. A full bath sits near the den so that it can double as guest space.

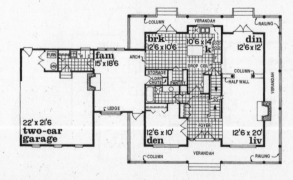

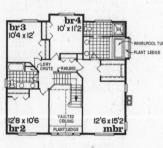

FOR PLAN ORDERING INFORMATION SEE PLAN

Design SHS010282

Square Footage: 2,758
Width: 81'-4" **Depth:** 76'-0"
Price Schedule: C2

This comfortable traditional home offers plenty of modern livability. A clutter room off the two-car garage is an ideal space for a workbench, sewing or hobbies. Across the hall is a media room. A spacious country kitchen to the right of the greenhouse (great for fresh herbs) is a cozy gathering place for family and friends, as well as a convenient work area. Both the formal living room, with its friendly fireplace, and the dining room provide access to the rear grounds. A spacious, amenity-filled owners suite features His and Hers walk-in closets, a relaxing whirlpool tub and access to the rear terrace. Two large secondary bedrooms share a full bath.

Design SHS010283

First Floor: 1,120 square feet
Second Floor: 1,083 square feet
Third Floor: 597 square feet
Total: 2,800 square feet
Width: 40'-0" **Depth:** 40'-0"
Price Schedule: C2

Covered porches to the front and rear, delicately detailed railings and an abundance of fireplaces give this farmhouse its character. Designed to accommodate a relatively narrow building site, the efficient floor plan delivers outstanding livability for the active family. Both the formal living room and dining room have corner fireplaces, as does the family room. The large tiled country kitchen has an abundance of work space, a planning desk and easy access to the utility room. On the second floor, the owners retreat features a fireplace and an expansive bathing and dressing suite.

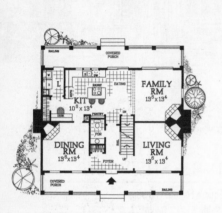

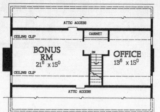

Design SHS010284

First Floor: 1,439 square feet
Second Floor: 1,419 square feet
Total: 2,858 square feet
Bonus Room: 241 square feet
Width: 63'-10" **Depth:** 40'-4"
Price Schedule: C3

Choose from one of two exteriors for this grand design—a lovely wood-sided farmhouse or a stately brick traditional. Plans include details for both facades. Special mouldings and trim add interest to the nine-foot ceilings on the first floor. The dining room features a tray ceiling and is separated from the hearth-warmed living room by decorative columns. A study is secluded behind double doors just off the entry. The private owners bedroom has a most exquisite bath with His and Hers walk-in closets, a soaking tub, a separate shower and a make-up vanity.

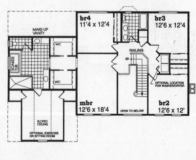

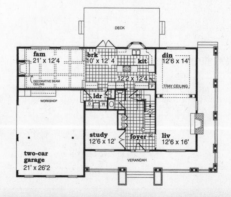

SELECT HOME DESIGNS

Design SHS010286

First Floor: 1,580 square feet
Second Floor: 1,232 square feet
Total: 2,812 square feet
Width: 74'-8" **Depth:** 38'-8"
Price Schedule: C1

This stately design features classic exterior details: circle-head windows, an arched entry, shutters, corner quoins and brick veneer. The foyer is vaulted with a dominating curved staircase to the second floor. The living room contains a fireplace and pocket doors that lead to the formal dining room. The den is to the front of the plan, across from a full bath. The vaulted family room offers a fireplace and an audiovisual center. Four second-floor bedrooms include three family bedrooms with a shared full bath. The owners suite features a walk-in closet and a bath with a separate shower, a double-bowl vanity and a whirlpool tub accented by columns.

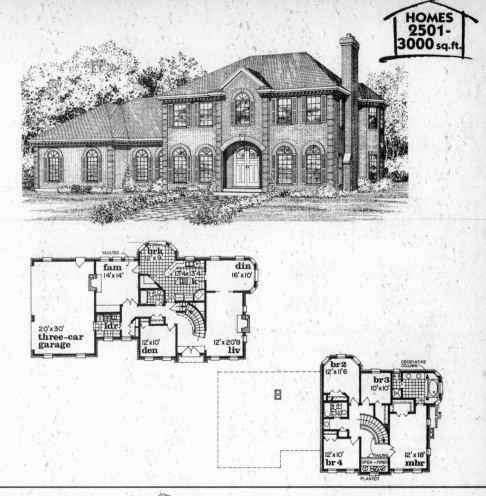

Design SHS010285

First Floor: 1,581 square feet
Second Floor: 1,344 square feet
Total: 2,925 square feet
Width: 74'-0" **Depth:** 46'-0"
Price Schedule: C2

Here's a traditional farmhouse design that's made for down-home hospitality, casual conversation and the good grace of pleasant company. The star attractions are the large covered porch and terrace, perfectly relaxing gathering points for family and friends. Inside, the design is truly a hard worker: separate living and family rooms, each with their own fireplace; a formal dining room; a large kitchen and breakfast area with bay windows; a private study; a workshop and a mudroom. The second floor contains a spacious owners suite with twin closets, and three family bedrooms that share a full bath.

Available reverse — *right reading*

Design SHS010287

Square Footage: 2,916
Width: 77'-10" Depth: 73'-10"
Price Schedule: C2

Intricate details make the most of this lovely one-story home. Besides the living room/dining room area to the rear, there is a large conversation area with a fireplace and plenty of windows. The kitchen is separated from living areas by an angled snack-bar counter. Three bedrooms grace the right side of the plan. The owners suite features a tray ceiling and sliding glass doors to the rear terrace. The dressing area is graced by His and Hers walk-in closets, a double-bowl lavatory and a compartmented commode. The shower area is highlighted with glass block and is sunken down one step. A garden whirlpool tub finishes off this area.

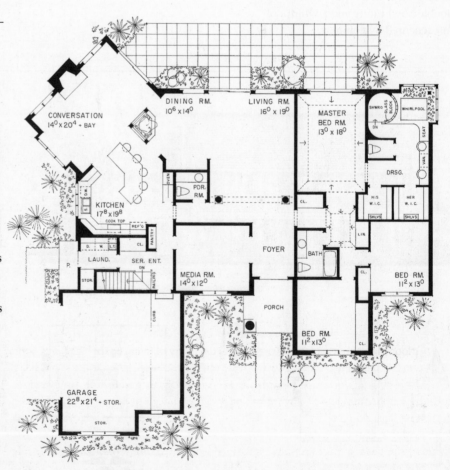

HOMES
2501-
3000 sq.ft.

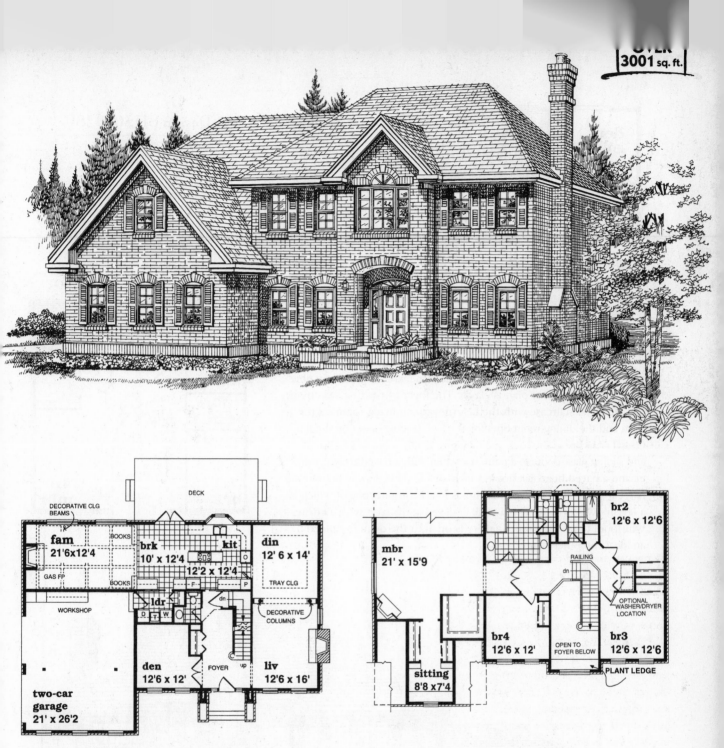

DECK

DECORATIVE CLG BEAMS

fam 21'6 x 12'4

BOOKS

GAS FP

WORKSHOP

BOOKS

brk 10' x 12'4

12'2 x 12'4

kit

F

ldr

D T W

dn

P

din 12'6 x 14'

TRAY CLG

DECORATIVE COLUMNS

den 12'6 x 12'

FOYER

up

liv 12'6 x 16'

two-car garage 21' x 26'2

mbr 21' x 15'9

br2 12'6 x 12'6

RAILING

dn

OPTIONAL WASHER/DRYER LOCATION

br4 12'6 x 12'

OPEN TO FOYER BELOW

br3 12'6 x 12'6

sitting 8'8 x7'4

PLANT LEDGE

A floor plan of over 3,000 square feet holds plenty of living space. The living room and dining room are separated by decorative columns; the dining room has a tray ceiling. Decorative beams and built-in bookcases adorn the family room. Both the family room and the living room have fireplaces. The island kitchen is open to the breakfast nook, which has double doors opening to the rear deck. A den with double-door access is found at the front of the plan. Upstairs are four bedrooms. The owners suite has a corner fireplace, walk-in closet and sitting room. The three family bedrooms share a full bath. If you choose, there is a laundry alcove on the second floor.

Design SHS010288

First Floor: 1,439 square feet
Second Floor: 1,576 square feet
Total: 3,015 square feet
Width: 63'-10" **Depth:** 40'-4"
Price Schedule: C4

OVER 3001 sq. ft.

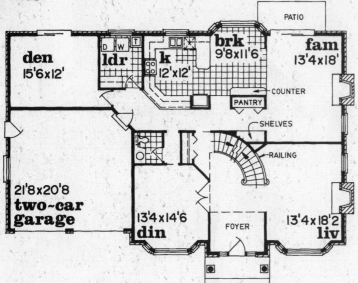

den 15'6x12'

ldr

D W T

k 12'x12'

brk 9'8x11'6

fam 13'4x18'

PATIO

COUNTER

PANTRY

SHELVES

RAILING

21'8x20'8 **two~car garage**

13'4x14'6 **din**

FOYER

13'4x18'2 **liv**

Design SHS010289

First Floor: 1,728 square feet
Second Floor: 1,316 square feet
Total: 3,044 square feet
Width: 60'-8" **Depth:** 43'-3"
Price Schedule: C2

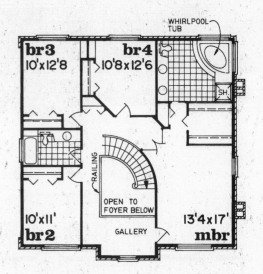

br3 10'x12'8

br4 10'8x12'6

WHIRLPOOL TUB

SH.

RAILING

10'x11' **br2**

OPEN TO FOYER BELOW

GALLERY

13'4x17' **mbr**

Elegance personified, this traditional plan is the home of a lifetime. Inside, the floor plan is classic. The foyer opens to a sweeping, curved staircase with the hearth-warmed living room on the right and the dining room opening through double doors on the left. Casual areas are at the back and include a family room with a fireplace and sliding glass doors to a patio, a kitchen with a pass-through counter, and a bayed breakfast nook. A cozy den is tucked away behind the two-car garage. The second floor holds four bedrooms, one of which is a lavish owners suite with a walk-in closet and a bath with a corner whirlpool tub. The upstairs gallery is open to the owners suite and is an ideal computer station.

Design SHS010290

Square Footage: 3,018
Width: 74'-0" **Depth:** 82'-0"
Price Schedule: C2

The entry is grand and allows for a twelve-foot ceiling in the entry foyer. Open planning calls for columns to separate the formal living room and the formal dining room from the foyer and central hall. Both rooms have tray ceilings; the living room has a fireplace and double-door access to the skylit lanai. The modified, U-shaped kitchen has an attached breakfast room and steps down to the family room with its fireplace and optional wet bar. A lovely octagonal foyer introduces family bedrooms and their private baths. A den with a tray ceiling and full bath sits to the right of the foyer and doubles as a guest room when needed. The owners suite is separated from family bedrooms. It has double-door access to the rear yard, a walk-in closet and a full bath with a whirlpool tub, double vanity, compartmented toilet and separate shower.

fam 15'x19'6 (SUNKEN) 11' CEILING

SKYLIGHT

LANAI

brk 12'x11'4

OPT. WET BAR

br3 14'x11'8 10' CEILING

lk 13'6x11'6 10'CEILING

liv 17'x15' 12' DOUBLE TRAY CEILING

mbr 16'6x16'6 10' TRAY CEILING

DROP CEILING

WHIRLPOOL TUB

PRIVATE GARDEN

PRIVACY WALL

10' CEILING

12'6x12'6 **br2**

dr

FOYER 12' CEILING

12' TRAY CEILING 14'x13' **din**

12' TRAY CEILING 11'x13' **den**

GLASS BLOCK

22'x25'8 **two-car garage**

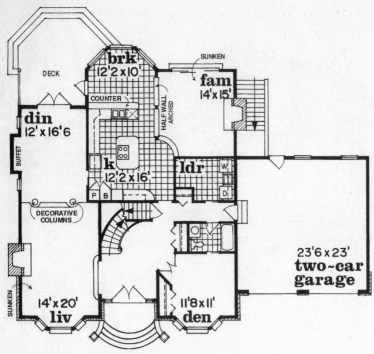

DECK

brk 12'2 x 10

SUNKEN

fam 14'x 15'

COUNTER

din 12'x 16'6

HALF WALL ARCHED

BUFFET

k 12'2 x 16'

ldr

W

D

P B

DECORATIVE COLUMNS

23'6 x 23' **two-car garage**

SUNKEN

14'x 20' **liv**

11'8 x 11' **den**

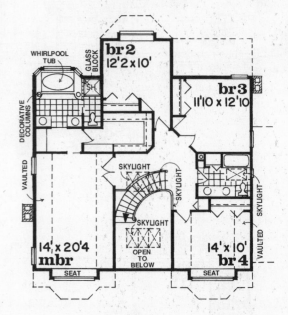

WHIRLPOOL TUB

GLASS BLOCK

SH

br2 12'2 x 10'

br3 11'10 x 12'10

DECORATIVE COLUMNS

VAULTED

SKYLIGHT

SKYLIGHT

SKYLIGHT

SKYLIGHT

SKYLIGHT

14'x 20'4 **mbr**

OPEN TO BELOW

14'x 10' **br4**

SEAT

SEAT

VAULTED

Skylights illuminate this home's vaulted foyer and curved staircase. The formal dining room has a niche for a buffet and French doors to the rear deck. Decorative columns help define the living room, which offers a fireplace. A quiet den provides a bay window and a nearby full bath. The gourmet kitchen overlooks the family room, which has a hearth.

Design SHS010291

First Floor: 1,725 square feet

Second Floor: 1,364 square feet

Total: 3,089 square feet

Width: 64'-4" **Depth:** 50'-4"

Price Schedule: C2

Design SHS010292

First Floor: 2,300 square feet
Second Floor: 812 square feet
Total: 3,112 square feet
Width: 83'-0" **Depth:** 69'-6"
Price Schedule: C2

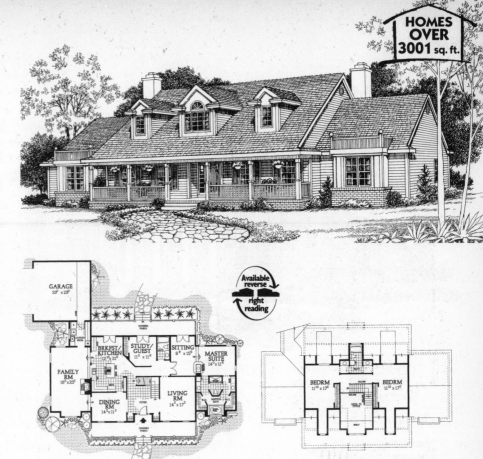

Dormered windows, a covered porch and symmetrical balustrades provide a warm country welcome. Inside, formal living and dining rooms flank the foyer. To the left of the dining room, and down a step, is a spacious family room with a raised-hearth fireplace. The nearby breakfast/kitchen area features an island cooktop, a pantry and a planning desk. French doors in the breakfast area, the study (or optional guest room) and the owners suite's sitting area provide access to the rear porch. The owners bath is complete with a whirlpool tub and separate His and Hers dressing areas. The second floor contains two family bedrooms and a full bath with separate vanities.

Design SHS010293

First Floor: 2,347 square feet
Second Floor: 1,087 square feet
Total: 3,434 square feet
Width: 93'-6" **Depth:** 61'-0"
Price Schedule: C3

Dutch gable rooflines and a gabled wraparound porch provide an extra measure of farmhouse style. The foyer opens to the study or guest bedroom on the left. To the right is the formal dining room, and the massive great room is in the center. The kitchen combines with the great room, the breakfast nook and the dining room for entertaining options. The owners suite includes access to the covered patio, a spacious walk-in closet and a private bath with a whirlpool tub.

SELECT HOME DESIGNS

Design SHS010294

Square Footage: 3,462
Width: 100'-2" **Depth:** 58'-10"
Price Schedule: C3

The white-pillared one-story house is a significant Kentucky contribution to the architectural heritage of the South. This imposing design recalls Rose Hill, built near Lexington, Kentucky, around 1820. The living room, dining room (positioned on either side of the foyer) and library each have a fireplace flanked by built-in cabinets. The large country kitchen, with a fourth fireplace, provides an efficient work station that includes an island cooktop. A clutter room with a workbench and a potting counter is a welcome amenity. Terrace access and a large bow window are highlights in the owners bedroom; a sumptuous bath with His and Hers walk-in closets and a large, step-up platform with a whirlpool tub completes the suite. Two additional bedrooms with walk-in closets are located at the front of this home. A fourth bedroom, which could double as a sewing room, is placed at the opposite end.

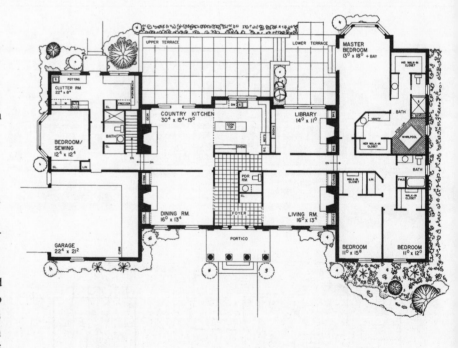

ecorative latticework and circle-head windows combine to make the exterior of this home unique. The long entry hall is flanked by the living and dining rooms. An island kitchen acts as a hub for the circular breakfast area and the family room with a fireplace. Bedrooms are at the right of the plan with the luxurious owners suite at the back and two family bedrooms sharing a hall bath. Bonus space above the kitchen could be developed as an office, guest bedroom or studio.

HOMES OVER 3001 sq. ft.

7Design SHS010295

Square Footage: 3,555
Width: 80'-0" Depth: 109'-6"
Price Schedule: C3

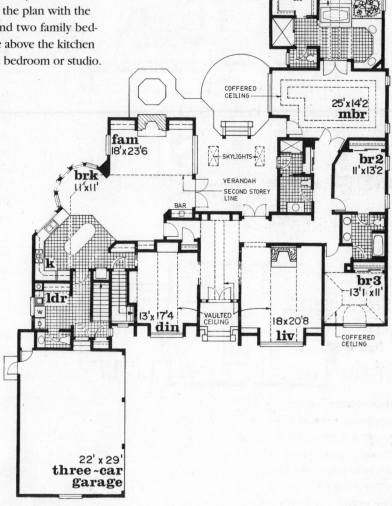

FACTS AT THE BEGINNING OF THIS ISSUE

SELECT HOME DESIGNS

223

Design SHS010296

First Floor: 2,126 square feet
Second Floor: 1,882 square feet
Total: 4,008 square feet
Width: 92'-0" **Depth:** 32'-8"
Price Schedule: L1

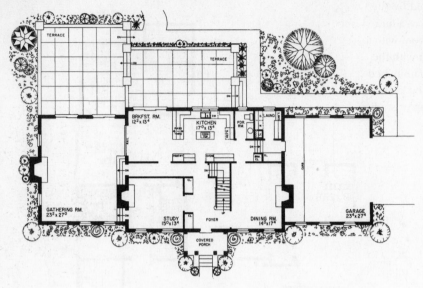

This historical Georgian home has its roots in the 18th Century. The full two-story center section is delightfully complemented by the 1½-story wings. An elegant gathering room, three steps down from the rest of the house, has ample space for entertaining on a grand scale. Guests and family alike will enjoy the two rooms flanking the foyer—the study and the formal dining room. Each of these rooms has a fireplace as its highlight. The breakfast room, kitchen, powder room and laundry room are arranged for maximum efficiency. The second floor houses the family bedrooms. Take special note of the spacious owners suite. It enjoys a deluxe bath, a fireplace, a sunken lounge with a dressing room and a walk-in closet.

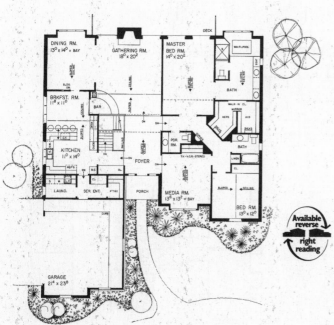

This plan has the best of both worlds—a traditional exterior and a modern, multi-level floor plan. The central foyer routes traffic effectively to all areas: the kitchen, gathering room, sleeping area and media room. The lower level can be developed later. Plans include space for a summer kitchen, activities room and bedroom with a full bath. The owners suite features a luxurious bath and His and Hers walk-in closets.

Available reverse right reading

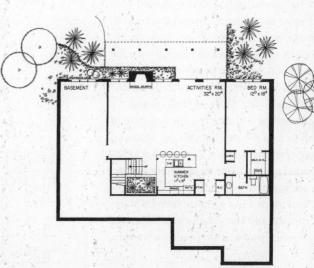

Design SHS010297

Main Level: 2,673 square feet

Lower Level: 1,389 square feet

Total: 4,062 square feet

Width: 60'-0" Depth: 72'-0"

Price Schedule: L1

Design SHS010298

First Floor: 2,403 square feet
Second Floor: 1,684 square feet
Total: 4,087 square feet
Width: 77'-10" **Depth:** 55'-8"
Price Schedule: L1

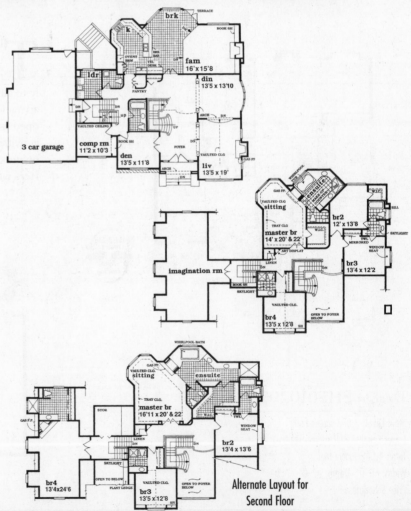

Alternate Layout for
Second Floor

With an elegant entry, this dramatic two-story home is the essence of luxury. Double doors open to a foyer with a sunken living room on the right and a den on the left. An archway leads to the formal dining room, mirroring the curved window in the living room and the bowed window in the dining room. The den and nearby computer room have use of a full bath, making them handy as extra guest rooms when needed. The family room, like the living room, is sunken and warmed by a hearth, but also has built-in bookcases. A snack-bar counter separates the U-shaped kitchen from the light-filled breakfast room. The second floor can be configured in two different ways. Both plans allow for a gigantic owners suite with His and Hers vanities, an oversized shower, a walk-in closet and a sitting area.

Design SHS010299

First Floor: 2,348 square feet
Second Floor: 1,872 square feet
Total: 4,220 square feet
Width: 90'-4" **Depth:** 44'-8"
Price Schedule: L1

This classic Georgian design contains a variety of features that make it outstanding: a pediment gable with cornice work and dentils, beautifully proportioned columns, and distinct window treatment. The first floor contains some special appointments: a fireplace in the living room, a wet bar in the gathering room and sliding glass doors from the study to the rear terrace. Upstairs, an extension over the garage allows for a huge walk-in closet in the deluxe owners suite and a full bath one in of the family bedrooms. Two other family bedrooms share a full bath.

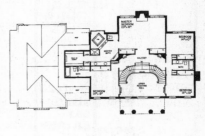

Design SHS010300

First Floor: 2,995 square feet
Second Floor: 1,831 square feet
Total: 4,826 square feet
Width: 95'-0" **Depth:** 99'-3"
Price Schedule: C4

A magnificent, finely wrought covered porch wraps around this impressive Victorian estate home. The two-story foyer provides a direct view past the stylish banister and into the great room with a large central fireplace. To the left of the foyer is a bookshelf-lined library, and to the right is an octagonal-shaped dining room. The island cooktop completes a convenient work triangle in the kitchen, and a pass-through connects this room with the morning room. A butler's pantry, walk-in closet and broom closet offer plenty of storage space.

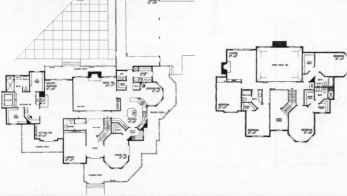

Opening with a main foyer this plan proceeds to the main living area on the second level. The living room/dining room combination is separated from the staircase by a half-wall and graced by a bay window and fireplace. The L-shaped kitchen is to the rear and contains plenty of space for a breakfast table and sliding glass doors to a rear deck. Three bedrooms find space on the right side of the plan: an owners bedroom with a walk-in closet and two family bedrooms. Unfinished space on the lower level can be developed into a family room with a fireplace and an extra bedroom with a bath.

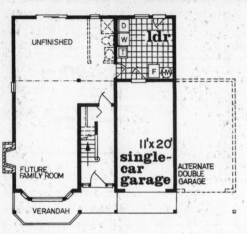

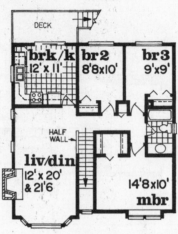

Design SHS010302

Square Footage: 1,018
Unfinished Lower Level: 693 square feet
Width: 31'-6" **Depth:** 36'-6"
Price Schedule: A2

Design SHS010301

Square Footage: 1,074
Unfinished Lower Level: 710 square feet
Width: 35'-0" **Depth:** 37'-0"
Price Schedule: A2

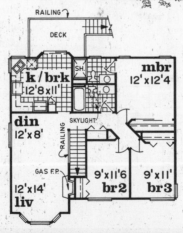

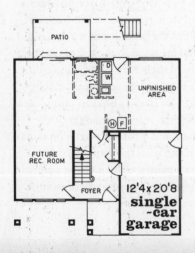

This classic stucco model offers a covered archway at its entry, which opens to a 125-square-foot foyer leading up to the main level. A living room and dining room area features a bay window and fireplace and sits adjacent to an efficient kitchen with a breakfast area and access to a deck. Three bedrooms include an owners suite with a private bath and two family bedrooms sharing a full bath. The lower level is unfinished but can be developed later into a family room and an additional bedroom with a bath.

Design SHS010304

Square Footage: 1,293
Unfinished Lower Level: 905 square feet
Width: 40'-0" Depth: 41'-4"
Price Schedule: A2

The main level of this home—on the second floor—includes a beautiful sun deck to allow views and outdoor enjoyment in the front of the plan. This level is reached via a foyer in the lower level of 67 square feet. Additional lower-level space may be finished at a later time to include a family room and bedrooms with a bath. Second-level space is complete with a dining room and a bayed living room with a fireplace. The kitchen has an attached breakfast room with etched-glass corner windows separating it from the main hall. Bedrooms line the rear of the plan. Family bedrooms have walk-in closets and share a full bath.

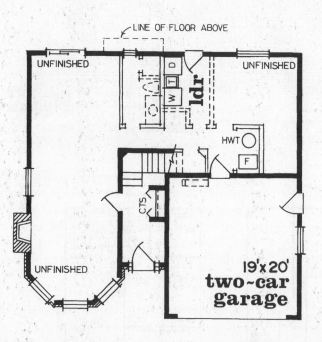

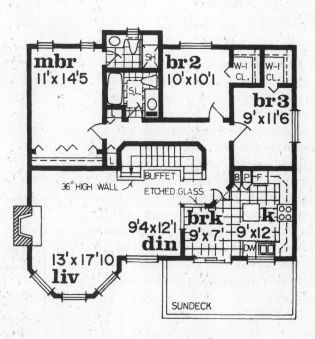

Design SHS010306

Square Footage: 1,311
Unfinished Lower Level: 1,038 square feet
Width: 44'-0" Depth: 49'-0"
Price Schedule: A2

Choices abound with this plan: two exterior options and unfinished space on the lower level that can become a family room, bedrooms and a full bath at a later time. The main floor holds a living room with a fireplace and window seat, a dining room, an island kitchen with an attached breakfast room and a family room with a fireplace. A rear deck opens from the breakfast room. Three bedrooms and an owners suite with a private bath reside on the right side of the plan. A two-car garage sits to the front of the plan.

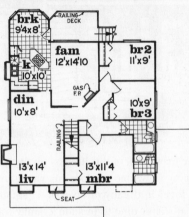

Design SHS010305

Square Footage: 1,190
Unfinished Lower Level: 874 square feet
Width: 36'-0" Depth: 39'-0"
Price Schedule: A2

A quaint covered porch on the front of this unusual home opens to a 256-square-foot den and a foyer leading up to the main level. A railed staircase accents the living/dining area in addition to a box-bay window and fireplace. The nearby kitchen and breakfast room have access to a rear deck. Down an angled hall are three bedrooms—one an owners suite with a private bath and His and Hers closets. Family bedrooms share a full bath. Unfinished space on the lower level can be made into a recreation room, extra bedrooms and a full bath.

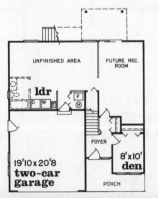

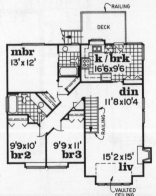

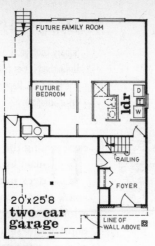

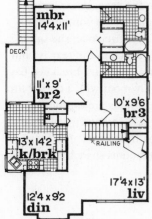

Design SHS010307

Square Footage: 1,221
Unfinished Lower Level: 651 square feet
Width: 38'-0" Depth: 46'-2"
Price Schedule: A2

This traditional home, with its slim footprint, is perfect for a narrow lot or in-fill project. The foyer is on the lower level and provides stairs to the main living area. The open floor plan features a corner fireplace in the living room that can be enjoyed from the dining bay and roomy kitchen/breakfast area. A deck can be accessed through the kitchen. Two family bedrooms share a full bath. The owners suite features a walk-in closet and private, full bath. Unfinished space on the lower level is ideal for future expansion.

Design SHS010308

Square Footage: 1,266
Unfinished Lower Level: 799 square feet
Width: 38'-0" Depth: 41'-0"
Price Schedule: A2

This delightful plan begins small, but can be expanded later on the lower level. The foyer—132 square feet—leads up to the main living level, which holds a living and dining room area with a fireplace and window seat. An L-shaped kitchen and bayed breakfast room take advantage of a rear deck. Bedrooms include an owners suite with a private bath and walk-in closet. When you're ready to expand, develop the lower level into a recreation room, a den and an additional bedroom with a bath.

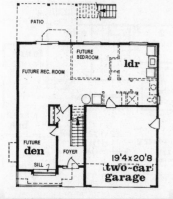

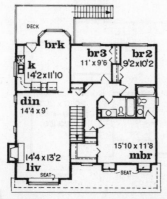

Design SHS010309

Square Footage: 1,324
Unfinished Lower Level: 999 square feet
Width: 47'-0" Depth: 44'-0"
Price Schedule: A2

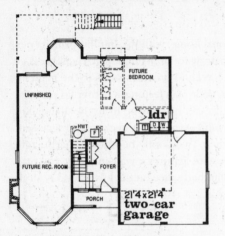

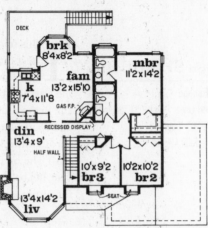

Using the second floor as the main living level allows for a deck in the back and future space for development into a recreation room and bedroom—or an entire in-law suite. A classic floor plan reigns on the second level with a living/dining room combination warmed by a fireplace. The open gathering space in the rear is comprised of a kitchen, a breakfast bay and a family room with a corner fireplace. Bedrooms are on the right. They include an owners suite with private bath and walk-in closet. Family bedrooms share a full bath.

Design SHS010310

Square Footage: 1,391
Unfinished Lower Level: 932 square feet
Width: 47'-0" Depth: 36'-0"
Price Schedule: A3

Build this interesting design where second-floor living space can take advantage of a great view. The lower level can remain unfinished until needed. The foyer contains 132 square feet of finished space and leads up to the living areas and bedrooms on the second floor. Living areas here are comprised of a living room/dining room combination with wide windows overlooking the front, plus a cozy fireplace. A smaller family room is to the rear with sliding glass doors to a deck. Three bedrooms sit quietly to the rear of the plan. The owners suite features a walk-in closet and a private bath.

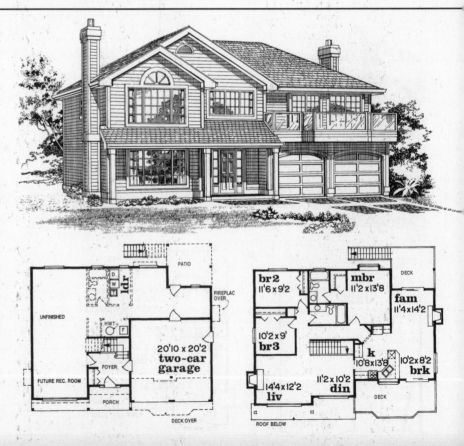

SELECT HOME DESIGNS

Design SHS010312

Square Footage: 1,286
Unfinished Lower Level: 704 square feet
Width: 38'-0" Depth: 45'-6"
Price Schedule: A3

Country charm prevails with a covered front porch and double chimneys in this design. The floor plan is unusual in that main living areas are on the second floor. The entry leads up a staircase that opens into the living/dining room combination. A vaulted window seat and a fireplace adorn this area. The U-shaped kitchen, family room and bayed breakfast nook sit to the rear and enjoy access to a deck. An owners suite is also to the rear and has a walk-in closet and private bath. Two family bedrooms share a bath.

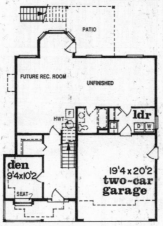

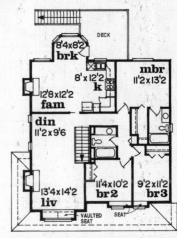

Design SHS010311

Square Footage: 1,816
Unfinished Lower Level: 1,223 square feet
Width: 64'-0" Depth: 41'-0"
Price Schedule: A3

This is a grand design with superb livability on the second floor. A wide deck surrounds the living areas on this level as well as the owners bedroom. The living room is vaulted and features a corner fireplace and double-door access to the deck. A corner fireplace also graces the family room. An adjoining breakfast room shares a pass-through counter with the kitchen. Three bedrooms include an owners suite with a luxurious bath and walk-in closet. Finish lower-level space into a game room, extra bedrooms, a workshop and a full bath.

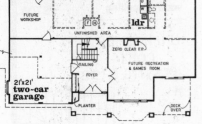

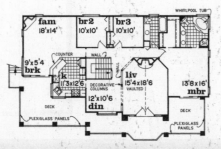

COTTAGE COUNTRY

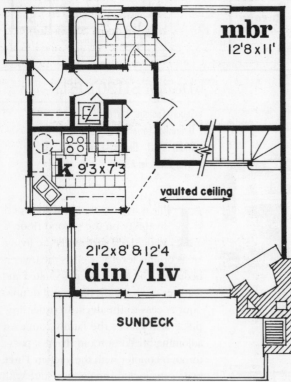

mbr
12'8 x 11'

k 9'3 x 7'3

vaulted ceiling ←→

21'2 x 8' & 12'4
din / liv

SUNDECK

Design SHS010313

Square Footage: 680
Width: 26'-6" Depth: 28'-0"
Price Schedule: A1

F ull window walls provide the living and dining rooms of this rustic vacation home with natural light. A full sun deck with a built-in barbecue sits just outside the living area and is accessed by sliding glass doors. The entire lliving space has a vaulted ceiling to gain spaciousness and to allow for the full-height windows. The efficient U-shaped kitchen has a pass-through counter to the dining area and a corner sink with windows overhead. An owners bedroom is on the first floor and has the use of a full bath. A loft on the second floor overlooks the living room. It provides an additional 419 square feet not included in the total. Use it for an additional bedroom or as a studio. It has a vaulted ceiling.

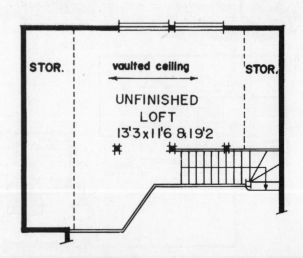

STOR.

vaulted ceiling

STOR.

UNFINISHED LOFT
13'3 x 11'6 & 19'2

SELECT HOME DESIGNS

FOR PLAN ORDERING INFORMATION SEE PLAN

Design SHS010314

First Floor: 616 square feet
Second Floor: 300 square feet
Total: 916 square feet
Width: 22'-0" **Depth:** 28'-0"
Price Schedule: A1

Rustic details such as a stone fireplace work well for this country cottage. A floor-to-ceiling window wall accents the living and dining rooms and provides an expansive view past a wide deck. Twin sliding glass doors access the deck from the living space. The U-shaped kitchen offers roomy counters and is open to the dining room. Behind it is a laundry room and a full bath serving the owners bedroom. An additional bedroom sits on the second floor and may be used as a studio.

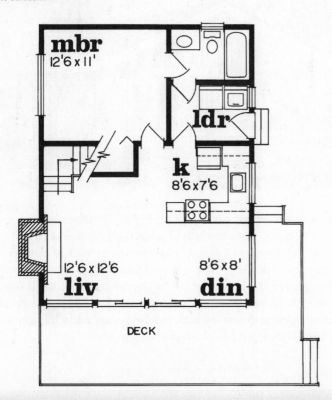

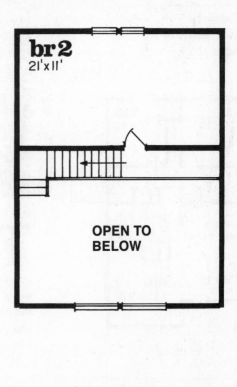

Design SHS010315

First Floor: 936 square feet
Second Floor: 358 square feet
Total: 1,294 square feet
Width: 30'-0" **Depth:** 32'-0"
Price Schedule: A2

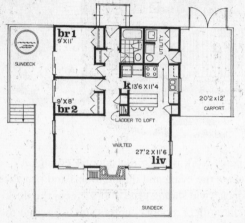

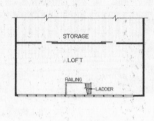

This space-efficient leisure home offers many extras. Adding the optional carport adds an extra 12 feet to the width of the home. The sun deck wraps around two sides and features a built-in barbecue and hot tub. The living room boasts a soaring vaulted ceiling, a large fireplace and sliding glass doors to the sun deck. The galley-style kitchen has a breakfast bar that connects it to the living area. Two bedrooms on the first level share the use of a full bath. A ladder to the second level reaches to a loft area that works as additional bedroom space.

Design SHS010316

Square Footage: 817
Width: 24'-0" **Depth:** 36'-0"
Price Schedule: A1

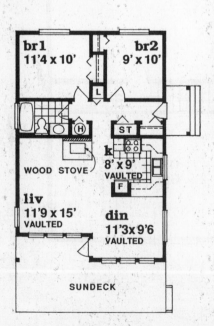

This compact, economical cottage is perfect as a getaway retreat or a cozy retirement home. Abundant windows overlook the sun deck and capture the views beyond for panoramic enjoyment. Vaulted ceilings and an open floor plan throughout the living and dining rooms enhance the feeling of spaciousness on the inside. For colder months, there is a wood stove in the living room. The kitchen is also vaulted and features a U-shaped workspace and countertop open to the dining area. Two bedrooms are to the rear; each has a wall closet. They share a full bath and a linen closet.

FOR PLAN ORDERING INFORMATION SEE PLAN

Design SHS010317

Square Footage: 825
Width: 30'-0" Depth: 30'-0"
Price Schedule: A1

Compact and economical to build, this vacation home is nonetheless quite comfortable. It will fit easily into just about any vacation setting, from seaside to mountainside. A sun deck to the front stretches the width of the home and opens to a vaulted living room/dining room area with a corner wood stove and full-height window wall. The kitchen has a raised bar with seating space open to the living area and also features a U-shaped workspace, a window over the sink and a large pantry or broom closet. Two bedrooms are to the back. They have wall closets and share a full bath that includes a soaking tub.

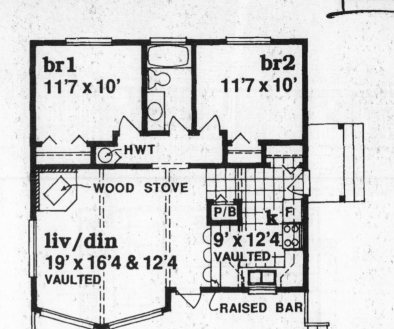

Design SHS010319

Square Footage: 950
Width: 38'-0" Depth: 25'-0"
Price Schedule: A1

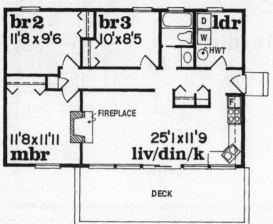

br2
11'8 x 9'6

br3
10'x8'5

D W ldr
HWT

FIREPLACE

11'8x11'11
mbr

25'1x11'9
liv/din/k

F

DECK

This open-plan cottage is perfect for family living—or as a getaway for relaxing vacations. The living area is totally open and acts as living room/dining room and corner kitchen. A fireplace at one end adds a warm glow on chilly evenings. Sliding glass doors here open to a wide deck for outdoor enjoyment or alfresco dining. Three bedrooms allow plenty of sleeping space. The owners bedroom overlooks views beyond the deck. All three bedrooms share a full bath with a soaking tub and separate vanity area. The laundry room is large enough to hold a washer and dryer and also to serve as a mudroom.

Design SHS010318

Square Footage: 988
Width: 38'-0" Depth: 26'-0"
Price Schedule: A1

This cozy design serves nicely as a leisure home for vacations or as a full-time retirement residence. Horizontal siding and a solid-stone chimney stack are a reminder of a rustic retreat. A spacious living/dining area has a full wall of glass overlooking a deck with views beyond. A masonry fireplace warms the space in the cold months. A U-shaped kitchen is nearby and has a pass-through counter to the dining room. A large laundry/mud room is across the hall and holds storage space. Sleeping quarters are comprised of a large owners suite and smaller family bedroom, both with hall closets.

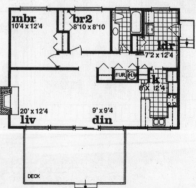

mbr
10'4 x 12'4

br2
8'10 x 8'10

ldr
7'2 x 12'4

FUR HW

k
8'x 12'4

20' x 12'4
liv

9' x 9'4
din

DECK

Design SHS010320

First Floor: 593 square feet
Second Floor: 383 square feet
Total: 976 square feet
Width: 22'-8"   **Depth:** 26'-8"
Price Schedule: A2

A stunning arch-top window sets off this charming European cottage. An angled entry and open planning allow a sense of spaciousness from the moment one enters the home. A voluminous bedroom on this floor adjoins a full bath. The staircase leads to a second-floor mezzanine, which overlooks the living area and may be used as a study area or an extra bedroom. This home is designed with a basement foundation.

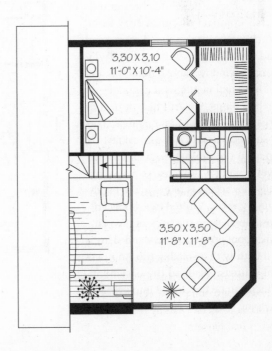

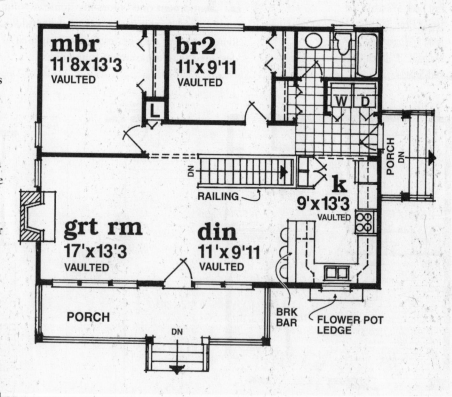

COTTAGE
COUNTRY

Design SHS010321

Square Footage: 1,064
Width: 38'-0" **Depth:** 34'-0"
Price Schedule: A2

This farmhouse design squeezes space-efficient features into its compact design. A cozy front porch opens into a vaulted great room and its adjoining dining room. Twin dormer windows above flood this area with natural light and accentuates the high ceilings. A warm hearth in the great room adds to its coziness. The U-shaped kitchen has a breakfast bar open to the dining room and a sink overlooking a flower box. A nearby side-door access is found in the handy laundry room. Vaulted bedrooms are positioned along the back of the plan. They contain wall closets and share a full bath with a soaking tub. An open-rail staircase leads to the basement, which can be developed into living or sleeping space at a later time, if needed.

mbr 11'8x13'3 VAULTED

br2 11'x 9'11 VAULTED

L

W D

PORCH DN

k 9'x13'3 VAULTED

DN RAILING

grt rm 17'x13'3 VAULTED

din 11'x 9'11 VAULTED

PORCH

DN

BRK BAR

FLOWER POT LEDGE

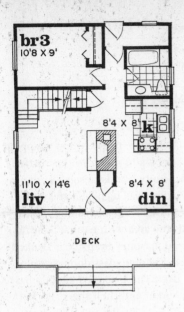

br3
10'8 X 9'

8'4 X 8' k

11'10 X 14'6 liv

8'4 X 8' din

DECK

Design SHS010322

First Floor: 672 square feet
Second Floor: 401 square feet
Total: 1,073 square feet
Width: 24'-0" **Depth:** 36'-0"
Price Schedule: A2

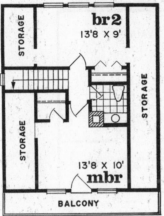

STORAGE

br2
13'8 X 9'

STORAGE

STORAGE

STORAGE

13'8 X 10'
mbr

BALCONY

This chalet plan is enhanced by a steep gable roof, scalloped fascia boards and fieldstone chimney detail. The front-facing deck and covered balcony add to outdoor living spaces. The fireplace is the main focus in the living room. It separates the living room from the dining room, which is near the U-shaped kitchen. One bedroom is found on the first floor. Two additional bedrooms and a full bath are upstairs. The owners bedroom has a walk-in closet. Three large storage areas are also found on the second floor.

Design SHS010323

First Floor: 878 square feet
Second Floor: 262 square feet
Total: 1,140 square feet
Width: 35'-0" **Depth:** 30'-6"
Price Schedule: A2

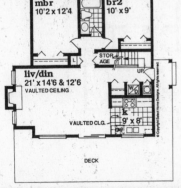

mbr
10'2 x 12'4

br2
10' x 9'

STORAGE

liv/din
21' x 14'6 & 12'6
VAULTED CEILING

UP

k
9' x 8'

VAULTED CLG.

DECK

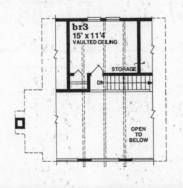

br3
15' x 11'4
VAULTED CEILING

STORAGE

DN

OPEN TO BELOW

Windows galore and sliding glass doors take advantage of views in this vacation home. A full deck wraps around to the side to a covered side entry. Vaulted ceilings throughout the living and dining rooms and the large upstairs bedroom give a feeling of spaciousness to the plan and allow for tall, bright windows. The galley-style kitchen is open to the dining room. Two bedrooms line the rear of the plan—an owners bedroom and a secondary bedroom. They share the full bath, as does Bedroom 3. Convenient storage is found under the stairs.

Design SHS010325

Square Footage: 1,197
Loft: 497 square feet
Width: 31'-6" **Depth:** 38'-0"
Price Schedule: A2

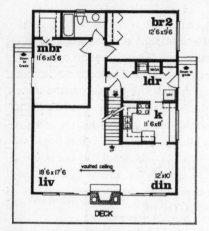

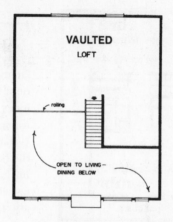

A fieldstone fireplace and wrapping deck add much to the rustic beauty of this design. An expansive window wall highlights the vaulted ceiling in the living and dining rooms and fills the area with natural light. An oversized masonry fireplace is flanked by a set of sliding glass doors opening to the deck. The U-shaped kitchen has great counter and shelf space. Pocket doors seclude it from the dining room and the laundry room at the back. Behind the laundry room is a bedroom with a wall closet. It shares a bath with the owners bedroom, which has a walk-in closet. A vaulted loft can serve as additional sleeping space.

Design SHS010324

Square Footage: 1,230
Width: 55'-6" **Depth:** 30'-0"
Price Schedule: A2

This is a grand vacation or retirement home, designed for views and the outdoor lifestyle. The full-width deck complements the abundant windows in rooms facing its way. The living room is made for gathering with a vaulted ceiling, a fireplace and full-height windows overlooking the deck. Open to this living space is the dining room with sliding glass doors to the outdoors and a pass-through counter to the U-shaped kitchen. Two family bedrooms sit in the middle of the plan. They share a full bath. The owners suite has a private bath and deck views.

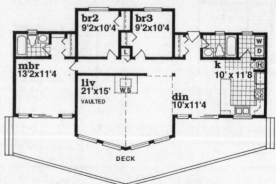

FOR PLAN ORDERING INFORMATION SEE PLAN

Design SHS010326

First Floor: 843 square feet
Second Floor: 370 square feet
Total: 1,213 square feet
Bonus Room: 217 square feet
Width: 32'-4" Depth: 44'-1"
Price Schedule: A2

This country-style vacation home is economical to build and offers additional space for future development. A bonus room may be used as an extra bedroom, playroom or media center. The front veranda opens to a living room with a wood stove and vaulted ceiling. The kitchen and breakfast room are nearby; the kitchen has an L-shaped work counter. The owners bedroom is on the first floor for privacy and has its own deck, accessed through sliding glass doors, and a private bath. Note the storage room just beyond the carport. Family bedrooms are on the second floor as is the bonus room.

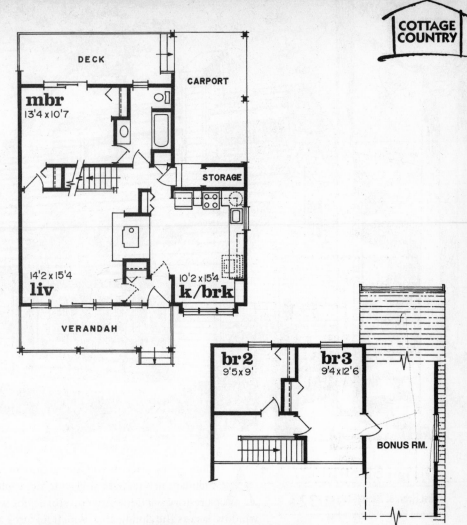

COTTAGE
COUNTRY

Design SHS010327

First Floor: 852 square feet
Second Floor: 400 square feet
Total: 1,252 square feet
Width: 32'-0" **Depth:** 28'-0"
Price Schedule: A2

An interesting array of window treatments distinguish this three-bedroom home. Abundant natural light spills into the vaulted living room through skylights and clerestory windows. A wood stove adds warmth. The kitchen, with a greenhouse window, serves the dining area, which features a full window wall on the rear yard. A bedroom or den is tucked into a corner and has the use of a full bath near the laundry room. The second-floor family bedroom and owners suite share a full bath that contains a shower.

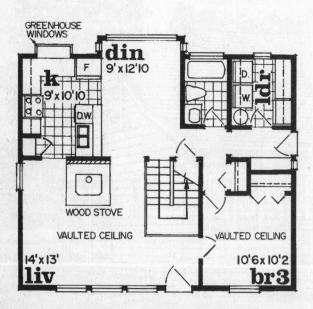

GREENHOUSE WINDOWS

din 9' x 12'10

k 9' x 10'10

F

D.

W.

ldr

D.W.

WOOD STOVE

VAULTED CEILING

liv 14' x 13'

VAULTED CEILING

br3 10'6 x 10'2

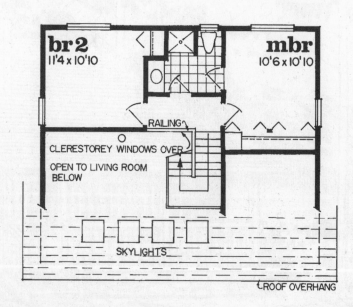

br 2 11'4 x 10'10

mbr 10'6 x 10'10

RAILING

CLERESTOREY WINDOWS OVER

OPEN TO LIVING ROOM BELOW

SKYLIGHTS

ROOF OVERHANG

FOR PLAN ORDERING INFORMATION SEE PLAN

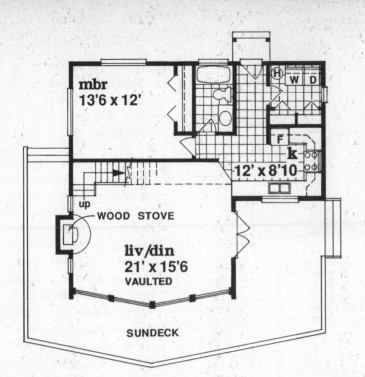

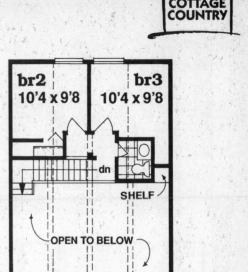

Design SHS010328

First Floor: 898 square feet
Second Floor: 358 square feet
Total: 1,256 square feet
Width: 34'-0" **Depth:** 32'-0"
Price Schedule: A2

A surrounding sun deck and expansive window wall capitalize on vacation-home views in this design. The full-height windows flood the living and dining rooms with abundant natural light and bring attention to the high vaulted ceilings. A wood stove in the living area warms cold winter nights. The efficient U-shaped kitchen has ample counter and cupboard space. Behind it is a laundry room and rear entrance. The owners bedroom sits on this floor and has a large wall closet and full bath. Two family bedrooms are on the second floor and have use of a half-bath.

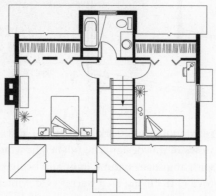

Design SHS010329

First Floor: 753 square feet
Second Floor: 505 square feet
Total: 1,258 square feet
Width: 30'-0" **Depth:** 25'-0"
Price Schedule: A2

Bay windows and a columned entry accent the facade of this charming cottage. Inside, the family room features a fireplace and combines with the dining room for a feeling of spaciousness. The efficient kitchen includes an eat-in breakfast area. A bedroom is also on this level, as is a large powder room with laundry facilities. Two additional bedrooms are upstairs and share a full bath. This home is designed with a basement foundation.

Available reverse right reading

Design SHS010330

First Floor: 725 square feet
Second Floor: 561 square feet
Total: 1,286 square feet
Width: 25'-0" **Depth:** 36'-6"
Price Schedule: A2

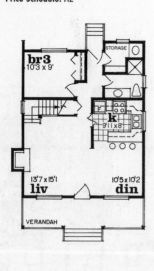

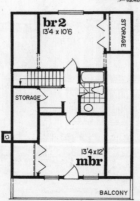

This cozy chalet design begins with a railed veranda opening to a living room with a warm fireplace and a dining room with a snack-bar counter through to the kitchen. The kitchen itself is U-shaped and has a sink with window over. A full bath and large storage area sit just beyond the kitchen. One bedroom with a roomy wall closet is on the first floor. The second floor holds two additional bedrooms—one an owners suite with a private balcony—and a full bath. Additional storage is found on the second floor, as well.

This home's covered front porch provides a warm welcome. Inside, a beam-ceilinged living room delights with a raised-hearth fireplace. The projecting bay window in the dining room offers a picturesque window seat. Upstairs, the owners bedroom suite includes a raised-hearth fireplace, a walk-in dressing area and plenty of privacy. Additional livability can be developed over the garage as a den, guest room or hobby area.

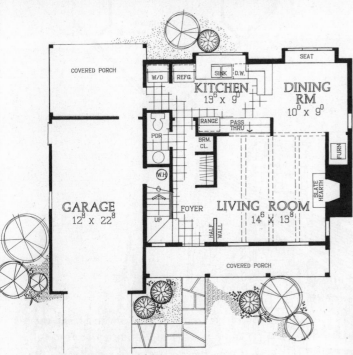

Design SHS010331

First Floor: 663 square feet

Second Floor: 624 square feet

Total: 1,287 square feet

Width: 40'-0" **Depth:** 32'-0"

Price Schedule: A4

SELECT HOME DESIGNS

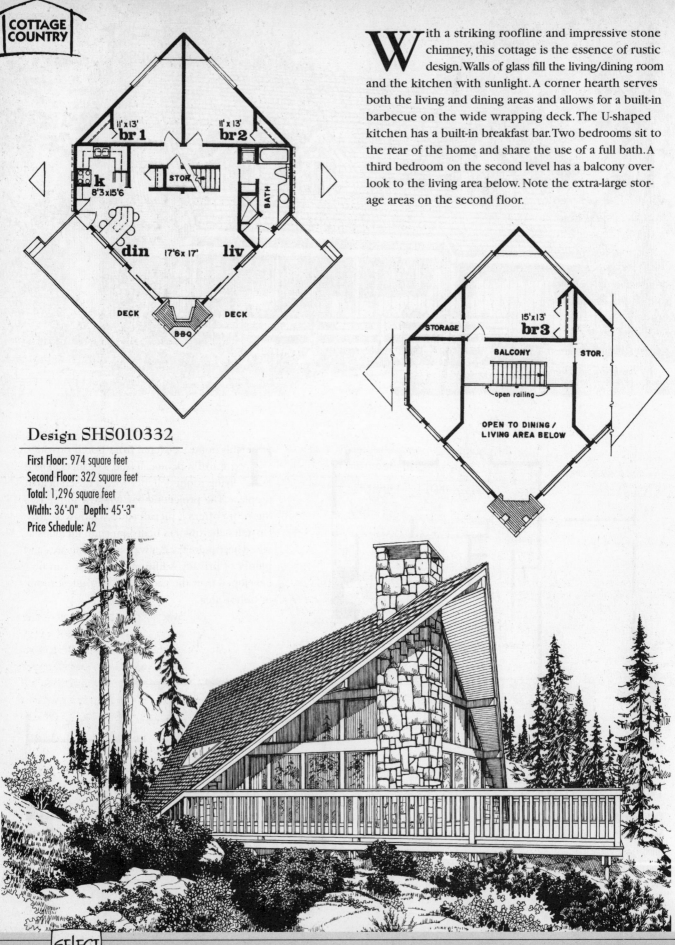

COTTAGE COUNTRY

With a striking roofline and impressive stone chimney, this cottage is the essence of rustic design. Walls of glass fill the living/dining room and the kitchen with sunlight. A corner hearth serves both the living and dining areas and allows for a built-in barbecue on the wide wrapping deck. The U-shaped kitchen has a built-in breakfast bar. Two bedrooms sit to the rear of the home and share the use of a full bath. A third bedroom on the second level has a balcony overlook to the living area below. Note the extra-large storage areas on the second floor.

Design SHS010332

First Floor: 974 square feet
Second Floor: 322 square feet
Total: 1,296 square feet
Width: 36'-0" **Depth:** 45'-3"
Price Schedule: A2

FOR PLAN ORDERING INFORMATION SEE PLAN

Design SHS010334

Square Footage: 1,292
Width: 52'-0" Depth: 34'-0"
Price Schedule: A2

This three-bedroom cottage is cozy and comfortable, yet roomy enough for the whole family. Its vertical wood siding and massive chimney stack grace the facade. Inside, a wall of windows in the living area allows for wonderful views; a vaulted ceiling and a wood stove further enhance its appeal. Double glass doors lead to a full-width deck that surrounds the living/dining area. The owners bedroom leaves nothing to chance, with deck access, a walk-in closet and a full private bath. Family bedrooms share a full bath that separates them.

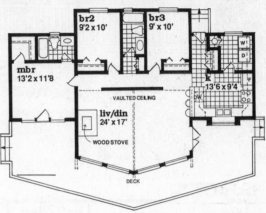

Design SHS010333

Square Footage: 1,312
Width: 69'-0" Depth: 39'-6"
Price Schedule: A2

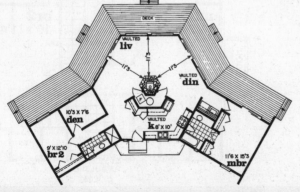

A large wrapping deck across the rear of this home makes it a very special vacation spot. Wide windows and sliding glass doors capture the views beyond. The living and dining rooms and the kitchen form a hexagon around a central wood stove to create one comfortable gathering area. Vaulted ceilings abound throughout. The owners bedroom is in the right wing and features His and Hers wall closets and a private bath. A den and one family bedroom are in the left wing and share a full bath. Use the den as extra sleeping space, if you choose.

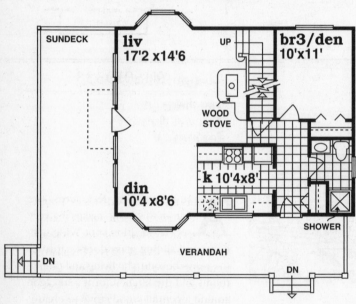

SUNDECK

liv 17'2 x14'6

UP

br3/den 10'x11'

WOOD STOVE

k 10'4x8'

din 10'4 x8'6

SHOWER

VERANDAH

DN

DN

Design SHS010335

First Floor: 792 square feet

Second Floor: 573 square feet

Total: 1,365 square feet

Width: 42'-0" **Depth:** 32'-0"

Price Schedule: A2

This distinctive vacation home is designed ideally for a gently sloping lot, which allows for a day-light basement. It can, however, accommodate a flat lot nicely. An expansive veranda sweeps around two sides of the exterior and is complemented by full-height windows. Decorative woodwork and traditional multi-pane windows belie the contemporary interior. An open living/dining room area, with a wood stove and two bay windows, is complemented by a galley-style kitchen. A bedroom, or den, on the first floor has the use of a full bath. The second floor holds an owners bedroom with a balcony and one family bedroom. Both second-floor bedrooms have dormer windows and share a full bath that has a vaulted ceiling.

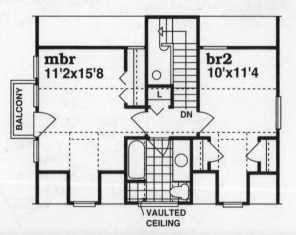

mbr 11'2x15'8

BALCONY

L

br2 10'x11'4

DN

VAULTED CEILING

Design SHS010336

First Floor: 780 square feet
Second Floor: 601 square feet
Total: 1,381 square feet
Width: 26'-0" **Depth:** 30'-0"
Price Schedule: A2

This A-frame cottages takes advantage of a front view from a deck and a balcony. The side entrance has direct access to the laundry/mud room, which connects directly into the galley kitchen. The open living and dining rooms are warmed by a wood stove and stretch out to enjoy the deck. The owners bedroom is to the rear and has a walk-in closet and a bath nearby. Two bedrooms upstairs have large wall closets and share a full bath. Bedroom 3 has double doors to the balcony.

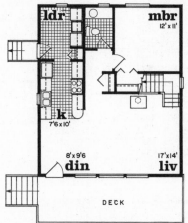

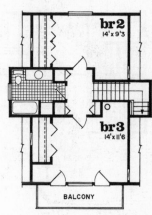

Design SHS010337

Square Footage: 1,405
Width: 62'-0" **Depth:** 29'-0"
Price Schedule: A2

This three-bedroom leisure home is perfect for the family that spends casual time out of doors. An expansive wall of glass gives a spectacular view to the great room and accentuates the high vaulted ceilings throughout the design. The great room is also warmed by a hearth and is open to the dining room and L-shaped kitchen. A triangular snack bar graces the kitchen and provides space for casual meals. Bedrooms are split, with the owners bedroom on the right side of the plan and family bedrooms on the left.

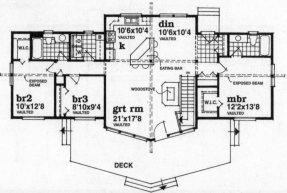

COTTAGE COUNTRY

Design SHS010338

First Floor: 1,084 square feet
Second Floor: 343 square feet
Total: 1,427 square feet
Width: 37'-0" Depth: 36'-0"
Price Schedule: A2

Vertical siding and a wide deck grace the exterior of this plan. Inside, the floor plan features a secluded second-floor owners suite with a private bath and walk-in closet. Extra-high vaulted ceilings and a wall of windows make the living/dining room a comfortable gathering area. It is warmed by a fireplace and open to the U-shaped kitchen. A laundry room is just beyond. The back entrance has a closet and opens to a rear deck. Two family bedrooms are on the first floor and share a full bath.

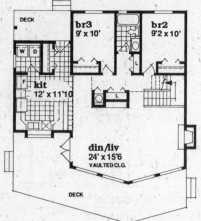

DECK

br3
9' x 10'

br2
9'2 x 10'

W D

F

kit
12' x 11'10

din/liv
24' x 15'6
VAULTED CLG.

DECK

mbr
13'4 x 12'4

PLANT LEDGE

Design SHS010339

Square Footage: 1,495
Width: 58'-6" Depth: 33'-0"
Price Schedule: A2

This three-bedroom cottage has just the right rustic mix of vertical wood siding and stone accents. Inside, the living is pure resort-style comfort. High vaulted ceilings are featured throughout the living room and owners bedroom. The living room also has a fireplace and full-height windows overlooking the deck. The dining room includes double-door access to the deck; the owners bedroom has a single door that opens to the deck. Two family bedrooms share a bath that is situated between them.

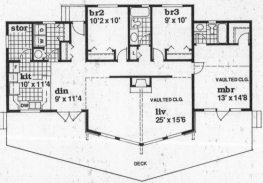

stor

br2
10'2 x 10'

br3
9' x 10'

F

kit
10' x 11'4

din
9' x 11'4

DW

VAULTED CLG.

liv
25' x 15'6

VAULTED CLG.

mbr
13' x 14'8

DECK

SELECT HOME DESIGNS

FOR PLAN ORDERING INFORMATION SEE PLAN

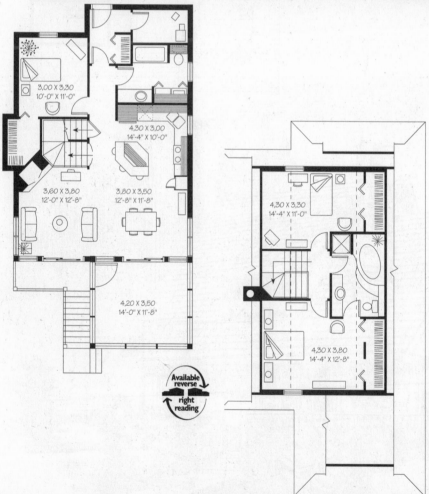

3,00 x 3,30
10'-0" X 11'-0"

4,30 x 3,00
14'-4" X 10'-0"

3,60 x 3,80
12'-0" X 12'-8"

3,80 x 3,50
12'-8" X 11'-8"

4,20 x 3,50
14'-0" X 11'-8"

4,30 x 3,30
14'-4" X 11'-0"

4,30 x 3,80
14'-4" X 12'-8"

Available
reverse
right
reading

Design SHS010340

First Floor: 895 square feet
Second Floor: 576 square feet
Total: 1,471 square feet
Width: 26'-0" **Depth:** 36'-0"
Price Schedule: A3

A lovely sun room opens from the dining room and allows great views. An angled hearth warms the living and dining areas. The gourmet kitchen has an island counter with a snack bar. The main-level owners bedroom enjoys a walk-in closet and a nearby bath. A daylight basement allows a lower-level portico.

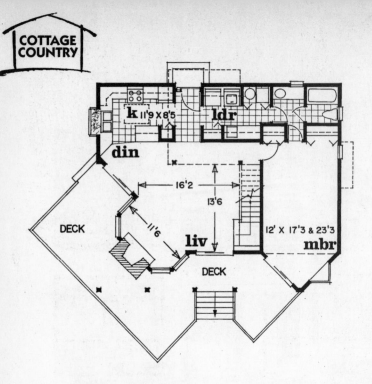

k 11'9 x 8'5   **ldr**

din

DECK

16'2

13'6

11'6

liv

12' X 17'3 & 23'3

mbr

DECK

This quaint cottage works equally well in the mountains or by the lake. Its entry is sliding glass and opens to a vaulted living room with a fireplace tucked into a wide windowed bay. The dining room has sliding glass access to the deck. The skylit kitchen features a greenhouse window over the sink and is just across from a handy laundry room. The owners bedroom captures views through sliding glass doors and a triangular feature window. It has the use of a full bath. The second floor holds another bedroom, a full bath and a loft area that could be used as a bedroom, if you choose.

SKYLIGHT

LOFT
10'-5" x 10'-8"
& 12'-11"

RAILING

OPEN TO LIVING
BELOW

DN

BEDRM. 2
12' x 14' & 16'-11"

CEILING
HAUNCH

Design SHS010341

First Floor: 1,022 square feet

Second Floor: 551 square feet

Total: 1,573 square feet

Width: 39'-0" **Depth:** 32'-0"

Price Schedule: A3

FOR PLAN ORDERING INFORMATION SEE PLAN

Design SHS010343

First Floor: 1,042 square feet
Second Floor: 456 square feet
Total: 1,498 square feet
Width: 36'-0" Depth: 35'-8"
Price Schedule: A2

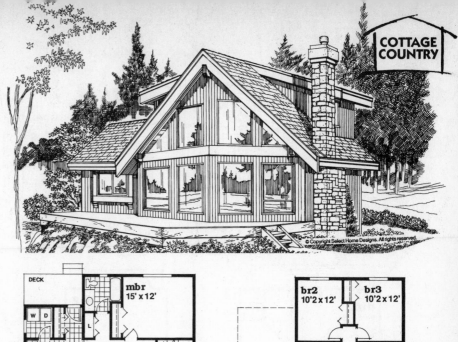

With a deck to the front, this vacation home is sure to provide outdoor fun. The living and dining rooms are dominated by a window wall to take advantage of the view. A high vaulted ceiling and wood-burning fireplace create a warm atmosphere. The U-shaped kitchen, with an adjoining laundry room, is open to the dining room with a pass-through counter. The owners bedroom to the rear has the use of a full bath with a large linen closet. Two family bedrooms upstairs share a full bath that has a skylight.

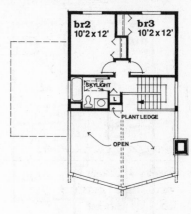

Design SHS010342

First Floor: 1,061 square feet
Second Floor: 482 square feet
Total: 1,543 square feet
Width: 28'-0" Depth: 39'-9"
Price Schedule: A3

A sun deck makes this design so popular, but it is enhanced by views through an expansive wall of glass in the living and dining rooms. They are warmed by a wood stove and enjoy vaulted ceilings, as well. The kitchen is also vaulted and has a prep island and breakfast bar. Behind the kitchen is a laundry room with side access. Two bedrooms and a full bath are found on the first floor. A skylit staircase leads up to the owners bedroom and its walk-in closet and private bath on the second floor.

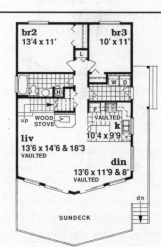

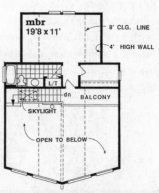

Design SHS010345

First Floor: 922 square feet
Second Floor: 683 square feet
Total: 1,605 square feet
Width: 27'-7" **Depth:** 39'-5"
Price Schedule: A3

This charming cottage is the perfect size and configuration for a leisure-time home. A weather-protected entry opens to a mudroom and serves as a storage space and airlock. The gathering area is comprised of a living room and a dining room and is warmed by a wood-burning stove. An entire wall of glass with sliding doors opens to a rear deck. The owners bedroom is on the first floor and features a main-floor bath with an attached sauna. Two bedrooms and a full bath are on the second floor. Bedroom 2 has a private balcony.

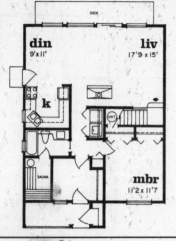

din 9'x11'
liv 17'9 x 15'
k
SAUNA
mbr 11'2 x 11'7

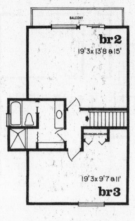

BALCONY
br2 19'3x13'8 a 15'
19'3x9'7 a 11'
br3

Design SHS010344

First Floor: 1,113 square feet
Second Floor: 543 square feet
Total: 1,656 square feet
Width: 44'-0" **Depth:** 32'-0"
Price Schedule: A4

For a lakeside retreat or as a retirement haven, this charming design offers the best in livability. The gathering room with a corner fireplace, the U-shaped kitchen with an attached dining room, the lovely deck and the first-floor owners suite make a complete and comfortable living space. Two bedrooms with a full bath and a balcony lounge upstairs complement the design and provide sleeping accommodations for family and guests.

Available reverse
right reading

CL.
DRSG. RM.
BATH
KIT. 8'0 x12'6
DINING RM. 12'0 x 11'4
DECK
STOR. LINEN
CL.
MASTER BED RM. 11'6 x 16'8
DN UP
ENT. HALL
GATHERING RM. 15'6 x 15'0
PORCH

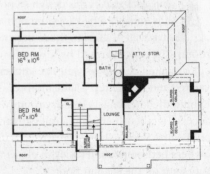

ROOF
BED RM. 16'4 x 10'6
ATTIC STOR.
CL.
BATH
SLOPED CEILING
BED RM. 11'0 x 10'6
DN
LOUNGE
RAILING
SLOPED CEILING
ROOF
ROOF

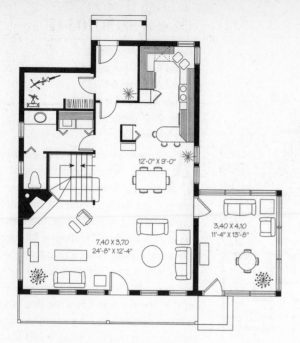

12'-0" X 9'-0"

7,40 X 3,70
24'-8" X 12'-4"

3,40 X 4,10
11'-4" X 13'-8"

Design SHS010346

First Floor: 1,074 square feet
Second Floor: 565 square feet
Total: 1,639 square feet
Width: 38'-0" **Depth:** 36'-0"
Price Schedule: A3

Available reverse right reading

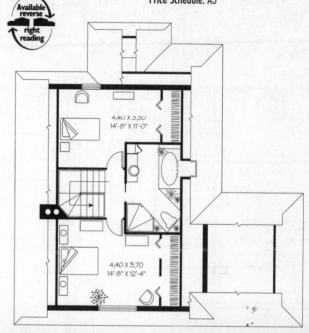

4,40 X 3,30
14'-8" X 11'-0"

4,40 X 3,70
14'-8" X 12'-4"

This four-season Cape Cod cottage is perfect for a site with great views. A sun room provides wide views and good indoor/outdoor flow. The living area boasts a corner fireplace. A well-organized kitchen serves a snack counter as well as the dining room. This home is designed with a basement foundation.

SELECT HOME DESIGNS

Design SHS010347

First Floor: 1,094 square feet
Second Floor: 576 square feet
Total: 1,670 square feet
Storage Area: 105 square feet
Width: 43'-0" **Depth:** 35'-4"
Price Schedule: A3

A covered veranda with a covered patio above opens through French doors to the living/dining area of this vacation cottage. A masonry fireplace with a wood storage bin warms this area. A modified U-shaped kitchen serves the dining room; a laundry room is just across the hall with access to a side veranda. The owners bedroom is on the first floor and has the use of a full bath. Sliding glass doors in the owners bedroom and the living room lead to still another veranda.

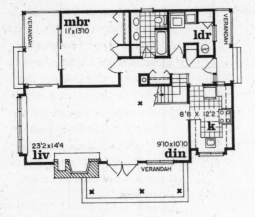

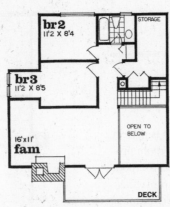

Design SHS010348

First Floor: 1,093 square feet
Second Floor: 580 square feet
Total: 1,673 square feet
Width: 36'-0" **Depth:** 52'-0"
Price Schedule: A4

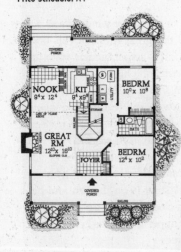

Brackets and balustrades on front and rear covered porches spell old-fashioned country charm on this rustic retreat. Warm evenings will invite family and guests outdoors for watching sunsets and stars. In cooler weather, the raised-hearth fireplace will make the great room a cozy place to gather. The nearby kitchen serves the snack bar and breakfast nook. Two family bedrooms and a full bath complete the main level. Upstairs, an owners bedroom with a sloped ceiling offers a window seat and a complete bath. The adjacent loft/study overlooks the great room.

Design SHS010349

First Floor: 1,093 square feet
Second Floor: 603 square feet
Total: 1,696 square feet
Width: 46'-0" **Depth:** 52'-0"
Price Schedule: A4

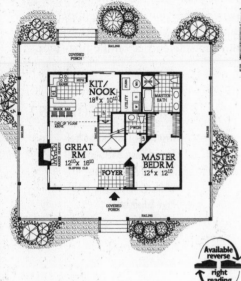

Available reverse / right reading

This home's rustic design reflects thoughtful planning, including a porch that fully wraps around the house, providing lots of room for rocking. A stone chimney and arched dormer windows further enhance this home's country appeal. Inside, the great room's raised-hearth fireplace radiates warmth into the nearby kitchen/nook. The first-floor owners suite includes plenty of closet space and a bath filled with amenities. The second floor contains two family bedrooms, a full bath and a loft/study with a window seat.

Design SHS010350

First Floor: 1,375 square feet
Second Floor: 284 square feet
Total: 1,659 square feet
Width: 58'-0" **Depth:** 32'-0"
Price Schedule: A3

An expansive window wall across the great room of this home adds a spectacular view and accentuates the high ceiling. The open kitchen shares an eating bar with the dining room and features a convenient U shape. Sliding glass doors in the dining room lead to the deck. Two family bedrooms sit to the back of the plan and share the use of a full bath. The owners suite is on the left and has a walk-in closet and private bath. The loft on the upper level adds living or sleeping space.

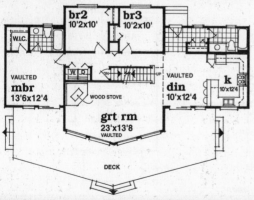

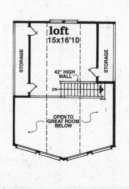

An expansive sun deck with an optional spa wraps around this design to highlight outdoor living. Tall windows accent the living and dining rooms' vaulted ceiling. Both areas are warmed by a central fireplace flanked by doors to the deck. A U-shaped kitchen is open to the dining room. Two bedrooms with walk-in closets sit to the back of the first floor. They share the use of a full bath. The owners suite dominates the upper level and has a full bath and large wall closet. Note the laundry room and side entries on the first floor.

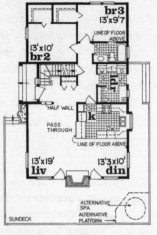

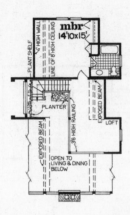

Design SHS010352

First Floor: 1,235 square feet
Second Floor: 543 square feet
Total: 1,778 square feet
Width: 27'-6" **Depth:** 46'-0"
Price Schedule: A3

Design SHS010351

First Floor: 986 square feet
Second Floor: 722 square feet
Total: 1,708 square feet
Width: 36'-6" **Depth:** 53'-6"
Price Schedule: A3

This charming four-bedroom home is dramatic on the outside and comfortable on the inside. Large glass sliding doors and floor-to-ceiling windows flood the interior with natural light. A vaulted living room has an oversized fireplace and connects to the dining area. A galley kitchen features a sink overlooking the deck. The owners bedroom and a secondary bedroom are to the rear and share the use of a full bath. The second floor holds two additional bedrooms and a gallery area with front and side decks. Use this area as a playroom or studio.

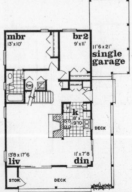

FOR PLAN ORDERING INFORMATION SEE PLAN

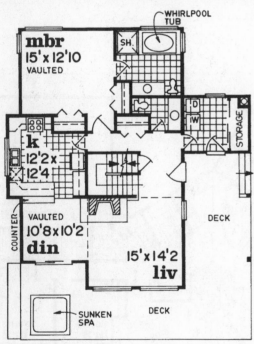

mbr
15' x 12'10
VAULTED

WHIRLPOOL TUB

SH.

k
12'2 x 12'4

D

W

STORAGE

COUNTER

VAULTED
10'8 x 10'2
din

15' x 14'2
liv

DECK

DECK

SUNKEN SPA

Design SHS010353

First Floor: 1,186 square feet

Second Floor: 597 square feet

Total: 1,783 square feet

Width: 39'-4" **Depth:** 41'-4"

Price Schedule: A3

A partially covered, wraparound deck on this vacation home allows for outdoor relaxation; a sunken spa adds to the enjoyment. The living room and dining room are vaulted and warmed by a central fireplace situated between the two. The kitchen offers a breakfast counter as separation from the dining room. The owners suite is luxurious and sits to the rear of the first floor. Its bath contains a whirlpool spa. An additional half-bath is found near the entry, just to the left of a laundry/storage area. The second floor holds two additional bedrooms—one with a built-in desk—and a full bath.

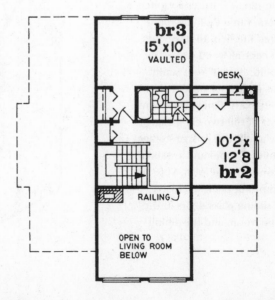

br3
15' x 10'
VAULTED

DESK

10'2 x 12'8
br2

RAILING

OPEN TO LIVING ROOM BELOW

COTTAGE
COUNTRY

Design SHS010354

Square Footage: 1,803
Width: 65'-8" Depth: 55'-7"
Price Schedule: A3

A hexagon forms the hub of living space in this clever design. It features a vaulted living room, vaulted dining room and vaulted kitchen, all revolving around a central wood stove. The owners suite is split from family bedrooms and has a walk-in closet and private bath. Family bedrooms sit in front of the two-car garage and share a full bath. A large storage area, a laundry room and a walk-in pantry complete the plan. Note the wide wrapping deck, accessed through sliding glass doors in the owners bedroom and the dining room.

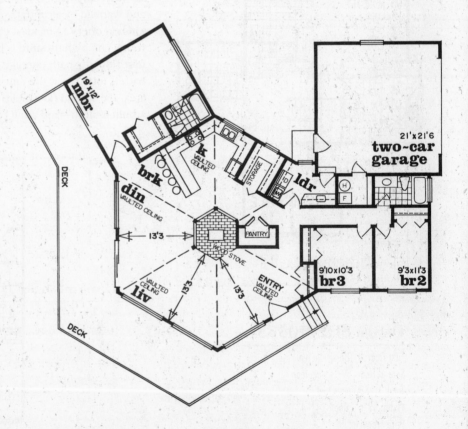

SELECT
HOME DESIGNS

Design SHS010355

First Floor: 1,328 square feet
Second Floor: 503 square feet
Total: 1,831 square feet
Width: 44'-0" **Depth:** 52'-0"
Price Schedule: A3

Thoughtful planning creates open, flowing spaces on the main level. Here, a living room warmed by a fireplace shares space with an efficient eating nook and kitchen. Two bedrooms—one an owners suite—complete this level. The upper level contains two family bedrooms, a full bath and an open loft that overlooks the main-level living room.

This leisure home is perfect for outdoor living with French doors opening to a large sun deck and sunken spa. The open-beam, vaulted ceiling and high window wall provide views for the living and dining rooms, which are decorated with wood columns and warmed by a fireplace. The step-saving U-shaped kitchen has ample counter space and a bar counter to the dining room. The owners bedroom on the first floor features a walk-in closet and a private bath. A convenient mudroom with an adjoining laundry room accesses a rear deck. Two bedrooms on the second floor share a full bath.

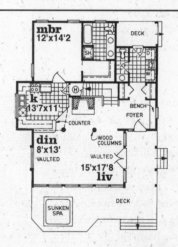

Design SHS010356

First Floor: 1,157 square feet
Second Floor: 638 square feet
Total: 1,795 square feet
Width: 36'-0" **Depth:** 40'-0"
Price Schedule: C1

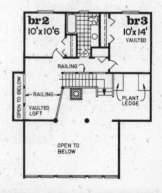

COTTAGE COUNTRY

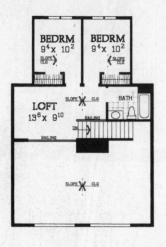

BEDRM
9⁴ x 10²

BEDRM
9⁴ x 10²

SLOPE CLG

SLOPE CLG

LOFT
13⁶ x 9¹⁰

BATH

SLOPE X CLG

RAILING

DN

RAILING

SLOPE X CLG

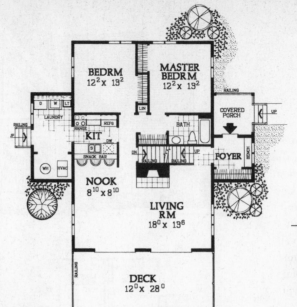

BEDRM
12² x 13²

MASTER BEDRM
12² x 13²

D W LT

LAUNDRY

REFG

RANGE

KIT

DW

SNACK BAR

WH

HVAC

NOOK
8¹⁰ x 8¹⁰

LIN

BATH

COVERED PORCH

UP

FOYER

BENCH

RAILING

DN

LIVING RM
18⁰ x 13⁶

RAILING

DECK
12⁰ x 28⁰

RAILING

RAILING

BATH

STORAGE

UP

RAILING

BASEMENT
14⁰ x 26⁴

PATIO
12⁰ x 28⁰

Available reverse right reading

Design SHS010357

First Floor: 1,328 square feet
Second Floor: 503 square feet
Total: 2,234 square feet
Width: 44'-0" **Depth:** 52'-0"
Price Schedule: C2

Expansive views enhance this floor plan. Thoughtful planning creates open, flowing spaces on the main level. Here, a living room warmed by a fireplace shares space with an efficient eating nook and kitchen. Two bedrooms—one an owners suite—complete this level. The upper level contains two family bedrooms, a full bath and an open loft that overlooks the main-level living room.

This home, as shown in photograph, may differ from the actual blueprints. For more detailed information, please check the floor plans carefully.

Photo by Andrew P. Lautman

Design SHS010358

First Floor: 1,356 square feet
Second Floor: 490 square feet
Total: 1,846 square feet
Width: 50'-7" **Depth:** 38'-0"
Price Schedule: A4

Split-log siding and a rustic balustrade create country charm with this farmhouse-style retreat. An open living area features a natural stone fireplace and a cathedral ceiling with exposed rough-sawn beam and brackets. A generous kitchen and dining area complement the living room and share the warmth of its fireplace. An owners suite with a complete bath, and a nearby family bedroom with a hall bath complete the main floor. Upstairs, a spacious loft affords extra sleeping space—or provides a hobby/recreation area—and offers a full bath.

FACTS AT THE BEGINNING OF THIS ISSUE

Design SHS010359

Studio: 428 square feet
Width: 23'-4" **Depth:** 13'-2"
Price Schedule: P5

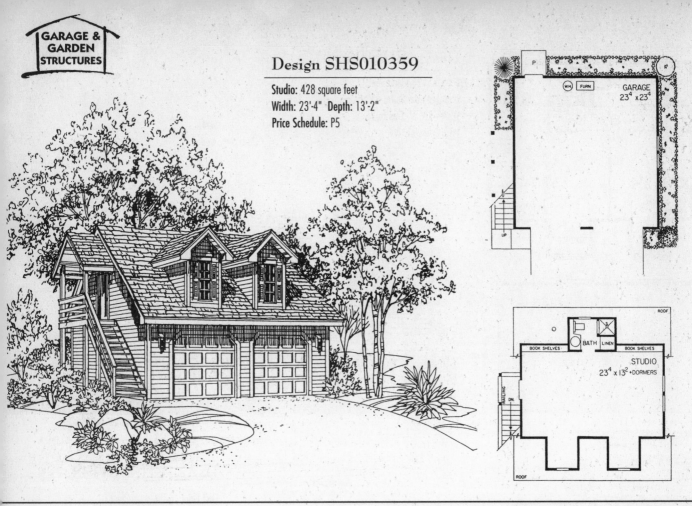

GARAGE
23⁴ x 23⁴

WM FURN

BOOK SHELVES   BATH LINEN   BOOK SHELVES

STUDIO
23⁴ x 13² +DORMERS

ROOF

RAILING

Design SHS010360

Garage: 528 square feet
One-Bedroom Suite: 484 square feet
Width: 27'-6" **Depth:** 22'-0"
Price Schedule: P6

two-car garage

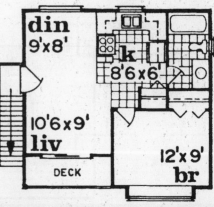

din
9'x8'

k
8'6x6'

10'6x9'
liv

DECK

12'x9'
br

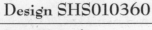
SELECT HOME DESIGNS

GARAGE &
GARDEN
STRUCTURES

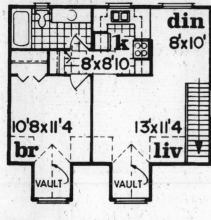

din
8'x10'

k
8'x8'10

10'8x11'4
br
VAULT

13x11'4
liv
VAULT

two~car garage

Design SHS010361

Garage: 728 square feet
One-Bedroom Suite: 652 square feet
Width: 28'-0"   Depth: 26'-0"
Price Schedule: P6

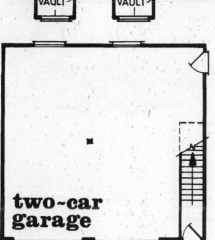

YARD TOOL HANGING
STORAGE CABINETS
WASH SINK
WORK COUNTER

GARAGE
35'4 x 24'4

OPTIONAL WORK PIT BY OWNER

AIR COMP.

Available
reverse
right
reading

Design SHS010362

Garage: 900 square feet
One-Bedroom Suite: 690 square feet
Width: 36'-0"   Depth: 25'-0"
Price Schedule: P5

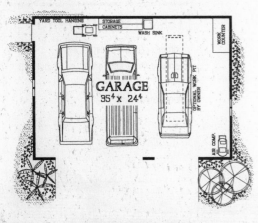

ROOF
BATH
LINEN
REFG
KIT
11'x 7'8
RANGE
SHWR
SKYLITES
RAILING

BEDRM
13'0 x 13'10
+ DORMER

WASH
DRY

LIVING ROOM
10'0 x 13'5
+ DORMER

NOOK
7'0 x 7'10

DOWN
RAILING

BLT.
CLO.

W.I.C.

BLT
CLO.

BOOK SHELVES

SEAT
ROOF
SEAT

SELECT
HOME DESIGNS

GARAGE & GARDEN STRUCTURES

Design SHS010363

Garage: 672 square feet
Loft Space: 320 square feet
Width: 28'-0" **Depth:** 27'-0"
Price Schedule: P5

two~car garage

LOFT

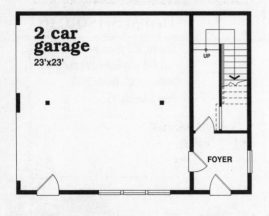

2 car garage 23'x23'

UP

FOYER

Design SHS0103364

Garage: 728 square feet
Carriage House Apartment: 652 square feet
Width: 28'-6" **Depth:** 26'-0"
Price Schedule: P6

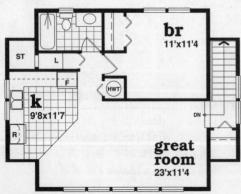

ST
L
F
k 9'8x11'7
R
HWT
br 11'x11'4
DN
great room 23'x11'4

SELECT HOME DESIGNS

FOR PLAN ORDERING INFORMATION SEE PLAN

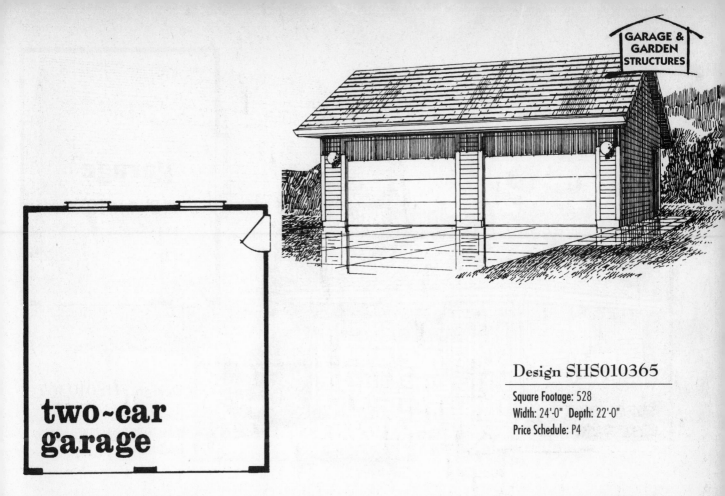

**two~car
garage**

Design SHS010365

Square Footage: 528
Width: 24'-0" Depth: 22'-0"
Price Schedule: P4

LOFT

LINE OF
8' CEILING

**three~car
garage**

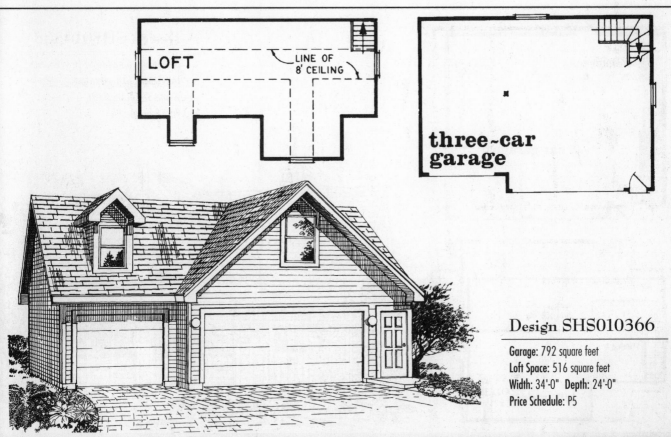

Design SHS010366

Garage: 792 square feet
Loft Space: 516 square feet
Width: 34'-0" Depth: 24'-0"
Price Schedule: P5

SELECT
HOME DESIGNS

garage

15'-4 x 19'-4

Design SHS010367

Square Footage: 320
Width: 16'-0" **Depth:** 20'-0"
Price Schedule: P4

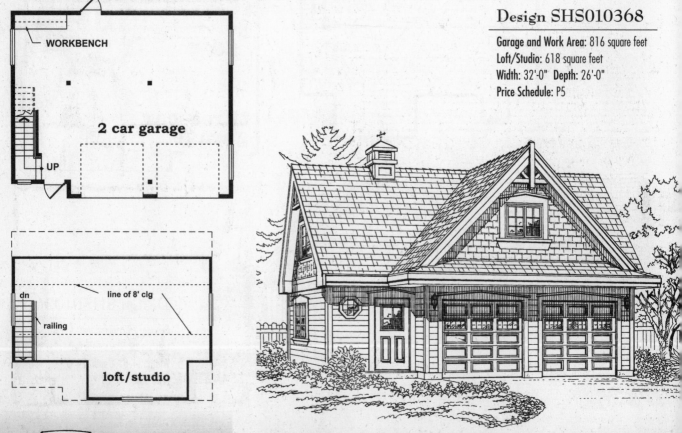

WORKBENCH

2 car garage

UP

dn

line of 8' clg

railing

loft/studio

Design SHS010368

Garage and Work Area: 816 square feet
Loft/Studio: 618 square feet
Width: 32'-0" **Depth:** 26'-0"
Price Schedule: P5

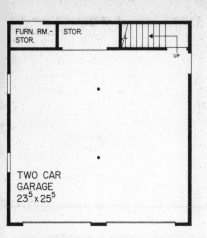

FURN. RM.- STOR.   STOR.   UP

TWO CAR GARAGE 23⁵ x 25⁵

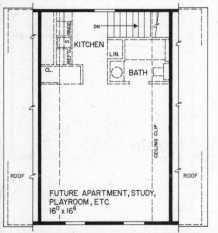

KITCHEN
DN
REFG. RANGE
CL.
LIN.
BATH
ROOF
CEILING CLIP
ROOF

FUTURE APARTMENT, STUDY, PLAYROOM, ETC. 16⁰ x 16⁶

Design SHS010369

Garage: 624 square feet
Loft/Studio: 431 square feet
Width: 24'-0" **Depth:** 26'-0"
Price Schedule: P4

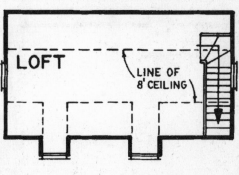

LOFT

LINE OF 8' CEILING

two~car garage

HANDRAIL

Design SHS010370

Garage: 664 square feet
Loft Space: 478 square feet
Width: 28'-0" **Depth:** 24'-0"
Price Schedule: P5

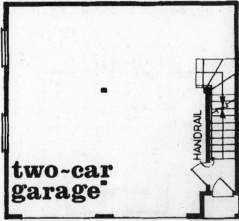

Design SHS010372

Square Footage: 794

Width: 52'-0" Depth: 34'-0"

Price Schedule: P6

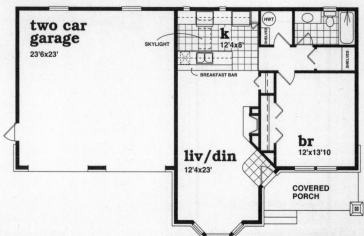

two car garage
23'6x23'

SKYLIGHT

k
12'4x8'

HWT

SHELVES

BREAKFAST BAR

SHELVES

br
12'x13'10

liv/din
12'4x23'

COVERED PORCH

Design SHS010371

Square Footage: 604

Width: 48'-0" Depth: 28'-0"

Price Schedule: P6

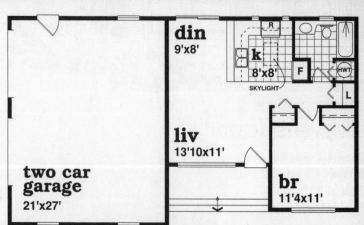

din
9'x8'

R

k
8'x8'

F

HWT

SKYLIGHT

L

liv
13'10x11'

two car garage
21'x27'

br
11'4x11'